DISCLOSURE AND CONCEALMENT IN CONSUMER INSURANCE CONTRACTS

Cavendish
Publishing
Limited

London • Sydney

DISCLOSURE AND CONCEALMENT IN CONSUMER INSURANCE CONTRACTS

Dr Julie-Anne Tarr
BA (Wisconsin), JD (Cornell)
LLM (Monash), PhD (Queensland)
Senior Lecturer in Law,
TC Beirne School of Law,
University of Queensland

Cavendish
Publishing
Limited

London • Sydney

First published in Great Britain 2002 by Cavendish Publishing Limited,
The Glass House, Wharton Street, London WC1X 9PX, United Kingdom
Telephone: +44 (0)20 7278 8000 Facsimile: +44 (0)20 7278 8080
Email: info@cavendishpublishing.com
Website: www.cavendishpublishing.com

British Library Cataloguing in Publication Data

Tarr, Julie-Anne
Disclosure and concealment in consumer insurance contracts
1 Insurance, products liability – Great Britain
2 Disclosure of information – law and legislation – Great Britain
I Title
346.4'1'086562

ISBN 1 85941 712 4

Printed and bound in Great Britain

FOREWORD

In addition to this work's manifestly profound and extensive research on technical aspects, it is an important contribution to the theoretical foundation of insurance and insurance law generally and, in particular, to its most prolific sources of controversy. It deserves to be read by any serious practitioner, teacher or researcher who has an interest in the direction and substance of the development of this branch of commerce and its relevant law; and it is very readable. It must enlarge the breadth of any reader's perception of the topics discussed and, incidentally, but on a wider scale, of important influences on the law as an instrument for the resolution of competing interests in an organic society. Any sophisticated discussion of disclosure and concealment in insurance contracts demands an understanding of the features that it reveals.

It ventures into the economic, social and consumer dimensions in its study of relevant and very practical aspects of the technical law of its subject matter, which it also handles with meticulous accuracy and extensive detail. This combination of practical application with original ideas and inquiry into new theoretical lines is valuable on both fronts. In relation to those matters that are encountered frequently in practice where the development of the law or insurance practices should be considered, it provides lawyers and insurers with a deep and interesting identification of issues that must be considered. It then expands the discussion of the points identified, and the author does not flinch from suggesting her preferred resolution – with well argued reasons.

Plainly, because of the breadth of the policy issues involved and their controversial nature, not all of these suggested conclusions will receive universal endorsement, and some may finally be rejected; but even these will have served the process well by leading identification, analysis and informed and enlightened discussion in the process. Conversely, failure to advert to the issues raised in this work would constitute a serious deficiency in any relevant controversy or development.

The author has the distinction of direct working knowledge of the United States legal system in insurance law as well as intimate knowledge of the Australian and English systems. In a comparative exercise of considerable quality, she is able to draw felicitously on these diverse streams of progressive and cautious policy considerations and their resolution of competing elements. Her preferences, clearly and strongly explained, are supported by this direct experience and an understanding based on a suitably strong foundation, and no doubt they will receive appropriate respect. It is to be hoped that American jurisprudence will profit from this work as much as does its Anglo-Australian counterpart.

The Honourable Desmond Derrington,
BA, LLB, LLD (Honoris Causa), QC
Adjunct Professor of Law, TC Beirne School of Law,
University of Queensland,
Justice of the Supreme Court of Queensland (1982–2000),
Medal of L'Association Internationale du Droit des Assurances

CONTENTS

TABLE OF CASES

TABLE OF LEGISLATION

Australia

Malaysia

New South Wales

New Zealand

Singapore

Thailand

United Kingdom

United States of America

TABLE OF ABBREVIATIONS

All ER	All England Reports
BCLC	Butterworths Company Law Cases
CLJ	Cambridge Law Journal
Conv	Conveyancer and Property Lawyer
EGCS	Estates Gazette Case Summaries
FCR	Family Court Reporter
FLR	Family Law Reports
HKLJ	Hong Kong Law Journal
JBL	Journal of Business Law
LMCLQ	Lloyd's Maritime Commercial Law Quarterly
LQR	Law Quarterly Review
LS	Legal Studies
MLR	Modern Law Review
NILQ	Northern Ireland Law Quarterly
NLJ	New Law Journal
NPC	New Property Cases
NZLR	New Zealand Law Reports
OJLS	Oxford Journal of Legal Studies
P & CR	Property and Compensation Reports
RLR	Restitution Law Review
SJ	Solicitors Journal
VUWLR	Victoria University of Wellington Law Review
WLR	Weekly Law Reports

CHAPTER 1

INTRODUCTION

> Insurance is a contract upon speculation. The special facts upon which the contingent chance is to be computed, lie most commonly in the knowledge of the insureds only: the underwriter trusts to his representations, and proceeds upon confidence that he does not keep back any circumstances in his knowledge, to mislead the underwriter into a belief that the circumstance does not exist, and to induce him to estimate the risque, as if it did not exist.
> *Carter v Boehm* (1766) 3 Burr 1905; 97 ER 1162.

For the vast majority of consumers, insurance arrangements are regarded at best as a necessary evil. An Israeli writer who observed that '[i]nsurance policies are not likely to emerge, even at the present, as a major source of recreational reading'[1] remains unlikely to be accused of understatement.

The complaints made not only are that policies are drafted in terms that are intelligible only to experts, but also that the information may be contained in a combination of any two – or more – of the proposal form, the preamble, the definition section, clauses dealing with exclusions or conditions, and the schedule.[2] Compounding such difficulties are 'fine print' legibility problems which led one American judge to observe that 'seldom has the art of typography been so successfully diverted from the diffusion of knowledge to the suppression of it'.[3] Consequently, while insurance in many respects closely parallels gambling,[4] consumers' enthusiasm for insurance transactions cannot be said to rival their response to the Melbourne Cup, the Grand National or the Kentucky Derby.

In many ways, as is discussed below, this reality is far removed from the early days of modern insurance history.[5] Seafarers and insurers nutting out

---

1 Procaccia, 'Readable insurance policies: judicial regulation and interpretation' (1979) 14 Israel L Rev 74.

2 See, for example, *Guardian Insurance Co Ltd v Underwood Constructions Pty Ltd* (1974) 48 ALJR 307, at 308, where Mason J describes a policy as a 'jumble of ill-assorted documents expressed in the distinctive style which insurance companies have made their own'; more recently in *Forsikringsaktieselskapet Vesta v Butcher* [1989] 1 Lloyd's Rep 331, Lord Bridge of Harwich commented on a Lloyd's reinsurance policy in the following terms: '... the only people who can expect to profit from the obscurities of the present form ... are the lawyers.'

3 See *Delancy v Insurance Co* (1873) 52 NH Rep 581, 587–88.

4 In the 18th century wagers on the lives of famous people and 'insurance' on whether there would be a war or some other contingency were commonly effected by persons with no insurable interest in the subject matter. See, for example, Brown, 1973, pp 26–27; Clayton, 1971, p 58; Merkin, 'Gambling by insurance – a study of the Life Assurance Act 1774' (1980) 9 Anglo-American L Rev 331.

5 The history of insurance can be traced back past 2000 BC. See, for example, (the Honourable Mr Justice) Derrington, 'Insurance as a cornerstone of civilisation – and another cornerstone' (1994) 7 Corporate and Business Law Journal 1.

the terms of deals at the tables of Edward Lloyd's Edwardian coffee shop were well aware of the nature of risks being undertaken and the graphic repercussions for deals gone bad. Sunken ships, pirates, exotic ports and bad straits presumably made for more romantic discussion (and contemplation) than the average subrogation clause in household contents policies.

Although Lloyd's remains, a few centuries have made a dramatic difference to the way contemporary would-be contractors approach the acquisition of insurance. Mechanisms for obtaining and verifying background information for actuarial risk calculations of individual policies would be unrecognisable to the 18th century underwriters who were more reliant on the word of the shipowners and captains as to what risks lay in the remote ports to which their vessels would sail. In addition, they depended upon the proponent to identify the vessel, the captain, the number of crew and the cargo, which was entirely the proponent's particular knowledge. In contrast, few insurers are reliant on their car owning clients to advise them of the likely ordinary risks to which the family Sedan will be exposed daily in the suburbs. Moreover, should an accident happen, the ability to obtain first hand information on the circumstances surrounding the loss is different from that attaching to a deep water loss of a marine vessel several thousand miles removed from London in the 1700s.

Despite these changes for the better for actuarial insurance calculation purposes, a variety of legal precedents still remain under contemporary insurance law that have the potential to skew what is desirably the equitable allocation of risk between insurer and insured. Such precedents rest specifically on the question of disclosure of information and the extent to which parties to a potential contract are compelled to exchange information. Unduly onerous or inappropriate requirements for disclosure can impose unfair burdens on consumers and, in a broader context, unnecessary costs to society itself. As an Australian Law Reform Commission Report notes:

> Fairness between the parties to an insurance contract demands the ready availability of information concerning the nature and incidents of that contract. The insured must know what he is purchasing if he is to be able to judge its value to him. Yet insurance is a subject in respect of which there is widespread ignorance.[6]

There is significant asymmetry of information and knowledge between insurers and insureds in relation to consumer contracts of insurance; that is, contracts of consumer insurance involving home buildings, home contents, motor vehicle cover, travel, personal accident and consumer credit. In some respects the insured is in a superior position – he or she is aware of the particular circumstances surrounding the subject matter of the insurance contract and any specific risks to which the property is exposed or where

6 *Report on Insurance Contracts* (No 20, 1982), at para 31.

liability may be incurred. Conversely, the insurer is in an advantageous position as regards the scope and content of the insurance cover being sought. The insured is aware of the primary features of the transaction (such as the type of cover, the quantum of cover and the premium payable) but is unlikely to have a clear (or any) understanding of subordinate terms such as average clauses, subrogation provisions and the myriad of exclusions, excesses and limitations upon liability.

This monograph considers whether the current regulatory framework of statutes and regulations and the common law provide a just and efficient set of standards for the exchange of information between insurer and insured in the pre-contract stage of insurance contract formation. There is a critical balance to be maintained to ensure that consumers receive adequate information about the insurance cover they are acquiring while retaining a system of fair information procedures to protect the insurer from excessive or extraordinary risk. Particular focus will be upon the approaches adopted in the United Kingdom, Australia, New Zealand and the United States of America.

Consumer insurance contracts[7] are selected for consideration as it is in the context of these most widely used types of general insurance contracts that the disparity in knowledge and bargaining power between insured and insurer is most acute. Insured parties in other forms of insurance are usually better informed, better advised or more equally placed to negotiate and bring about settlement. Accordingly, any legal framework erected, the balance struck between insured and insurer, and the efficacy of that framework is most appropriately assessed by reference to consumer insurance contracts. Consumer insurance contracts in this context are contracts where the insured or one of the insureds is a natural person and which are for:

- motor vehicle insurance – cover in respect of one or more of the following: (a) loss of, or damage to, a motor vehicle; (b) liability for loss of, or damage to, property caused by or resulting from impact of a motor vehicle with some other thing;
- home buildings insurance – cover in respect of loss or destruction of, or damage occurring to a building used principally and primarily as a place of residence;
- home contents insurance – cover in respect of loss of, or damage to the contents of a residential building, but not including a contract that provides cover only or primarily in respect of specified personal effects;
- sickness and accident insurance – cover in respect of the insured contracting sickness or disease or sustaining injury, other than: (a) a life policy or a continuous disability insurance contract incorporated within a

7 Defined below.

life policy; (b) sickness and accident policies which are guaranteed renewable at the option of the insured or where the insurer guarantees not to cancel the policy in response to a change in the risk and the policy has been effected for a predetermined period in excess of one year;

- consumer credit insurance – cover in respect of the death of the insured, or the insured contracting a sickness or disease, sustaining an injury or becoming unemployed, and the amount of liability under the contract is ascertained by reference to a liability of the insured under an agreement to which the insured is a party;
- travel insurance – cover in respect of financial loss for fares or accommodation in the event that a specified journey is not commenced or completed, and loss or damage to personal belongings or sickness or disease contracted, or injury sustained, in connection with a specified journey.[8]

The passage of time and technological advances have had dramatic impacts upon how insurance transactions are effected, especially in the case of consumer insurance contracts. Contemporary insurers have recourse to information and resources far superior to their 18th century counterparts. Access to detailed statistical data relevant to a wide range of risks and sophisticated investigative facilities and personnel for example, are now readily available to examine claims and to detect fraud; the tyranny of distance is no longer a problem with modern communications and technological advances; actuarial analysis has refined the process of estimating risk/loss and setting premiums with appropriate regard to a range of variables; and, prudential margins are incorporated into loss forecasts to cater for unforeseen contingencies. Perhaps most importantly, use of standard form proposals and policy documents prescribes closely what information is to be provided, what risks are assumed and upon what terms that risk is accepted. Having regard to these factors, asymmetry of information relative to the particular transaction being negotiated is less significant. The only knowledge that the insurer does not have is particular knowledge that the insured may have or be aware of in relation to the specific property or potential liability that he or she wishes to insure. This deficiency can be cured by the insurer asking particular questions. In consequence, the legal requirements of disclosure, deriving from the utmost good faith doctrine in insurance contracts, and the provision of information in the pre-contractual setting generally, have in certain areas arguably become outmoded.

---

8 See Insurance Contracts Act 1984 (Australia), ss 34, 35 and the Insurance Contracts Regulations (SR No 162 of 1985, as amended). The definitions of consumer insurance contracts given above vary slightly from jurisdiction to jurisdiction but in substance the contracts described above represent the principal classes of consumer insurance contract. See, for example, Ivamy, 1993, at pp 7–10.

At a micro level, the implication of this is unduly onerous disclosure provisions for consumers wishing to take out insurance contracts. In a broader context, society is potentially burdened with unnecessary transaction costs arising from inappropriate enforcement of regulations and excessive litigation over ambiguous legal standards. The appropriate approach to information disclosure in the formation of consumer insurance contracts will be examined and recommendations made.

CHAPTER 2

ECONOMIC ISSUES

> An Act concerning matters of Assurances, amongst Merchants.
>
> Whereas it has been the policy of this Realm by all good means to comfort and encourage the Merchant, thereby to advance and increase the general wealth of the Realm, Her Majesty's Customs and the strength of shipping ... [through the issuing of a policy of assurance] it has come to pass, upon the loss or perishing of any ship there follows not the undoing of any Man, but that the loss falls rather easily upon many, as opposed to heavily upon few, and preferably upon those who do not venture forth rather than upon those who do, whereby all merchants, especially the younger, are lured to venture more willingly and freely.[1]
>
> – *Elizabethan Statute of 1601*, 43 Eliz C 12

2.1 INTRODUCTION

This chapter examines the economic underpinning of the evolution of information disclosure standards in the formation of insurance contracts. Proponents of the 'law and economics' strain of jurisprudence have long maintained that common law doctrine is a reflection of the principles of economic efficiency underlying market function.[2] Left to its own devices, free market philosophies hold that the unfettered interplay between buyers and sellers will naturally produce optimal outcomes in terms of production and

1 *The Statutes of the Realm*, Vol IV, Part II (London: Dawsons, 1819), 978. The original text provides:

> Whereas it hasthe bene the Plicie of this Realme by all good meanes to comforte and encourage the Merchante, therebie to advance and increase the generall wealth of the Realme, her Majesties Customes and the strengthe of shippinge, which consideracon is nowe the more requisite, because Trade and Traffique is not at this psente soe open as at other tymes it hathe bene: And whereas it hathe bene tyme out of mynde an usage amongst Merchantes, both of this Realme and of forraine Nacyons, when they make any greate adventure (specialie into remote partes) to give some consideracon of Money to other psons (which comonlie are in noe small number) to have from them assurance made of their Goodes Merchandizes Ships and Things adventured, or some parte thereof, at suche rates and in suche sorte as the Parties assurers and the Parties assured can agree, whiche course of dealinge is comonlie termed a Policie of Assurance; by means of which Policies of Assurance it hathe come to passe, upon the losse or perishinge of any Shippe there followethe not the undoinge of any Man, but the losse lightethe rather easilie upon many, than heavilie upon fewe, and rather upon them that adventure not then those that doe adventure, whereby all Merchantes, specialie the younger sorte, are allured to venture more willinglie and more freelie.

2 Holmes, 1921: 'For the rational study of the law the black letter man may be the man of the present, but the man of the future is the man of statistics and the master of economics.' As cited in Cooter and Ulen, 1988, p 48.

supply or, in the more prosaic terms of the insurance market, will naturally reach optimal levels of risk allocation between the parties.

As is evidenced by the enabling statute cited above, its Elizabethan drafters believed that creating adequate incentive to stimulate the development of a nascent shipping industry was critical to England's economic and social development. Of paramount importance within this scheme was that of ensuring that the losses commonly associated with merchant marine activities were able to be spread sufficiently amongst those able to accommodate them so that the high cost of any given catastrophe did not prove fatal to the individual merchant involved, and so that fear of this would not inhibit the industry's development. This, of course, similarly became the basis for the expansion of the insurance industry generally and, with its growth, the development of the key principles of risk based heavily upon the initial disclosure of information between parties entering into insurance contracts. In this way, by reducing the uncertainty of risk as far as possible underwriters could be encouraged to participate while merchants would be assisted by keeping down premiums.

The financial relevance of disclosure as part of a successful risk pool assessment procedure is of perhaps even greater importance to the contemporary insurance industry. Unlike in earlier times when profit was generally deemed to be tied directly to premiums paid in, contemporary insurers generally are more reliant on the income earned on monies held between intake of premium and pay out of such. It is the careful fund management of these blocks of capital that in actuality generate profit. A poorly constituted risk pool – due to inadequate disclosure or appraisal of risk – will therefore precipitate earlier payout of funds than anticipated and with this, the loss of investment revenue and consequent profit.

This chapter identifies and considers economic factors relating to insurance contract law. The purpose is to identify the extent to which economic and legal developments in the industry have been efficient. Section 2.2 examines: (a) the economic principles generic to contract law; and (b) the implications that the widespread use of standard form contracts throughout this industry poses to this analysis. Section 2.3 then examines those aspects of law unique to insurance regulation in terms of the economic principles they similarly have either embraced or, in the course of development, diverged from in key respects. The historical context in which this transpires is interwoven in this section.

2.2 CONTRACT PARADIGM: THE ECONOMIC MODEL OF CONTRACT LAW

Analysis of the economic efficiency of insurance contracts presupposes an understanding of the economic principles underlying the operation of contract law in general. It is against these building blocks of economic argument that the legitimacy of doctrinal and regulatory variations inherent in insurance contract law can best be assessed. This section focuses on the basic principles advanced by economists in determining not only the existing efficiency of any given contract provision but also in predicting the long term viability of legal regulation of this field.

For economists, the mainspring of this type of analysis is the economic assumption that all individuals seek at all times to improve or maximise their own position. It is also assumed that such advancements are carried out in a rational – or informed and logical – manner. Hence, as a rational maximiser of personal satisfaction, an individual will choose from amongst those alternatives available, the course which in each circumstance extracts the most value.[3] A further assumption often applied by economists is that individuals are apprised of perfect information in relation to their interests in striking contractual bargains.[4] Individuals possessed of 'perfect information' are assumed to have knowledge about price, quality, competing products and the future.[5] This is, of course, only correct to the extent that information is available, is accurate and is able and likely to be (theoretically) factored into the reasoning process adopted. Knowledge in this context is therefore perfect to the extent that negative impediments do not obscure the process. Examples of the latter would include fraudulent representations or non-functioning marketplaces such as would be presented by a non-benign monopoly. Accordingly, parties that have access to the information they seek to evaluate their risks and who are sufficiently capable ('rational') of comprehending and applying the information are deemed to be operating in a market possessed of perfect information.[6]

In economic terms, such exchanges between knowledgeable rational maximisers are said to result in a Pareto superior outcome. In practice, this translates to an end result where at least one party perceives itself to be better off with no other party being, *de minimus*, worse off.[7] As it is assumed to be

3 Posner, 1977, p 3.

4 Cooter and Ulen, 1988, p 48.

5 Samuelson, 1992, p 28.

6 Standard supply and demand analysis have traditionally rested on the assumption that all buyers and sellers have perfect information about price, quality, competing products and the future. This assumption, however, has increasingly come under fire as failing to adequately address information imperfections, particularly as they apply to law. See Stigler (1961) 69 Journal of Political Economy 94; Arrow (ed), 1970; Akerlof (1970) 84 Quarterly Journal of Economics 488; Bishop, in Burrows and Veljanovski (eds), 1981 (arguing economic theorists' challenges to the presumption of perfect information 'are crucial to understanding the highly imperfect, implicit markets that constitute the subject matter of legal studies', p 170).

7 See, generally, Samuelson, 1992, p 28; Cooter and Ulen, 1988, p 48; Posner, 1977, p 3.

irrational for any individual to accept a deal that is contrary to his or her self-interest, what each party relinquishes in a bargain will be seen by that party to be of less value that that which is received. Voluntary negotiations, therefore, are presumed to achieve Pareto superior results because of the assumption of utility maximisation.[8] Put alternatively, voluntary negotiations produce efficient results.

Voluntary negotiations also produce efficient results for society as a whole. As Pareto superior outcomes result in parties to the transaction increasing their overall well being to some extent, by extension the cumulative welfare of society will similarly be enhanced through the movement of its resources to more highly valued uses. It is on this basis that contracts are deemed to be efficient and, according to proponents of law and economics, will be upheld not just by regulators but by society itself as efficient, and therefore desirable, law.

The intersection of common law precedent with principles of efficiency is born out by long standing prohibitions against certain categories of contracts. Specifically, contracts entered into by minors or legally incompetents are voidable at law as the participants are deemed to be insufficiently capable of comprehending and applying this information. Or, as Posner argues, such contracts are voidable 'because if someone cannot judge what is in his self-interest, there is no presumption that the contract he makes increases value'.[9] Similarly, contracts based on misrepresentations, fraud or duress are invalid because misinformation negates the premise that a party voluntarily entered into the deal.[10] In economic terms, this is appropriate in that a party misled about the utility to be derived from a proposed transaction cannot properly evaluate the true benefits of the deal. Hence, the assumption that the agreement will lead to a value increasing exchange is rebutted.

By parity of reasoning, in the context of this monograph, it will be subsequently argued that the same applies to the case where a party is virtually required by need to enter a contract; for example, insurance but where, by reason of its complexity and esoteric language, that party is without reasonable information as to the terms of the contract. Conversely, where the practical circumstances to which the contract relates are peculiarly within that party's knowledge, the same applies to the position of the other party in the absence of suitable information that would enable assessment of the value of the bargain.

The actual value of an exchange to its parties is comprised of the cumulative benefits and costs of the components that make up the deal.

8 Cooter and Ulen, 1988, p 49.

9 Posner, 1977, p 80.

10 At law, such contracts are 'voidable' – and are therefore enforceable only by the election of the party deemed to be incompetent. Knowledge on the part of both or either party, whether actual or constructive, is immaterial to enforcement of the contract as to do so would violate public policy interests.

Parties therefore can decide not only the value of a product or service overall, but also the value of individual contract clauses.[11] As most contract provisions serve to allocate any risks between the contracting parties, the value of a specific clause would be the known probability that an unfavourable outcome would occur multiplied by the magnitude of the loss that would be suffered if the risk materialised. How each party assesses this equation determines the price added to or subtracted from the overall contract and, consequently, the efficacy of the deal. Logically, in instances where the risk cannot be valued in such a way as to increase well being of each party, the contract would not come into being.[12]

In this context, the use of standard form contracts containing 'boiler plate language' which generally includes 'default' or 'gap filling' provisions can raise potential utility questions. Although fundamental economic principles lead to a conclusion that contracts entered into voluntarily tend to be efficient,[13] widespread industry use of standard form contracts attracts considerable criticism. Such criticism generally rests on two grounds: first, that inequity in – or elimination of – bargaining positions of consumers versus suppliers can create significant market imbalances; and, second, that the use of complex and extensive documents actually serves to hinder rather than enhance consumer access to information. Legislative intervention on the basis of free market principles in respect of either or both of the above carry significant implications for consumers and under economic theory would potentially provide the requisite grounds for judicial and legislative intervention to remedy market failure.

This said, it is incorrect to conclude that the use of standard form contracts in the insurance industry is in itself problematic. Indeed, economists contend the contrary.[14] Pre-settled clauses are efficient because they curtail negotiation

11 Schwartz and Wilde (1979) 127 University of Pennsylvania Law Review 630, p 668.

12 Polinsky, 1989, p 27. In the case of insurance, Polinsky notes that the price will be affected by the fact that parties seeking insurance are generally risk adverse – ie, by definition they are willing to pay substantial sums to avoid the uncertainty of loss.

13 Polinsky argues that fully specified contracts will be efficient. Polinsky, 1989, p 29; Posner, 1977, p 11. However, due to the myriad of conditions and contingencies inherent in even simple deals, no contract can be fully specified. Tullock, 1971, p 47.

14 As, under certain circumstances, does even the harshest judicial critic. Karl Llewellyn, who argued that standard form contracts often amounted to 'the exercise of unofficial government of some by others, via private law', also conceded that such contracts 'save trouble in bargaining. They save time in bargaining. They infinitely simplify the task of internal administration of a business unit, of keeping tabs on transactions, of knowing where one is at, of arranging orderly expectation, orderly fulfillment, orderly planning. They ease administration by concentrating the need for discretion and decision in such personnel as can be trusted to be discreet. This reduces human wear and tear, it cheapens administration, it serves the ultimate consumer. Standardising contracts is in this a counterpart of standardising goods and production processes, as well as a device for the adjustment of law to need'. Llewellyn (1939) 52 Harvard Law Review 700, p 701.

time involved in reaching a deal, remove uncertainties that might otherwise arise in unanticipated situations and, like terms of art, present a body of established precedent for clarification purposes.[15] Widely used standardised clauses can also minimise the transaction costs associated with educating consumers in that they can sometimes provide the insured with advance information of their contents through news of the experience of others; for example, public news that may surface that flood victims have found that their household policies did not cover flood damage. For an economist, therefore, standard form contracts, *per se*, serve a valuable function by minimising transaction costs otherwise inherent in reducing uncertainties.[16]

The loss of a party's ability to negotiate individual clauses in such contracts also does not in itself make a standard form contract unfair. To the extent that default rules approximate what the parties would otherwise have agreed upon had they negotiated the issue, the resultant deal would be deemed efficient.[17] This follows logically from the premise of parties as rational maximisers: such parties would be presumed to have negotiated efficient terms.[18] Inefficient default rules would be struck out as being cost inefficient to the bargain – higher transaction costs leading necessarily to lower profits.[19]

It has not escaped the notice of both economists and jurists however that this theoretical position does not always replicate itself in practice. The elimination of one party's bargaining strength has, it has been argued, led to market failure sufficient enough to justify regulatory intervention. In his seminal work on standard contracts in 1943, Kessler sets forth jurisprudential concerns in this respect by arguing that:

> Standard contracts are typically used by enterprises with strong bargaining power. The weaker party, in need of the goods or services, is frequently not in a position to shop around for better terms, either because the author of the standard form contract has a monopoly (natural or artificial) *or because all competitors use the same clauses* ... With the decline of the free enterprise system due to the innate trend of competitive capitalism towards monopoly, the meaning of contract has changed radically ... Standard contracts in particular could thus become effective instruments in the hands of powerful industrial

15 See, for example, Kronman and Posner, 1979, p 4; Polinsky, 1989, p 29 (arguing that the cost of negotiations leads parties to ignore relatively unimportant contingencies).

16 See, for example, Posner, 1977, p 11; Polinsky, 1989, p 29.

17 Polinsky, 1989, p 25; see also note 16. Polinsky characterises contract law generally as a method for filling in missing terms parties find too costly to negotiate themselves.

18 Kronman and Posner, 1979, p 6.

19 Coase (1960) 3 Journal of Law and Economics 1, p 8. Coase argues that given perfect information and zero transaction costs parties will achieve efficient results despite an inefficient rule of law, by one party paying the other a sum less that the cost of the inefficiency.

and commercial overlords enabling them to impose a new feudal order of their own making upon a vast host of vassals. (Emphasis added.)[20]

Although vassaldom has perhaps not extensively been wrought upon most insurance consumers, concerns raised over the use of similar clauses in a situation where consumers are unable in a practical sense[21] to negotiate or vary terms with suppliers are legitimate. This position is discussed further below[22] with empirical examples drawn from a range of standard form contracts; however, assuming this to be the case, such an impairment of free market function raises several economic concerns.

The lack of ability to negotiate does not in itself make a contract of adhesion unfair. The merits of such contracts necessarily go to the question of the positioning of the consumer in the market or, alternatively put, to the information available to the consumer. In instances where sufficient competition exists for the consumer to determine the subjective value of the product and it can be purchased through alternative sources (or not at all, if so desired), the presumption that resources will move towards their most valued use is preserved.

Genuine issues of market failure in the insurance industry therefore would seem to centre more on concerns that information supplied to parties is asymmetric as opposed to 'perfect'. In instances where consumers do not read standard form contracts, or do not understand the terms, thereby being effectively unaware of the contents, this premise is defeated. That the industry is aware that their potential consumers do not read the contracts and therefore draft prescribed contracts in this knowledge further undercuts the likelihood of values being maximised.

This is not to say that consumers are usually unaware of certain contract terms. They generally understand the central terms – such as price and the sum insured in the case of house or house contents insurance for example – but do not know or do not understand subordinate terms, particularly, it is surmisable, those which typical experience does not commonly reveal. For

20 Kessler (1943) 43 Columbia Law Review 629, pp 632–40.

21 Many standard form policies can be added to by extensions, sometimes overriding standard exclusions or conditions, at the cost of a higher premium. The problem is largely that the ordinary insured is uninformed of the gap or deficiency in his or her cover or, if it is revealed by enquiry, unwilling to pay the higher premium. Many consumers buy on the strength of the reputation of the insurer, much as most buyers of a new car when they have no technical knowledge. However the literature on insurance services is not as popular and widespread as that on cars. The partial solution may be an insurance information service provided by government, the industry or consumer groups to which consumers can turn to evaluate the respective responses to their needs. (See discussion below.)

22 See Section 6.2 below.

example, few average consumers are aware of average clauses.[23] Or, in the case of this discussion, the extent to which disclosure colours the likelihood of recovery.

The types of concerns outlined above that are raised by standard form contracts for complex products such as insurance has stimulated a significant body of literature. Economic theorists[24] have divided attributes of products or goods into three categories: (1) search qualities – those factors that are readily apparent to a consumer before purchase (such as size and colour); (2) experience qualities – those qualities readily discoverable after purchase with little time or cost involved (such as taste, effectiveness); and (3) credence qualities – those factors which are difficult to evaluate after normal use and are likely to require time and/or considerable expense to test. Products such as legal services are generally cited as illustrative of this last category in that the average consumer of legal advice is rarely well placed to assess its actual merits and/or is often unlikely to need to do so at the immediate time of purchase.

The range of standard form contracts in use reflects this spectrum. Search goods[25] would equate to those standard form contracts that, upon immediate examination are clear and self-encompassing. Experience goods would take in the more complex type of standard form contracts that while not immediately comprehensible on first perusal are readily understood through the experience of use. Trebilcock describes this category as encompassing contracts 'which are impenetrable to the layman, but where repeated use of the contract will quickly reveal the nature and consequence of the terms contained therein'.[26] Such contracts would include, for example, simple rental agreements or typical car hire documents. Credence goods, therefore, in this context extend to those contracts which contain terms or, which taken as a whole, are never totally understood by the buyer. Again, Trebilcock illustrates this category of contract by reference to 'some elements of an estate plan which come into force only after the party has died'.[27]

---

23 Average clauses provide that, if at the time of the loss the value of the subject matter of insurance exceeds the amount of cover, the insured is deemed to be his or her own insurer for the difference in value and must bear a rateable proportion of the loss accordingly. The Australian Law Reform Commission *Report on Insurance Contracts* (No 20, 1982), para 272, regarded average clauses as 'incomprehensible to most insureds, particularly those who take out houseowners'/householders' insurance'.

24 See, for example, Trebilcock and Dewees, in Burrows and Veljanovski (eds), 1981; Schwartz and Wilde (1979) 127 University of Pennsylvania Law Review 630; Darby and Karni (1973) 16 Journal of Law and Economics 67.

25 By definition, goods or products that have evolved out of the search qualities classification defined above: a search good is one with characteristics that can be identified upon examination.

26 Trebilcock and Dewees, in Burrows and Veljanovski (eds), 1981, p 108.

27 *Ibid*, p 109.

Consumer insurance contracts are in this last class and, like legal services, frequently form a category of goods the efficacy of which is often only called into effect if something subsequent to the transaction goes wrong. Even at that time the consumer is rarely in a position to assess their purchased product against what might otherwise have been available at the time. Interpretation of the efficacy of a given product, therefore, is not only polycentric but also generally costly (for example, the transaction costs of evaluating the position are high).

Classification of goods into these three categories traditionally arose out of economists' attempts to identify those types of goods most likely to lead to dishonest dealings in consumer transactions.[28] While fraud and deception are not in question in this context, aspects of standard form contracts raise analogies in that the assumption of perfect information is challenged by the fact that the insured is unlikely to determine the merits of contractual terms without incurring loss of considerable time or money. Some central contract terms could be classified as having search qualities because consumers can learn of them easily prior to purchase. The price and item being purchased are examples of this category. Many subordinate terms, however, are equivalent to credence terms, in that they will not be known to the typical consumer even after repeated purchases. Most often, these subordinate terms serve to shift risk away from the seller and on to the consumer.

Faced with this type of shift, most consumers of insurance contracts will inevitably fall into the uninformed basket. This is surmisable in part as the cost of acquiring the necessary information to understand subordinate terms will exceed the expected gains to the consumer from that information.[29] Moreover, the reading of complicated forms in detail denies the principal virtue of standard form contracts – reduced transaction costs.[30]

This, however, ignores a potentially more fundamental obstacle: consumers are unlikely to be able to work out what the given clauses are likely to mean for their own situation. The problem is not understanding what particular clauses mean in the sense of how they allocate risk but rather

28 Darby and Karni (1973) 16 Journal of Law and Economics 67, pp 68–69.

29 Schwartz and Wilde (1979) 127 University of Pennsylvania Law Review 630, p 643.

30 The first cost of acquiring such information is that of the amount of time required in reading the document. As consumers are subject daily to significant numbers of these contracts, the amount of time overall to function effectively would be substantial. While this does not pertain directly, *per se*, to the insurance form contract, the general anaesthetisation this barrage of material has is likely to reduce substantially the extent of concern the average consumer may otherwise have had about simply signing a form. See, for example, Murray (1982) 67 Cornell Law Review 735, p 740 ('the pain and suffering of attempting to read and understand every printed form would be greater than the pain suffered as a result of occasionally being bound by unread and uncomprehended printed terms').

recognising how this information applies to their own situation. As Trebilcock observes:

> In the case of an insurance policy which allocates risks in different ways between a consumer and his insurance company, he may understand perfectly how the policy allocates those risks, but what he may have difficulty assessing is how likely it is that certain risks may materialise and, if they do, what kinds of costs are likely to be entailed. Thus, how likely is it, as a matter of probability, that his house will catch on fire, and if it does how much damage is likely to be done? If there are exemptions for earthquakes, Acts of God, fires caused in certain ways, certain classes of property, etc, his problem lies in assessing whether his personal circumstances at any given time during the currency of the policy will fall within one of those clauses and what costs will be entailed for him if they do.[31]

Some sellers, moreover, may even attempt to increase this cost through the use of fine print or obscure (or disjointed) placement.[32] Indeed, legalese and Latin have long been suspected to serve this hallowed function – as noted wryly by Lord Bridge of Harwich when he observed in relation to a Lloyd's policy that 'the only people who can expect to profit from the obscurities of the present form ... are the lawyers'.[33] Such concerns for consumer well being have not gone unaddressed by precedent and legislative intervention in many jurisdictions. Lord Denning's famous caveat in *Thornton v Shoe Lane Parking* that an abnormally egregious clause *might* be validly incorporated into contracts of adhesion *if* notice requirements were sufficiently satisfied by a clause 'printed in red ink on the face of a document with a red hand pointing to it ...' has not only been underscored in this respect by the Court of Appeal's decision in *Interfoto Picture Library v Stiletto Visual Programs Ltd*,[34] but has been echoed in the UK through provisions in its Unfair Terms in Consumer Contracts Regulations 1999.[35] Similarly, most US States have not only a parallel matrix of 'plain English' and good faith requirement provisions but have, in a minority of jurisdictions, judicially recognised the consumer oriented doctrine of reasonable expectations.[36] However, even in so called 'plain English' contracts, it is apparent that considerable cost would be incurred by any average consumer intent on understanding the actual legal application of individual subordinate clauses.

Conversely, the bulk use of these types of contracts ensures that it is cost-effective for an insurer regularly using these documents to employ legal

31 Trebilcock and Dewees, in Burrows and Veljanovski (eds), 1981, p 115.

32 Posner, 1977, pp 85–86.

33 See *Forsikringsaktieselskapet Vesta v Butcher* [1989] 1 Lloyd's Rep 331, at 341.

34 [1989] 1 QB 433.

35 Sections 5, 6 and 7 of this Act.

36 See Chapter 5.2.4 for further discussion of this point.

expertise in their formation.[37] The aggregate value to the business of the potential profit from each individual transaction justifies the initial expense.[38] Moreover, not only will the benefit likely to accrue to the seller from correctly understanding a specific contract clause be far greater but, through economies of scale, its costs in ascertaining any subsequent information will be far less.[39] Given that the costs of drafting the clauses have already been expended, the marginal cost to the insurer of this additional information is small. By contrast, the marginal cost to the insured of obtaining the same information would be considerable. By implication, therefore, only the seller will typically have the necessary legal knowledge to evaluate such contracts fully, or, at least with the same efficiency.

The transaction costs to a potential purchaser of understanding individual subordinate clauses are further increased by the adhesion nature of an insurance contract. As discussed earlier, standard form contracts are used to save transaction costs; their fundamental characteristic therefore is that they are offered on a 'take it or leave it basis'.[40] A consumer armed with an understanding of an individual clause who then wishes to find an alternative will be forced to go through similar processes in relation to the provisions offered by rival companies. That the vast preponderance of competitors in the insurance market offer similar provisions also on a non-negotiable basis[41] adds further discounting to the value of this knowledge to a consumer.[42] The real risks are significant as material difference to one or more subordinate clauses can have a major impact upon the nature and extent of cover and consequently the risk that the insurer accepts. For example, a contents policy currently on the Australian market – a policy which makes up a significant

37 In a somewhat wry, albeit lyrical, summation of the relative advantage large firms that make extensive use of custom drafted standard form contracts possess in relation to cost efficient legal advice, Karl Llewellyn concludes: 'the great bargainor, defeated once and again, recurs to the attack. After each case he can redraft and fight again. A single victory, if achieved, has good chance of being permanent.' Llewellyn (1931) 40 Yale Law Journal 704, pp 732–34.

38 Seita (1984) 46 University of Pittsburg Law Review 75, p 135.

39 *Ibid*, p 138. An extension of this argument explains the somewhat perplexing practice insurers have of litigating seemingly small disputes. Cost-effectiveness is more readily explainable in this context where the sunken costs of developing the clause are combined with the potential costs likely to arise through the administration and payout of widespread challenges to the provision. Whereas the payout of small claims in the context of a few contracts may appear sensible compared with the costs of extended litigation, the clarification of a given point is likely in the long term to substantially curtail or even eliminate subsequent questions arising in other contracts.

40 This statement is subject to the exception of extensions asked for and paid for. Special policies will also be written to cover required contingencies, but at a price.

41 It is assumed that the rational seller is unlikely to forego the savings inherent in the use of their standard contract form by agreeing to an individual waiver for a specific customer unless the value of that individual deal is sufficient to exceed the loss expended in transaction time and precedent.

42 See below.

percentage of market sales in this area[43] – offers similar price/coverage clauses as well as a number of seemingly similar subordinate clauses to competitors. Part of the way through p 34 of the document, however, the (very) informed reader might be surprised to encounter an average clause. Presumably consumers of this product might have justified higher transaction costs in information and comparison shopping if they had been aware of this provision.

This latter case, however, may arguably be one of the exceptions that proves the rule. Generally, the benefit from acquiring adequate knowledge of contract terms is usually low and is likely to be far exceeded by the significant costs of acquiring that information. It is therefore rational for even a conscientious consumer to pay little attention to subordinate contract terms.

One constraint generally on the complexities subordinate clauses can introduce is that imposed by what numerous theorists have dubbed 'the marginal consumer'.[44] This elusive character is credited in economic literature with providing essentially the ballast that keeps standard form contract transactions on an even keel despite the propensity for the preponderance of consumers not to read the actual document. As Trebilcock and Dewees argue:

> … even where a consumer has not read or understood the terms of a standard form contract, it will not necessarily follow that a supplier is an unconstrained term-setter. One of the most important determinants of whether contract terms in such circumstances might be considered fair, in the sense of having been effectively disciplined by market forces, is the role of the marginal consumer … With respect to the determination of the initial terms of a contract, the issue will be whether, at the margin of the market, there are enough consumers who are sensitive to the content of these terms to bring effective pressure to bear on suppliers, eg, by threatening to switch business, to modify then in an acceptable way. Thus, it is conceivable that if only 10% of the buyers of a particular class of goods or services studied all terms scrupulously before contracting and were influenced in their choices of contractual offerings by their evaluation of the so called fine print clauses, this might create effective competitive pressures on each supplier in the relevant market to adjust the terms of all his contracts so as to minimise the risk of losing the potential business.

The vast preponderance of uninformed consumers therefore may be protected by the competition of sellers for the marginal buyers who are informed and

43 *Choice Magazine* November 1998, p 24; NRMA Home Contents Insurance Policy (Edition 10 NRMA NSW & ACT, Edition 3 Qld P100707 8/99).

44 Schwartz and Wilde (1979) 127 University of Pennsylvania Law Review 630; Priest (1981) 90 Yale Law Journal 1267, pp 1304–06 (manufacturers may be forced to respond to the demands of a small number of informed consumers despite the general ignorance of all contract terms held by the vast majority of consumers); Beales, Craswell and Salop (1981) 24 Journal of Law and Economics 491, p 503; Trebilcock and Dewees, in Burrows and Veljanovski (eds), 1981, p 105.

base their purchase decisions on this information. For consumers of standard form insurance contracts, however, this safeguard is minimised by its seeming inapplicability to subordinate contract terms.[45] Priest argues that while some consumers may research to find the best price and quality of products thereby passing on a 'pecuniary externality' to the uninformed, the far greater transaction costs inherent in searching for, reading, understanding and finally comparing the aggregate value of different sets of insurance contract terms will outweigh any benefit of doing so.[46] Accordingly, faced with rapidly rising information costs and equally diminishing returns, it is unlikely that a pool of marginal consumers would materialise sufficient to provide the counterweight necessary to produce a competitive market for contract terms.

It is theoretically arguable that contracts containing such one sided clauses will, through competition, be forced out of the market. Consumer dissatisfaction with the inefficiency such inequities render will stimulate rival companies (or provide sufficient incentive for new competitors to enter the market) to offer better-balanced terms. This argument, however, ignores two fundamental realities. First, consumers must be sufficiently informed in respect of these 'preferred' terms to be able to make this determination and hence influence demand.[47] As argued above, however, subordinate clauses that constitute credence provisions generally do not provide consumers with the requisite familiarity and/or understanding to stimulate sufficient consumer concern. Regardless of competitive offerings, therefore, consumers cannot express a preference for subordinate terms they do not understand. Further, as competitors attempting to offer more 'efficient' variants would necessarily have to do so at the cost of increasing the overall price of the contract it is likely that this higher price would result in an overall decrease in demand and profit. In consequence, Schwartz and Wilde argue that contrary to the pattern that would emerge in relation to search and experience goods, the existence of consumer ignorance in relation to this type of information actually forces suppliers to offer products of lower quality than would otherwise be the case.[48]

45 Schwartz and Wilde (1979) 127 University of Pennsylvania Law Review 630.

46 Priest (1981) 90 Yale Law Journal 1267, pp 1346–47; Schwartz and Wilde (1979) 127 University of Pennsylvania Law Review 630, p 643 (the efficient search strategy will continue until the marginal cost of further searching exceeds the marginal gain – so the efficient search stops when the cost of the next step in the search process exceeds a sum that is the product of the likelihood that the next step will reveal a better price, multiplied by the amount of savings).

47 Indeed, experience would tend to indicate that the greatest downfall of such clauses seems to arise more in the wake of disasters (such as floods) where consumers' poor experiences with given policy provisions are sufficiently dramatic to merit negative news coverage (or some other equally widespread form of word of mouth).

48 Schwartz and Wilde (1979) 127 University of Pennsylvania Law Review 630, pp 376–78.

Secondly, it is unlikely that competitors would choose to remedy this through an 'educational' advertising campaign. Unlike readily graspable provisions such as price and quantity of cover, the elucidation of the contents of many subordinate clauses is not a straightforward exercise. For the average consumer, the explanation of an average clause would require substantially more time than the 30 and 60 second television spots (or the five panel brochures) employed for advertising. Accordingly, the preponderance of advertisers focus on positive qualities associated with their product.[49] To attempt more would necessarily give rise to substantial transaction costs associated with educating consumers as to the legal implications of such subordinate clauses. This potentially creates a free rider problem, in that the costs of educating the public while carried by one firm is likely to have spin off benefits to competitors.[50] Additionally, the relative wisdom of publicising such negative provisions (for example, 'we won't bury this *particular* nasty clause that reduces your overall cover by half in our multi-page contracts') has the potential for generating more alarm than assurance in the average target consumer. By alerting consumers to hidden negative risks of which they were previously unaware, insurers run the risk of creating an overall disincentive to purchase the product, or at least of heightening cynicism towards the safety of making such complex purchases. Finally, as one set of economists have pragmatically pointed out, there is a market reluctance on the part of competitors to publicise the disadvantages associated with the products of their competitors for fear of retaliation.[51]

Thus, consumers signing standard form contracts will generally not know the value of the contract terms either before or after purchase. Normal competitive pressures will neither force the disclosure of these terms nor create the externality of informed consumers protecting the uninformed majority. So, although the classic contract paradigm provides that voluntary negotiations between knowledgeable and rational consumers produce efficient contracts, the presupposition that perfect information exists for consumers of heterogenous products such as complex standard form insurance contracts potentially undercuts the assumption of an efficient market in operation.

49 Such is the extent of this 'positiveness' thrust that Jordan and Rubin contend that it is taken to extremes in that '[m]uch advertising is patently uninformative; rational consumers should not care what sort of breakfast cereal is eaten by famous baseball players, nor should they expect any relationship between the cleanliness of their clothes and the catchiness of the tune used to advertise a wash powder' (1978) 8 Journal of Legal Studies 527, pp 528–29. A cursory scan of current commercial insurance advertising in Australia would immediately bring to light consumer choices between friendly attractive young women embodied as 'AAMI'; sporting figures playing against the backdrop of insurers' logos and humorous accident scenarios leading to reassuring messages about either price or friendliness of service.

50 Posner, 1977; Beales, Craswell and Salop (1981) 24 Journal of Law and Economics 491.

51 Green and Moore (1973) 82 Yale Law Journal 903, p 907.

2.3 ECONOMIC INFORMATION AND THE INSURER

Asymmetric information problems are not limited to consumers of insurance. Obtaining information about prospective insureds has traditionally been of even greater significance to insurers for whom adequate information underpins accurate risk assessment and product pricing. As profits depend upon the success with which initial risk probabilities of any given transaction are forecast – in that risk portfolios are necessarily a cumulative compilation of individual deals – defining optimal rate classes as accurately as possible is the key objective of industry members.[52] Accordingly, having access to accurate data about the nature of a risk to be undertaken is the cornerstone on which the industry is built. It is also the unifying force behind the evolution of the insurance industry's legal regulatory structure.

Despite misperceptions that insurance is simply a blue-chip form of gambling,[53] its reliance on actuarial forecasting is such that 'luck', *per se*, is of marginalised significance. One set of commentators leave little in doubt in this respect in noting that:

> [T]here is a common belief among non-specialists that insurers must be risk-seeking, as though they must stand in a mirror-like relationship to their risk adverse insurees. This view is incorrect. Insurance companies are presumed to be profit-maximising firms. They offer insurance contracts not because they prefer gambles to certainties but because of a mathematical theorem known as the law of large numbers. This law holds that what may seem random, unpredictable, and undependable to the individual becomes deterministic and predictable among large groups of individuals.[54]

Logically then, if an insured's individual risk of loss can be predicted, and that individual aggregated into an appropriate larger pool, the insurance premium can be tailored to reflect the likelihood of future payouts. The greater the extent to which an insurer can cost-effectively segregate and pool applicants according to the level of risk they present the more advantageous its end result is likely to prove. Apart from the economic benefit to the insurer, there is the benefit to the low risk insured to whom cover can be offered at a cheaper rate.

In the context of insurance risk covered by standard form contracts, predicting risk presented by each applicant for purposes of calculating individual premiums is generally cost-prohibitive or, at least, relatively expensive.[55] As a result, insurers relegate individuals to appropriate insurance classes where viable or, in some cases, into one single risk pool.[56] The premium charged to each member of the class would then reflect the average

52 Cooter and Ulen, 1988, p 65.

53 See, for example, Merkin (1980) 9 Anglo-American Law Review 331.

54 Cooter and Ulen, 1988, p 65.

55 Priest (1981) 90 Yale Law Journal 1297, p 1314.

56 Cooter and Ulen, 1988, p 65; Priest (1981) 90 Yale Law Journal 1297, p 1314.

level of risk of that class with the aggregate premium charged usually being roughly equal to the expected monetary value of the loss.[57] Some high risk individuals will therefore escape with a lower premium while relatively low risk individuals will be overcharged. At the margin, depending on the overall price, some low risk individuals may determine the purchase of a policy to be cost inefficient. Rather than acquire outside insurance, such individuals may prefer instead to shift to allocative investments that reduce the probability of the loss or may opt for self-insurance.[58]

The more accurate an insurer is in constructing classes of insured who present similar risk profiles, the smaller the gap will be between the premium and the value of insurance to the lower risk members of the pool.[59] The smaller this discrepancy therefore the smaller the rate of attrition of such members towards alternative measures of self-protection and, logically, the increased rate of sales likely to be achieved by the insurer.[60]

Appropriate classification however presupposes that insurers have sufficient information about applicants to develop an adequate risk profile. As will be discussed subsequently, the insurance industry has developed a number of ways of handling this demand ranging from incorporating a variety of questions into proposal forms through to structuring policies so as to enable consumer 'signalling' of their relative risk positioning.[61] Backing up

57 Cooter and Ulen, 1988, p 65; Gravelle (1991) 11 International Review of Law and Economics 23. Alternately put, the aggregate premium collected is calculated to be greater than the average loss while not being so excessive as to deter low risk insureds.

58 Cooter and Ulen, 1988, pp 66–67.

59 Gravelle (1991) 11 International Review of Law and Economics 23.

60 Cooter and Ulen, 1988, p 65.

61 Economic theorists hold that the relative merit of a product (in this case the insured) can be interpreted without extensive research costs based on the confidence a producer manifests in it as attested to by its willingness to carry the risk of repair/replacement (usually in the form of express or implied warranties). For further discussion, see below ('signalling'). Arising originally out of studies in consumer product warranties, signal theory rests on the premise that consumers can obtain data cost-effectively about products with which they are otherwise unfamiliar by looking to the nature of the warranty coverage offered. In situations where the costs of obtaining such information would otherwise to be too high to be efficient the extent to which manufacturers choose to backup their products can provide a short cut 'signal' as to their confidence in its quality. Because reliability is correlated negatively with the costs of warranty coverage, the longer the warranty, the lower the costs of warranty coverage for the manufacturer, and the more extensive the coverage to the consumer. Translated, this theory potentially enables insurers to infer information as to the likely level of risk unknown individuals present based on their choices in such particulars as policy options. 'Signals' such as the level of deductibles, the extent of coverage sought, and the willingness of would-be insureds to forego extra variables amongst other factors would be considered useful indicia of risk. Under this approach to obtaining information, insurers are relying on insureds to affirmatively volunteer key information about themselves by recognising through the pricing structure that class of risk best able to maximise their own welfare. See: Akerlof (1970) 84 Quarterly Law Journal of Economics 488, pp 488–500; Priest (1981) 90 Yale Law Journal 1297; Rothschild and Stiglitz (1976) 90 Quarterly Journal of Economics 629, pp 629–49; Schwartz and Wilde (1983) 69 Virginia Law Review 1387.

these search mechanisms is a fiduciary, or utmost good faith, duty of disclosure between insurer and insured which has accompanied the evolution of the insurance industry since its formation. Requiring a uniquely high information exchange between the parties, the doctrine of utmost good faith attempts to add, from an economic perspective, the necessary carrot (or stick, depending upon its use) to ensure that all information able to be identified by the parties as relevant to the transaction is brought to the table in as cost-efficient a manner as possible. The doctrine therefore has historically acted as an incentive to ensure that both 'good news' and 'bad news' variables are available for risk forecasting purposes.

For the most part such requirements weigh most heavily on a would-be insured on the basis that he or she is the better placed of the parties to know the good and bad factors attached to the risk against which insurance is being sought. For low risk candidates, the strength of this disclosure standard is relatively superfluous: like sellers anxious to pass on 'good news' about a product, in this case themselves or their possessions, low risk applicants already possess sufficient economic incentive, in the form of possible premium discounts, to volunteer such information. High risk candidates, however, pose greater difficulties in that disclosure of negative information is likely to result in higher premiums. Faced with negative incentive therefore these types of insureds are more analogous to sellers of homes with termites: they are happy to present general information but will be reluctant to provide (let alone volunteer) details of detrimental factors. It is in this latter context that the original merchants-cum-insurers of Lloyd's coffee house chose to shift the locus of risk[62] that would otherwise have been called for in consumer-seller relations by a *laissez-faire* market.[63]

For purposes of constructing efficient risk pools, failure to obtain sufficient information to identify accurately high risk consumers remains one of the principal problems of the insurance industry. Insurers that fall short in this respect and construct a risk pool top heavy in high risk insureds face the financial loss problems likely to be engendered by adverse selection. Adverse

62 See discussion below.

63 For roughly contemporaneous statements of this position, see, for example, the seminal case *Laidlaw v Organ* 15 US (2 Wheat) 167–88 in which the US Supreme Court, in being asked to consider a buyer's duty to disclose pre-knowledge of the end of the War of 1812 quotes Pothier (*Traite du Contract de Vente*):

> [The greater part of the writers on natural law] are of opinion, that the good faith which ought to govern the contract of sale, only requires that the vendor should represent the thing sold as it is, without dissimulating its defects, and not to sell it above the price which it bears at the time of the contract; that he commits no injustice in selling it at this price, although he knows that the price must soon fall; that he is not obliged to disclose to the vendee a knowledge which he may have of the circumstances that may produce a depression of the price; the vendee having no more right to demand that the vendor should impart this knowledge than that he should give away his property … (pp 187–88).

selection, in an economic context, is effectively a by-product of the high information cost insurers face in accurately distinguishing between high and low risk insureds for purposes of constructing optimal pools. As risk pool premiums are calculated on the average probability of loss, the overall result, if incorrectly gauged, can lead to a skewing of a pool's risk ratio. Where the imbalance between low and high risk insureds is such that low risk insureds, as noted above, opt instead to seek alternative means of self-protection[64] the possible implication is that only those most likely to have a loss seek insurance. Theoretically, if the problem is great enough, markets may emerge[65] in which insurance is not available because the cost to an insured company of distinguishing between good and bad risks is too high to justify the product.[66] Taken to the extreme, adverse selection can result eventually in 'the unravelling of the insurance market itself',[67] as the loss of short run profits leads to premium increases that stimulate ongoing attrition of the lowest risk members of the pool.

In recognition of the potentially mortal impact inadequate information has traditionally posed to the insurance industry's vitality, and because certain information may be peculiarly within the insured's knowledge and difficult to elicit the common law has, as noted below,[68] responded by respecting the industry's position; namely, that the risk and consequences attendant upon non-disclosure should fall upon the insured or consumer. As contrasted with other categories of commercial sales contracts therefore contracts of insurance historically bestow higher standards of information disclosure on its parties. Entrenched in legal precedent and codified in various statutory provisions as *uberrimae fidei*, the doctrine of utmost good faith requires parties not only to answer all queries put to them truthfully but further parties are compelled to volunteer all information that might be relevant to the other party's decision making process in entering into a contract. This is distinct from the lesser requirement that only that information given in response to questions posed be truthful – thereby respecting the rights of parties not to disclose information as supported by the doctrine of *caveat emptor*.[69] In practice, the result is that the party best placed to provide the information pertinent to the

---

64 See, for example, Cooter and Ulen, 1988, pp 66–67; Gravelle (1991) 11 International Review of Law and Economics 23; Rhea (1993) 13 International Review of Law and Economics 145, p 153.

65 Flood and earthquake insurance in areas prone to these natural disasters historically have constituted such examples. See, for example, New Zealand's *Earthquake and War Damage Regulations* 1984 SR 1984/71 (extending cover also for damage caused by volcanic eruption, hydro-thermal activity, and landslip).

66 Cooter and Ulen, 1988, p 67.

67 Gravelle (1991) 11 International Review of Law and Economics 23, pp 24–25.

68 See detailed discussion in Chapter 3.

69 Let the buyer beware. This maxim summarises the rule that purchasers must examine, judge and test for themselves: *Black's Law Dictionary*, 1979, p 202.

transaction legally carries the risk of its non-disclosure, thereby ensuring that transaction costs of getting information into the public domain are minimised.

In his seminal text on insurance law, Edwin Patterson offers the following differentiation of the unique pedigree of this rule:

> The doctrine of [disclosure] in relation to insurance contracts is, and long has been, an exceptional rule. In commercial contracts, and in others between persons dealing at arm's length, A, one party, is not required to volunteer, at the time of negotiating the contract, disclosure to the other, B, of A's knowledge of fact X, which he knows that B does not know and which A knows B would deem material to the making of the contract. For example, if A offers to sell B a large quantity of coffee beans, knowing, as B does not, that the report of a prospective coffee crop failure in Brazil was false, B, contracting to buy in ignorance of this fact, cannot avoid the contract on the grounds of A's silence. The policy supporting this rule is based on the economic function of 'the market', as a process whereby the best informed traders provide a medium for the selling and buying of property at the 'best' prices obtainable, and for this public service they are rewarded by being allowed to profit by their special knowledge. The bargaining processes on a 'free market' would become tedious and unstable if each bargainer had to tell the other all his reasons for the price he asks or bids.[70]

Tedious or otherwise, such is the position traditionally required of both parties to insurance contracts, although in practice it is usually only the insured against whom charges of non-disclosure are levied.[71] The free market general objective of encouraging entrepreneurial information gathering is therefore, in the case of insurance, held for the reasons described to be subordinate to the market specific objective of providing insurers with adequate recourse to full background information about the risks they may choose to insure.

Historically, the fiduciary standard of insurance law can be argued to owe much to the unique circumstances surrounding its 16th century maritime origins.[72] Aside from being the stuff of which great legal mythology is made, the existence of Edward Lloyd's Lombard Street coffee house served as a critical catalyst in launching the nascent English insurance market and in influencing the shape of its initial and subsequent legal regulatory infrastructure.[73] In its original form, Lloyd's operated as the clearing house for all maritime information and rumour. The locality of the shop made it the

70 Patterson, 1957, pp 446–47.

71 See Chapter 3 for detailed discussion.

72 (The Hon Justice) Kirby (1995) 13 Australian Bar Review 1, pp 9–10 ('... the nature of the insurance contract having remained basically the same throughout the ages, perpetuating the need for substantial disclosure').

73 See, generally, Clayton, 1971; Holdsworth, Vol 8, pp 273–98; Tarr and Kennedy, 1992, pp 2–3; Kirby (1995) 13 Australian Bar Review 1, p 9.

natural gathering place for seagoing venturers and shipowners. Recognising the value of this particular niche, Lloyd further cultivated the coffee shop's positioning as the hub of information through such promotions as holding vessel and cargo auctions on site and establishing a newspaper called *Lloyd's News* that carried information on foreign events, relevant parliamentary proceedings and shipping intelligence.[74] It was in this hub of activity that information and rumour about sailing conditions, ports, locations of pirates and other hazards endemic to marine venturing were exchanged. In short, Mr Lloyd's business acumen was such that his shop became the resource base for most 17th century risk assessment.[75]

Maritime insurance contracts written on the Lloyd's premises were done on an underwriting basis – the term 'underwriting' itself being literally the physical act that created the contract.[76] Accordingly, a merchant wishing to ensure a particular subject matter would pass a document around to fellow merchants detailing the nature of the voyage, the vessel and the cargo. The decision to accept that risk, and for what price, then rested upon the participant underwriters' evaluation of the chance of loss having regard to the details of the voyage provided to them.[77]

Proper assessment of such 'contingent chance' necessitated the comprehensive disclosure of all factors material to the risk.[78] The need to provide full information for this calculation was necessary in part because the knowledge of factors pertaining to the risk rested almost entirely with the person seeking the insurance (and those who sailed the designated routes). It was further strengthened by the fact that a loss incurred usually translated as a ship sunk at the bottom of an ocean in a remote location. The transaction costs inherent in following up on causation of loss or, indeed, even verifying the condition of a ship located in a remote port, were generally (if not technologically) cost-prohibitive. The imbalance in transaction costs associated

74 *Ibid*.

75 If anecdote is to be believed, Mr Lloyd himself refrained from participating in the underwriting world, keeping instead to the task of supplying those related to marine ventures with coffee and essential information.

76 The term 'underwriting' refers to the fact that signatures were affixed by merchants willing to take on the risk, or a percentage of it, specified in what was effectively the prospectus detailing the venture at risk. Once signed by initialling, the slip would then be passed on to the next merchant until such time as the full complement of risk was covered. The contract was then complete.

77 See, generally, Clayton, 1971; (Mr Justice) Derrington (1994) 7 Corporate and Business Law Journal 1.

78 See, for example, Lord Mansfield in *Carter v Boehm* arguing: 'Insurance is a contract based upon speculation. The special facts upon which the contingent chance is to be computed lie most commonly in the knowledge of the insured only: the underwriting merchants trusts to the representations, and proceeds upon the confidence that he does not keep back any circumstances in his knowledge, to mislead the underwriter into a belief that the circumstance does not exist, and to induce him to estimate the risque, as if it did not exist.' (1766) 3 Burr 1905 [97 ER 1162].

with being able to produce this information was therefore extreme as between the insured and the insurer, sufficiently so that both the parties to the transaction and its legal regulators accepted that a legal obligation to disclose information and 'to put one's cards on the table' was justified.

The reality of the underwriters' dependence upon the veracity of the insureds' risk declarations was recognised in the contractual provisions in early maritime insurance contracts. The law clearly stood behind the insurers' right to access all possible information either actually possessed by the insured or of which the insured could have been expected to have knowledge.[79] As the provisions of the original Lloyd's contract became a model for all subsequent insurance contracts – and statutory law – until as late as the middle of the 20th century, this approach to information disclosure between parties became entrenched in the Anglo-Australian insurance context.[80]

The passage of time, however, has brought with it dramatic changes to the way this industry now conducts business. In this respect, Mr Justice Kirby comments:

> In the time which has passed since Mr Edward Lloyd provided his customers with fragrant coffee, many things have changed. The relative bargaining position of marine underwriters and assureds has changed. In those early days it lay almost solely with the insured. The purpose of the rule was to rectify that imbalance. Today, prudent underwriters have largely redressed the information imbalance. The law has moved a great distance from the values that it embraced in the 18th and 19th centuries. The perceptions of contemporary society concerning conduct appropriate to a bargain have also changed since the infant days of marine insurance.

Contemporary insurers seeking to identify the level of risk exposure a prospective insured will bring to a pool have also advanced well beyond their Elizabethan counterparts in actuarial forecasting. The advent of sophisticated communication and computerisation systems has removed much of the advantage Lloyd's seafarers held over their underwriters in the knowledge stakes. Technological change has similarly added new dimensions to how insurers go about establishing the risk profile of would-be applicants.

79 An insured was required, by both Lloyd's provisions and the subsequent force of common law, to disclose not only all facts relating to the ships/cargo/venture that *they thought* likely to be influential to underwriters in taking on the risk (and if so, on what terms) but also to disclose all other possible factors, events and rumours surrounding the venture that the *insurer might* have wished to consider. Further, disclosure was not limited to matters the insured knew but also to matters insured ought to have known. See Tarr and Kennedy, 1992, pp 62–63.

80 The Marine Insurance Act 1909 (Australia) is, in substance, identical to the Marine Insurance Act 1906 (UK) which represented a 'partial codification of the common law' and incorporates almost in its entirety the original Lloyd's printed Policy of 1779 as the statutory form.

Actuarial forecasting has evolved over the last three centuries in ways that would have been unheralded to early underwriters.[81] Methods of selling and buying consumer insurance[82] bear as little correlation to the physical underwriting process of contract formation at the coffee shop as does contemporary loss investigation processes to those of its Elizabethan predecessors.[83] In short, the original dynamics that necessitated full disclosure by a would-be insured for the purpose of minimising transaction costs in risk assessment have therefore been radically altered.

Nevertheless, the acquisition of information in the most cost-effective manner has remained a constant of the industry with the utmost good faith standard underpinning its operation. Faced with negative incentives to disclose information, most applicants still remain unlikely to disclose this data freely in the absence of obligations to make such disclosure. Insurers offering cover therefore have chosen to protect themselves in this respect through the introduction of several mechanisms for ensuring that disclosure of critical information is affirmatively requested. Contemporary insurers are generally reliant upon a three fold approach to obtaining adequate disclosure. The first approach is that of building into the proposal inquiry/testing requirements; the second, a variant on signalling theory, goes to the structuring of the pricing and inclusions/exclusions offered in the policy; and the third – remains – the penumbra of utmost good faith disclosure.

Affirmative questioning and, in some cases, testing requirements are familiar provisions to consumers completing proposal forms. In addition to name, age and generic identity questions, insurers commonly solicit information pertaining to: the exact nature and extent of risk being applied for; an insured's past risk experience including prior losses and claims; and specific history in regard to other insurers, including, for example, if (and why) cover has been denied from alternative sources.[84] Complete and accurate responses to all questions are generally prerequisites to the completion of the contract. False or misleading statements made in this document give rise to actions based on misrepresentation or fraud and create a right of termination for the insurer, and avoidance of payment of claims (subject to legislative controls discussed below).

81 See, for example, Bernstein, 1997.

82 See below for further discussion.

83 Compare the position of a 17th century London underwriter who is advised that an insured vessel has sunk in the Bass Strait. His modern day counterpart can commission an agent in Sydney to investigate and to report immediately. Submersibles are utilised commonly to investigate 'suspect' losses, data on the financial performance of shipowners is readily available, the history of their vessels, and so forth.

84 These are areas of enquiry which, though coarse and insufficient to catch all material information, provide the best indications of the risk that might be obtained within the confines of the proposal.

Soliciting information in this manner carries with it transaction costs associated both with the development of the form and with clarifying any potential ambiguities in interpretation that may arise when completed.[85] As noted earlier, however, once written the use of a standard form contract creates economies of scale which lessen subsequent transaction costs on both the negotiation and interpretation fronts.[86] Well developed questions in the standard proposal can also help to minimise transaction costs by red-flagging unnecessarily high risk parties. As the vast number of these forms are administered and reviewed initially by agents for the company who potentially lack sufficient background for genuine risk assessment, these types of questions (and answers) can provide clear cut grounds for rejection, thereby minimising the use of discretion at this lower end and curtailing subsequently processing and consideration time that would otherwise be consumed.

Even in respect of the majority of forms that do not set off alarms,[87] well structured questions can make for more efficient consideration of proposals as they go through the bureaucratic infrastructure that characterises most large insurers. This is of particular relevance in that the nature of the industry is such that it is assumed a significant percentage of insureds will not make a claim during the life of the policy. With the exception of identifying unduly high risk candidates at the outset, it is logical that the most cost-effective approach to considering proposal forms is to reserve in depth analysis for such time as a claim is made. To waste administration time excessively at the front end of the contract is financially inefficient overall.

Moreover, given that the actuarial forecasting for a given risk pool is well cast, it is misplaced to assume that all forms containing misleading or fraudulent answers will necessarily incur a claim. As noted earlier, because the inclusion of such responses gives rise to a right of termination and/or avoidance of a claim on the part of the insurer it is inefficient for the insurer to consider acting on the inclusion of such responses until such time as a claim is

85 The fact that this information is pursued extensively reinforces the view that economically such information acquisition costs are justified by the resultant savings on the risks accepted and the respective premiums charged.

86 See above and see also Seita (1984) 46 University of Pittsburg Law Review 75, p 138. An extension of this argument explains the somewhat perplexing practice insurers have of litigating seemingly small disputes. Cost-effectiveness is more readily explainable in this context where the sunken costs of developing the clause are combined with the potential costs likely to arise through the administration and payout of widespread challenges to the provision. Whereas the payout of small claims in the context of a few contracts may appear sensible compared with the costs of extended litigation, the clarification of a given point is likely in the long term to substantially curtail or even eliminate subsequent questions arising in other contracts. This can be further exasperated if the questions posed can be interpreted ambiguously by respondents. Clarifying the relative rights of parties as a result of an unclear answer can generate significant transaction costs to both sides.

87 They may form the evidentiary basis to ground relief against claims following on misrepresentation.

actually lodged. In the case of minor ambiguities, for consumer relations purposes it might behove the insurer to seek early clarification – although, again, the relative size of such ambiguities is probably more efficiently taken into consideration in the context of achieving a settlement.

In those cases where claims are subsequently made, the presence of these forms of information readily able to be identified as false or misleading makes for a clearer interpretation of the relative rights of the parties, thereby minimising costs associated with either settlement or outright rejection of claims. Avoiding the ambiguities inherent in non-disclosure arguments carries substantial benefit not only for insurers but also serves to diminish externality costs carried by society in the form of administrative and judicial dispute resolution.[88]

Of particular concern to insurers in developing the interrogatories that will be included on a proposal form is striking an effective balance between the number of questions posed and the level of information produced. Although it may be attractive superficially to identify as comprehensively as possible all contingencies, the transaction costs to the insured in doing so will be high and assurance of a perfect result is still impossible. Perhaps of more significance in the long run, however, is that the efficiency benefits such forms provide can be lost if their use necessitates too much consumer time to complete. Not surprisingly, in situations where a document becomes too lengthy or detailed, would-be customers are likely to find more compact documents produced by competitors preferable.

Moreover, as discussed below, the implicit presence of the utmost good faith standard and its principal duty to disclose information invites the cost-effective option of including a more generalised query soliciting from the applicant any information likely to be pertinent to the insurer.[89] Again, breach of this provision similarly gives rise to rights of termination and/or avoidance of a claim. From the perspective of an insurer a combination of a limited list of interrogatories and one catch-all type of question is probably the most efficient. As only a limited percentage of applicants are likely to possess hidden information that would push them into the high risk category and, of that group, only a smaller percentage again will actually incur a loss, this approach presents a dual benefit. Potential consumers can fill in the form in a

88 Inclusive in this calculation would be, for example, costs such as court time, filing and administrative fees and costs associated with mediation and negotiations.

89 Potentially questions cast too broadly pose the type of query courts most dread. As Levmore points out, overly general questions can give rise to ambiguity in determining a 'truthful' answer, thereby creating substantial third party enforcement costs (which he argues are usually resolved in favour of the insured). On this basis, US courts have been known to prohibit some such questions as constituting 'fishing'. (Although, as noted earlier, in the US the utmost good faith standard did not survive the 1964 Uniform Commercial Code codification.) Levmore (1982) 68 Virginia Law Review 117, pp 137–42.

time effective manner, thereby avoiding potential deterrence problems and enabling the insurer – or, perhaps more importantly, its agent – to disqualify baldly inappropriate risks immediately. It also, however, allows an insurer to preserve the option to review the contents of the proposal for accuracy and completeness in the event that a claim should materialise. The insurer can then judge the merits of contesting the claim in light of its potential settlement difficulties as well as its overall value to the portfolio.

Use of direct questions can also act as a positive exercise for both sides by creating the potential for mutual gains through the minimisation of risks that might otherwise remain at large. By using questions aimed at identifying risk diminishing properties – smoking/drinking habits being common examples or, in the case of home contents, the presence/installation of anti-theft or safety devices – an insurer able to identify low risk individuals may increase its expected profits by offering a policy at a premium which, while below average, would still be greater than the discounted value to the insured's claim. The attractiveness of self-insurance or alternative cover would then be curtailed.

A second method of separating high and low risk applicants adopts a similar type of incentive based approach. By structuring policies in such a way that they will automatically be of less interest to high risk consumers, insurers can largely avoid the transaction costs inherent in the normal documentation requirements. Among the most common methods are co-insurance and deductible provisions. Under co-insurance the insured carries a fixed percentage of any potential loss; under a deductible plan, the insured retains and is the first to bear a fixed dollar amount of the loss, with the insurance company paying for all losses above that amount. Such provisions are much less attractive to high risk insureds so, like signalling theory in consumer transactions,[90] the willingness of an insured to take on those provisions may

90 Arising originally out of studies in consumer product warranties, signal theory rests on the premise that consumers can obtain data cost-effectively about products with which they are otherwise unfamiliar by looking to the nature of the warranty coverage offered. In situations where the costs of obtaining such information would otherwise to be too high to be efficient the extent to which manufacturers choose to backup their products can provide a short cut 'signal' as to their confidence in its quality. Because reliability is correlated negatively with the costs of warranty coverage, the longer the warranty, the lower the costs of warranty coverage for the manufacturer, and the more extensive the coverage to the consumer. Translated, this theory potentially enables insurers to infer information as to the likely level of risk unknown individuals present based on their choices in such particulars as policy options. 'Signals' such as the level of deductibles, the extent of coverage sought, and the willingness of would-be insureds to forego extra variables amongst other factors would be considered useful indicia of risk. Under this approach to obtaining information, insurers are relying on insureds to affirmatively volunteer key information about themselves by recognising through the pricing structure that class of risk best able to maximise their own welfare. See: Akerlof (1970) 84 Quarterly Law Journal of Economics 488, pp 488–500; Priest (1981) 90 Yale Law Journal 1297; Rothschild and Stiglitz (1976) 90 Quarterly Journal of Economics 629, pp 629–49; Schwartz and Wilde (1983) 69 Virginia Law Review 1387.

indicate to the insurer the likelihood of risk being proposed. Two similar additional mechanisms are the exclusion of benefits for losses arising from pre-existing conditions and the introduction of specifically constructed objective tests (such as health checks, etc) to enable more effective classifications.

This approach can also be used to help reduce the related insurance risk of moral hazard. Unlike adverse selection problems which undermine actuarial forecasting at the pre-contract formation stage, moral hazard problems pose a threat to accurate risk classification of insureds once the policy has been issued. The term 'moral hazard' refers to a moral character of the insured – or to that aspect of the insureds character/behaviour – that could potentially increase either the probability or size of the loss.[91] For example, if perfect insurance is assumed, an insured would become (theoretically) indifferent to the magnitude of the risk retained and would have no incentive to take precautions against it occurring.[92] In practice, therefore, the better the insurance the lower the incentive and the insured has to engage in behaviour that will prevent the loss transpiring. From the perspective of both parties this would result in preventable risks remaining at large and would reflect inefficient market terms in that insureds would presumably have to pay the increased premiums the added risk calculation carried.[93]

To mitigate this problem, insurers try to ensure that policy holders retain sufficient incentive to take reasonable precautions to prevent a loss occurring.[94] Again, as noted above, co-insurance and deductibles play a significant role in this respect. Both methods provide ongoing inducements to insureds to avoid making risk enhancing changes during the currency of the insurance agreement by having the insured participate in coverage of potential losses. Additional methods of minimising this problem include cancellation provisions and, as noted above, premium reduction for certain easily established acts by the insured such as non-smoking or the installation of anti-theft/safety systems.

The third mechanism used to promote efficient information compilation is the underlying duty of 'utmost good faith' and its principal manifestation the duty to disclose information. The effect of this requirement generally

91 Tangible examples go to any behaviour or habit that is likely to bring about a level of non-diligence on the part of the insured once a policy is entered into that increase the risks of loss: eg, lapsing into excessive smoking, drinking or failure to maintain health regimes or, on the security front, failure to pay adequate attention to security protection of a home such as failing to close windows, activate alarms, make necessary repairs, etc.

92 Polinsky, 1989, pp 56–57.

93 *Ibid*, p 56.

94 See, generally, Cooter and Ulen, 1988, p 66; Gravelle (1991) 11 International Review of Law and Economics 23.

manifests itself in two ways. The first, as discussed above, is the presence of open-ended questions on the proposal requiring disclosure of any other material information of which an insured may be aware. The second may arise through the inclusion of a requirement in the policy of notification of any material change.[95] Failure to comply with such a requirement may entitle an insurer to cancel the insurance cover to refuse to pay any claim or to reduce the quantum of any claims payment.

These remedies, as noted earlier, are unusual in that they seem to give rise to a situation where the insurer may be best placed if it does not consider closely the responses in a proposal until such time as a claim is actually made. If the contingency does not occur, the insurer keeps the premium; if the contingency does occur, the cancellation of cover and non-payment of the claim are likely outcomes.

The implications of a misleading or false statement, or even a mistake, therefore seem to lie particularly heavily with the insured. Indeed, Rhea, a Canadian economist, takes issue with the seemingly punitive nature of this remedy by suggesting 'an alternative remedy in which the benefit paid is reduced to account for the higher risk. [For example] Accident and sickness insurers in Intro are permitted by statute to vary either the premiums or the benefits in order to reflect a misstatement of the age of the insured'.[96] Rhea goes on to conclude that this may perhaps fail to satisfy the deterrence objective to the extent that some insureds who engage in misrepresentation are undetected, although his concern about the seemingly punitive undertone of the remedy remains.

As much of an anathema as punitive damages constitutes to the jurisprudence of contract law[97] the availability of these damages in the context of insurance would seem to recognise that a substantially greater level of deterrence is necessary in this instance than in other areas of contract law to dissuade prospective insureds from withholding information. Successful deterrence depends on the expected sanction being at least equal to the

95 See, for example, Australian Home Alliance provision policy (and related discussion, Chapter 5).

96 Rhea (1993) 13 International Review of Law and Economics 145, p 154.

97 Traditionally, contract law presents no opportunity for awarding punitive damages, the objective of all contracts being to ensure that individuals simply end up in the enhanced position which the contract they entered was to have delivered. Contract law generally encourages breach – under the 'efficient breach' doctrine – in circumstances where to do so would create greater returns than those provided by the existing contract (eg, the increase in value is assessed as value accruing over and above that amount paid out to compensate the party subject to the breach of the existing contract). This approach is distinct from that of tort law which awards punitive damages in addition to compensatory damages in order to create deterrence. See Calabresi and Melamed (1972) 85 Harvard Law Review 1089; Posner, 1977, pp 88–98.

expected gains from the wrongdoing.[98] To the extent that this enables insurers to deter fraud and adverse selection (and potentially fraudulent actions implicitly incorporated therein), this quasi-punitive approach seems a logical corollary to the utmost good faith standard. In more ambiguous cases, however, it is arguably unduly weighted towards the insurer.

As discussed further in para 3.2, the evolution of common law precedent in this respect results in disclosure being required of an insured under current law even when the insured does not know that the fact is material and, even when the fact is readily discoverable by the insurer. The origins of this rule, as it evolved from the days of Lloyd's and its merchant-cum-underwriter venturers, constituted a logical assignment of information disclosure for diminution of transaction cost purposes. With the passage of time, however, the relative positions of the parties has altered significantly. Accordingly, the current formulation of this rule potentially, in many instances, imposes excessive transaction costs on the insured in discovering what it is that the insurer needs to know. In contrast, the insurer is much better informed about the probability of certain risks eventuating and its opportunity to investigate losses is greatly facilitated by modern processes and communications. It is arguable, therefore, that, but for statutory intervention in this area, the burden of risk for non-disclosure would in a free market have shifted more towards the insurer as its own mechanisms and strategies for identifying key information have evolved. The question consequently arises as to whether the rules pertaining to mandatory disclosure of information are appropriate at this time.

98 The expected sanction would be calculated by multiplying the probability that the sanction will be imposed by its monetary equivalent. See Cooter and Freeman (1991) 66 New York University Law Review 1045, pp 1051–53, analysing the deterrence factor represented in the calculation of remedies for breach of fiduciary duties.

CHAPTER 3

DISCLOSURE: THE ANGLO-COMMONWEALTH CONTEXT

3.1 INTRODUCTION

The next two chapters examine the duty of disclosure upon insured and insurer and the closely related obligation not to misrepresent material facts. As distinct from the economic and historical dynamics that have motivated information disclosure in the insurance industry (outlined in Chapter 2), understanding the regulatory structure that has evolved to govern pre-contract disclosure between insured and insurer requires not only a familiarity with statutory provisions but also presupposes an understanding of the common law principles that these statutory provisions have abrogated, amended or merely supplemented.

This chapter examines, on a comparative basis, the approaches adopted in the Anglo-Commonwealth context of England, Australia, New Zealand and Singapore; it then looks to the statutory provisions introduced to bridge such inequities as regulators have felt appropriate. Chapter 4 examines the divergent path undertaken in the United States of America.

Insofar as it applies to consumer insurance contracts the law in this area has undergone significant change. For instance, the common law duty of disclosure that measures materiality by reference to the so called prudent insurer was perceived to impose an unreasonable burden upon the insured. Consequently many reforms have been proposed and/or implemented and the Insurance Contracts Act 1984 (Australia) is a good example of restating the duty by reference to matters known to the insured to be relevant, or a reasonable person in the circumstances, to lighten this burden. Moreover, this Act seeks also to ensure that the insured is aware of his or her obligation to disclose information by imposing a duty upon the insurer to clearly inform the prospective insured of his or her duty of disclosure.

3.2 THE COMMON LAW

3.2.1 Utmost good faith

The duty of disclosure derives from a common law requirement that insurer and insured act in the utmost good faith towards each other.[1] It has been

1 See, for example, *Banque Financière de la Cité SA v Westgate (UK) Insurance Ltd* [1991] 2 AC 249 (HL).

pointed out that 'the word "utmost" may add very little as it is the examination of "good faith" that goes to the heart of the concept'.[2] Good faith is impossible to define with any precision, but an anthology of meanings are provided by Lucke[3] in a recent essay:

> [Good faith means] fairness, fair conduct, reasonable standards of fair dealing, decency, reasonableness, decent behavior, a common ethical sense, a spirit of solidarity, community standards of fairness, decency and reasonableness.[4]

Scotford[5] comments that:

> ... in the contractual setting ... the parties to a contract must be loyal or committed to the contract itself and the law which governs it, and finally, in giving respect to the bargain, one party must have some commitment to the other party's purpose and objective in the contract.[6]

In *Kelly v New Zealand Insurance Co Ltd*,[7] Owen J cited with approval the New Zealand High Court decision in *Vermuelen v Simu Mutual Insurance Association*[8] where the duty of utmost good faith was described as having the essential element of honesty. But this is not enough. Consistent with the added element connoted by 'utmost', the insured must positively address the question as to what the insurer – having little or no knowledge of the insured's particular circumstances – would need to take into account so as to make a reasonable commercial decision as to the terms of the contract. Accordingly, in the insurance context the duty of utmost good faith finds its most common expression in the requirement to disclose all material facts pertaining to the insurance. However, as is discussed below, the duty is not limited to this particular area.

Although the duty of utmost good faith arises at law, not by contract, its origins have occasioned considerable debate. One view is that the duty arises from an implied term in a contract of insurance,[9] but this explanation has been severely criticised[10] particularly as it exists before any contract arises.

2 See Scotford (1988) 1 Insurance Law Journal 83.

3 Lucke, in Finn (ed), 1987.

4 *Ibid*, p 160. Bollen J in *Sheldon v Sun Alliance Insurance Ltd* (1988) 50 SASR 236; (1989) 53 SASR 97, expresses the view that 'good faith' is more exacting than this; namely, that it is more than the reasonable standard of fair dealing.

5 (1988) 1 Insurance Law Journal 83, at 84.

6 See also Pincott (1988) 1 Insurance Law Journal 110.

7 (1991) 9 ANZ Insurance Cases 61-317.

8 (1987) 4 ANZ Insurance Cases 60-812.

9 For example, *Blackburn Low & Co v Vigors* (1887) 12 App Cas 531; *Joel v Law Union & Crown Insurance Co* [1908] 2 KB 863.

10 See *Merchants & Manufacturers Insurance Co Ltd v Hunt* [1941] 1 KB 295, at 313; *Southern Cross Assurance Co Ltd v Australian Provincial Assurance Association Ltd* (1939) 39 SR (NSW) 174, at 187; *Claude R Ogden & Co Pty Ltd v Reliance Fire Sprinkler Co Pty Ltd* [1973] 2 NSWLR 7, at 21–22; *Kolokythas v Federation Insurance Ltd* (1980) 1 ANZ Insurance Cases 60-412; *Khoury v Government Insurance Office (NSW)* (1984) 58 ALJR 502, at 507.

The House of Lords' decision in *Banque Financière de la Cité SA v Westgate Insurance Co*[11] confirmed that at common law the duty of good faith, and consequently the duty of disclosure, is not given the status of an implied term. As Roberts J explained in *Iscor Pension Fund v Marine & Trade Insurance Co Ltd*:[12]

> In some contracts parties are required to place their cards on the table to a greater extent than others, but the determination of the extent of the disclosure does not depend on the label we choose to stick on the contract.

Thus, the more accepted view is that the duty of utmost good faith and the duty of disclosure is not based on an implied term in the contract, nor is it limited to insurance contracts. These duties, according to the accepted view, are common law duties arising outside of the contract and applicable to all contracts *uberrimae fidei*.[13]

The duty of utmost good faith applies to all aspects of the insurance relationship and a breach of this duty entitles the innocent party to avoid the contract. As mentioned above, the requirement that the insurer and insured act in the utmost good faith towards one another has usually been recognised in connection with the duty of disclosure. Failure to effect full disclosure, at common law, entitles the innocent party to avoid the contract.[14] The reason for the duty may, as noted by Lord Mansfield in *Carter v Boehm*[15] and as discussed in the previous chapter, be due to the speculative nature of the contract in which one party is in complete possession of facts material to the

11 [1990] 2 All ER 947; [1991] 2 AC 249.

12 (1961) 1 SA 178, at 185. Generally, see Turner and Sutton, 1990.

13 See, for example, *March Cabaret Club & Casino Ltd v London Assurance* [1975] 1 Lloyd's Rep 169, at 175; *Preece v State Insurance General Manager* [1982] 2 ANZ Insurance Cases 60-493. In *Khoury v Government Insurance Office (NSW)* (1984) 58 ALJR 502, the High Court held that the duty of disclosure was an obligation which was imposed by the common law as an incident of the relationship between insurer and insured. Their Honours pointed out that there were numerous conceptual difficulties in basing this duty on an implied term of the contract of insurance; for example, the duty of disclosure was logically anterior to the making of the contract and to treat it as a special implied term lay ill with the general rule that the dealings of parties preliminary to a formal contract were not part of the contract itself. See further Sutton (1985) 13 ABLR 108. *Khoury's* case is also noted in (1985) 59 ALJ 235. Reference should also be made to *Banque Financière de la Cité SA v Skandia (UK) Insurance Co Ltd* (1988) 5 ANZ Insurance Cases 60-881; [1988] 2 Lloyd's Rep 513; (1990) 6 ANZ Insurance Cases 60-987. Generally, see Davis (1991) 4 Insurance Law Journal 71.

14 See, for example, *Carter v Boehm* (1766) 3 Burr 1905 [97 ER 1162]; *Banque Financière de la Cité SA v Westgate Insurance Co Ltd* [1991] 2 AC 249; [1990] 3 WLR; [1990] 2 All ER 947.

15 (1766) 3 Burr 1905; 97 ER 1162.

risk calculation of the contract while the other is, absent such disclosure, largely ignorant of this information.[16]

Case law on the duty of utmost good faith is overwhelmingly concerned with the failure or alleged failure by the insured to disclose material facts in the pre-contract setting. However, recent cases, such as the House of Lords' decision in *Banque Financière de la Cité SA v Westgate (UK) Insurance Co Ltd*[17] confirm the application of this duty to all contractual matters. However, at least as regards the giving of information by the insured is concerned, the House of Lords in *Manifest Shipping Co Ltd v Uni-Polaris Shipping Co Ltd (The Star Sea)*[18] has restricted the scope of this duty. The House of Lords held that, after entry into an insurance contract, the duty of utmost good faith was only breached in cases where the insured failed to disclose a matter that was relevant to the variation of that contract, and in cases where the insured has made a fraudulent claim under it. They rejected the view that negligent or other culpable conduct by an insured short of fraud amounted to a breach of the duty of utmost good faith. Lord Hobhouse, in justifying this position, observes:

> ... there is a clear distinction to be made between the pre-contract duty of disclosure and any duty of disclosure which may exist after the contract has been made. It is not right to reason, as the defendants submitted that your Lordships should, from the existence of an extensive duty pre-contract positively to disclose all material facts to the conclusion that post-contract there is a similarly extensive obligation to disclose all facts which the insurer has an interest in knowing and which might affect his conduct. The courts have consistently set their face against allowing the assured's duty of good faith to be used by the insurer as an instrument for enabling the insurer himself to act in bad faith. An inevitable consequence in the post-contract situation is that the remedy of avoidance of the contract is in practical terms wholly one sided. It is a remedy of value to the insurer and, if the defendant's argument is accepted, of disproportionate benefit to him; it enables him to escape retrospectively the liability to indemnify which he has previously and (on hypothesis) validly undertaken. Save possibly for some types of reinsurance treaty, it is hard to think of circumstances where an assured will stand to benefit from the avoidance of the policy for something that has occurred after the contract has

16 (1766) 3 Burr 1905, at 1909; see also *London General Omnibus Co Ltd v Holloway* [1912] 2 KB 72, at 85; *Rozanes v Bowen* [1928] 2 Lloyd's Rep 98; *Barclay Holdings (Aust) Pty Ltd v British National Insurance Co Ltd* (1987) 4 ANZ Insurance Cases 60-770; (1987) 8 NSWLR 514.

17 [1990] 2 All ER 947; [1991] 2 AC 249 (HL). This decision and that of the Court of Appeal and Steyn J has been extensively noted. See, for instance, Scotford (1988); Pincott (1988); Birds (1988) Journal of Business Law 421; Birds (1990) Journal of Business Law 512, at 514; the Hon Justice Brownie (1993) 5 Insurance Law Journal 226.

18 [2001] 1 Lloyd's Rep 389.

> been entered into; the hypothesis of continuing dealings with each other will normally postulate some claim having been made by the assured under the policy.[19]

Interestingly, the Australian legislature in enacting the Insurance Contracts Act 1984 made it clear that the paramount obligation upon the parties was to observe utmost good faith towards one another with the only limitation upon this pervasive duty – that the insured's duty of disclosure as specified in s 21 of the Act is not to be rendered more onerous by reference to the provision requiring each party to act with utmost good faith.[20] Section 21 imposes obligations as to pre-contract disclosure of information, and the limitation precludes an insurer from arguing a breach of the duty of utmost good faith in circumstances where the insured failed to disclose a material circumstance which arose during the currency of the contract of insurance – success in such an argument would render the duty of disclosure more onerous.

Apart from this limitation, the legislation makes it clear that the duty of utmost good faith applies to all aspects of the relationship between insurer and insured. The duty arises 'in respect of any matter arising under or in relation to' a contract of insurance.[21] Consequently, pursuant to this Statute, the duty has potential application to wide range of relations including settlement of claims, admissions and denials of liability. Australian courts are given the opportunity to take a more interventionist and reconstructive role in relation to insurance contracts, their terms and conditions and the insured's reasonable expectations.[22] Particular mention should be made in this context to *Beverley v Tyndall Life Insurance Co Ltd*[23] where the Full Court of the Supreme Court of Western Australia decided that the insurer's duty of utmost

19 *Ibid*, at 401–02. See also *K/S Merc-Skandia XXXXII v Certain Lloyd's Underwriters (The Mercandian Continent)* [2001] Lloyd's Rep IR 802, where the English Court of Appeal endeavoured to clarify the scope of the duty of utmost good faith in the wake of the decision in *The Star Sea*. Longmore LJ held that in the post-contractual situation the rights of the parties were to be determined primarily by reference to their contract and not by rules of law. The Court of Appeal held that an insurer can avoid a policy for the continuing duty of utmost good faith only where: (a) the assured has been fraudulent; (b) the assured was in breach of some contractual obligation relating to the provision of information; and (c) the assured's breach was so serious that it conferred upon the insurer the right to terminate the policy for repudiation by the assured. See further the decision of the English Court of Appeal in *Agapitos v Agnew* [2000] EWCA Civ 247, 6 March.

20 Insurance Contracts Act 1984 (Australia), s 12.

21 *Ibid*.

22 See, for example, *Moss v Sun Alliance Australia Ltd* (1990) 6 ANZ Insurance Cases 60-967; *Gugliotti v Commercial Union Assurance Co of Australia* (1992) 7 ANZ Insurance Cases 61-104; *Australian Associated Motor Insurers Ltd v Ellis* (1990) 6 ANZ Insurance Cases 60-987; *Kelly v New Zealand Insurance Co Ltd* (1993) 7 ANZ Insurance Cases 61-197; *Ibrahim v Greater Pacific Life Insurance Co Ltd* (1996) 9 ANZ Insurance Cases 61-330; cf *Re Zurich Australian Insurance Ltd* (1999) 10 ANZ Insurance Cases 61-429.

23 (1999) 10 ANZ Insurance Cases 61-453.

good faith to an insured obliged it to follow rules of procedural fairness and to disclose to the insured all the material upon which the insurer intended to rely, in sufficient time to allow the insured to respond to any adverse material. The key issue in this case was the definition of 'disability' in an insurance contract and as this depended upon the insurer being satisfied that the insured was disabled, the insurer was in a very real sense acting as a judge in the insurer's own cause. This was, therefore, a particularly appropriate circumstance in which to apply the duty of utmost good faith.

Similarly in *Ibrahim v Greater Pacific Life Insurance Co*,[24] a sickness policy provided for benefits payable for total disability to be reduced for 'other benefits'. These 'other benefits' were defined to include social service benefits whether received or not. After the insurer ceased payment under the policy after seven months, the insured applied for and received social service benefits. In an action against the insurer to recover benefits under the policy, the insurer sought to reduce its liability by reference to the 'other benefits' clause, contending that the social service benefits should be deducted from any payment it had to make. The insured argued that had the insurer paid him the benefits to which he was entitled, he would not have been qualified to receive social service benefits, and if he succeeded in the case, he would have to refund the social service benefits. Brownie J read the policy subject to the legislation and rejected the insurer's argument. He held that it could not be right to say that because of the insurer's breach of contract, the insured was liable to repay social service benefits, but was not entitled to be paid by the insurer. Alternatively, he held:

> ... that by force of s 14 of the Insurance Contract Act the [insurer] would be failing to act with the utmost good faith in taking this point: it was only the [insurer's] failure to meet its contractual obligations that led to the [insured] claiming social security benefits, and therefore having to repay those benefits [at 76-668].

Accordingly, it is clear that ss 12–14 of the Insurance Contracts Act (Cth) gives the Australian courts considerable scope to control the post-formation conduct of parties to an insurance contract and to impose and modify matters relative to performance and discharge of obligations, payment of claims and other matters 'arising under or in relation to' the contract.

From the insured's perspective, the courts have affirmed that the duty of utmost good faith and the duty of disclosure are mutual and that the remedy for breach of the duty of utmost good faith is avoidance of the contract. In *Banque Financière de la Cité (SA) v Westgate Insurance Ltd*,[25] the House of Lords

24 (1996) 9 ANZ Insurance Cases 61-330.

25 [1990] 2 All ER 947; [1991] 2 AC 249. See also *Manifest Shipping Co Ltd v Uni-Polaris Shipping Co Ltd (The Star Sea)* [2001] Lloyd's Rep 389.

rejected the view that damages are available for a breach of the duty of utmost good faith. Whether or not a claim may be pursued in tort has been left open.[26] Avoidance of the contract is usually an ineffective remedy in the case of a breach of duty of utmost good faith by the insurer – it enables the insured to recover his or her premium, but does not enable the insured to recover for a loss.[27]

3.2.2 Duty of disclosure

(a) The prudent insurer

The common law duty of disclosure upon an insured in Singapore, England, Australia and New Zealand is to disclose all material facts. The materiality of information is a question of fact determined by reference to the judgment of a prudent insurer at the time when the insured is obliged to disclose.[28] The Marine Insurance Acts[29] of the jurisdictions being considered, in faithfully recording the common law position, state that: 'every circumstance is material which would influence the judgment of a prudent insurer in fixing the premium, or determining whether he will take the risk.'

The term 'prudent insurer' is nowhere defined but was considered in *Associated Oil Carriers Ltd v Union Insurance Society of Canton Ltd*.[30] The insurer in this case argued that it was material on 31 July 1914 for charterers of a vessel to disclose that they were of German nationality. Aitkin LJ pointed out that this fact had been held material in *British and Foreign Marine Insurance Co Ltd v Samuel Sanday & Co*,[31] but rejected the insurer's contention that a

26 See *Banque Financière de la Cité (SA) v Westgate Insurance Co Ltd* [1990] 2 All ER 947; [1991] 2 AC 249.

27 See Kelly and Ball, 1991, p 155. The authors argue convincingly that a remedy in damages should be available; see pp 156–60.

28 See, for example, *Thompson v Liverpool & London & Globe Insurance Co* 23 F Cas No 13, 966; *Babatsikos v Car Owners; Mutual Insurance Co Ltd* [1970] VR 297; *Avon House Ltd v Cornhill Insurance Co Ltd* (1980) 1 ANZ Insurance Cases 60-429; *Barclay Holdings (Australia) Pty Ltd v British National Insurance Co Ltd* [1987] 8 NSWLR 514.

29 See the Marine Insurance Act 1906 (UK), s 18; Marine Insurance Act 1908 (NZ), s 18; Marine Insurance Act 1909 (Australia), s 24; Marine Insurance Act, Cap 387, Singapore Statutes, rev ed, 1994, s 18. In *Lambert v Co-operative Insurance Society Ltd* [1975] 2 Lloyd's Rep 485, the English Court of Appeal stated that s 18 of the Marine Insurance Act 1906 (UK), which provides for the application of the prudent insurer test, in the case of marine insurance, codified the common law applicable to all types of insurance contracts.

30 [1917] 2 KB 184.

31 [1916] 1 AC 650.

prudent insurer must be taken to know the law as it was subsequently declared in *Sanday's* case. He stated:

> I think that this standard of prudence indicates an insurer much too bright and good for human nature's daily food. There seems no reason to impute to the insurer a higher degree of knowledge and foresight than that reasonably possessed by the more experienced and intelligent insurers carrying on business in that market at that time.[32]

Thus, the 'prudent insurer' corresponds closely to the 'reasonable insurer' and the terms may well be interchangeable.

(b) Inducement

The adoption of the 'prudent insurer' test as to materiality raised the issue as to whether the opinion of the particular insurer was relevant in deciding the issue of materiality. Until the decision of the House of Lords in *Pan Atlantic Insurance Co Ltd v Pine Top Insurance Co Ltd*,[33] the settled position was that even if a particular insurer did not regard an undisclosed fact as material (in the sense that it would not have influenced him or her in fixing the premium or deciding whether to take the risk), if a prudent insurer would have regarded it as material, that particular insurer was not precluded from avoiding the contract for non-disclosure.[34] However, following *Pan Atlantic Insurance Co Ltd v Pine Top Insurance Co Ltd*,[35] it is clear that a two stage approach should be adopted. The first stage requires an assessment of the impact of the non-disclosure upon the hypothetical prudent insurer in fixing the premium or determining whether he will take the risk. The second stage, which is anchored in the facts of the actual case, requires the court to determine whether the non-disclosure in fact induced the particular insurer who assumed the risk to issue the policy on the terms it did.[36] This curtails the possibility of a particular insurer avoiding a contract for non-disclosure even though he or she would not have been influenced had he or she been aware of the fact concealed. This importation of subjectivity does involve a difficult

32 [1917] 2 KB 184, at 192.

33 [1995] 1 AC 501. Although the issues in this case arose under a policy of non-marine insurance, the House of Lords considered that it was convenient to consider these issues by reference to the Marine Insurance Act 1906 (UK) since it was accepted that in relevant respects the common law relating to general and marine insurance was the same. See judgment at p 518.

34 See, for example, *Avon House Ltd v Cornhill Insurance Co Ltd* (1980) 1 ANZ Insurance Cases 60-429; *Container Transport International Inc v Oceanus Mutual Underwriting Association (Bermuda) Ltd* [1984] 1 Lloyd's Rep 476; *Elston v Phoenix Prudential Australia Ltd* [1987] 2 Qd R 354.

35 [1995] 1 AC 501.

36 See *Akedian Co Ltd v Royal Insurance Australia Ltd* (1997) 148 ALR 480, at 487 (*per* Byrne J). Cf *Tey Say Cheng v North British and Mercantile Insurance Co Ltd* (1921) FMSLR 248 (adverse comment on the practicality of the actual insurer test).

ex post facto judgment as to the attitude of the particular insurer, but it does close the door on the obvious anomaly of a negligent or careless insurer calling evidence to show that his or her more prudent counterpart would have been influenced by a non-disclosure, and thus avoid a contract on the basis of a non-disclosure the particular insurer would not consider material.[37]

(c) *Degree of influence*

There are conflicting views as regards the degree of influence that the undisclosed circumstance must have upon the prudent insurer. The House of Lords in *Pan Atlantic Insurance Co Ltd v Pine Top Insurance Co Ltd*[38] rejected the proposition that it must be shown that full and accurate disclosure would have led the insurer to a different decision on accepting or rating the risk, the so called 'decisive influence' test. Lord Goff observed:

> [T]he decisive influence test faces insuperable practical difficulties, because it ignores the fact that it is the duty of the assured to disclose every material circumstance which is known to him, with the result that the question of materiality has to be considered by the assured before he enters into the contact. At that time, it is not unreasonable to expect that an assured who is aware of, and understands, his duty of disclosure should be able to identify those circumstances, within his knowledge, which would have an impact on the mind of the insurer when considering whether to accept the risk and, if so, on what terms he should do so; but it appears to me to be unrealistic to expect him to be able to identify a particular circumstance which would have a decisive effect. Likewise it seems to me ... that an inquiry after the event as to whether the judgment of a prudent insurer would have been decisively influenced by the relevant circumstance, if disclosed, would in many cases be impracticable, because this must in the nature of things depend upon the reactions of the particular underwriter.[39]

The result of the application of the reasoning in *Pan Atlantic* is the continuation of the requirement that the insured disclose all matters which might be relevant to a prudent insurer. Clarke[40] refers to this approach as the 'awareness test of materiality' and points to the advantage of testing materiality in the market by reference to whether the non-disclosed circumstance would have had an 'effect on the thought processes' of the

37 This was what Kerr J was attempting to achieve in *Berger and Light Diffusers Pty Ltd v Pollock* [1973] 2 Lloyd's Rep 442, at 463. He resiled from this position in *Container Transport International Inc v Oceanus Mutual Underwriting Association (Bermuda) Ltd* [1984] 1 Lloyd's Rep 476, but *Pan Atlantic Insurance Co Ltd v Pine Top Insurance Co Ltd* [1995] 1 AC 501 vindicates his initial view that inducement of the actual insurer is required.

38 [1995] 1 AC 501, at 517 (*per* Lord Goff); at 531 (*per* Lord Mustill).

39 *Ibid*, at 517.

40 Clarke, 1997, pp 604, 606.

prudent insurer than to establish what would have influenced the prudent insurer decisively.[41]

The effect the *Pan Atlantic Insurance Co Ltd* decision will have on Australian law is, as yet, unknown. The decision seems to be at odds with the approach taken by Samuels J in *Mayne Nickless Ltd v Pegler*[42] and subsequently approved by the Privy Council in *Marene Knitting Mills Pty Ltd v Greater Pacific General Insurance Ltd*.[43] While Mustill LJ in *Pan Atlantic Insurance Co Ltd* considered that the 'general tenor' of the decision in *Mayne Nickless* was broadly in accord with his own opinion,[44] the test of materiality laid down by Samuels J is usually cited in support of an argument for the decisive influence test.[45] The use of the word 'affected' in the relevant passage set out below, suggests, from the insurer's perspective, a more stringent test of materiality than that propounded by the House of Lords:

> [A] fact is material if it would have reasonably affected the mind of a prudent insurer in determining whether he will accept the insurance, and if so, at what premium and on what conditions. The word 'reasonably' is necessary to maintain control over the evidence of possibly absurdly stringent insurance practice ... It achieves the purpose of the 'reasonable assured test', but fixes the area of judgment where it properly belongs – that is, with the insurer.[46]

This resonates closely with the reasoning of Kirby P, as he then was, in *Barclay Holdings (Australia) Pty Ltd v British National Insurance Co Ltd*[47] where he argues that the duty of disclosure at common law is 'already an onerous one' and therefore on policy grounds the duty of disclosure should be confined, not expanded. Accordingly, Kirby P was not in favour of a test that imposed on an insured an obligation to disclose endless material about the past and which left open to the insurer a denial of indemnity based upon some fact which of itself would not have been determinative of acceptance or rejection of insurance. The obligation of disclosure should not require the insured to 'volunteer a catalogue of background data ... to an insurance office'.[48]

---

41 A slightly broader test of materiality was later applied by the English Court of Appeal in *St Paul Fire & Marine Insurance Co (UK) v McConnell Dowell Constructions Ltd* [1995] 2 Lloyd's Rep 116, at 124, that a non-disclosed circumstance is material where, had it been disclosed, the prudent underwriter would have appreciated that it was a different risk.

42 [1974] 1 NSWLR 228.

43 [1976] 11 ALR 167.

44 [1995] 1 AC 501, at 541.

45 See *Barclay Holdings (Aust) Pty Ltd v British National Insurance Co Ltd* (1987) 8 NSWLR 514, Glass JA at 523 and Kirby P at 517. See also Kirby (1995) Aust Bar Rev 1, at 8 and Sutton (1995) 23 ABLR 64, at 67.

46 *Mayne Nickless Ltd v Pegler* [1974] 1 NSWLR 228 *per* Samuels J at 239. See also *Elston v Phoenix Prudential Australia Ltd* [1987] 2 Qd R 354 *per* Derrington J.

47 (1987) 8 NSWLR 514.

48 *Ibid*, at 518. See also *General Accident Insurance Co Australia Ltd v Kelaw Pty Ltd* (1997) 9 ANZ Insurance Cases 61-369, at 77-049 (Supreme Court of Western Australia, Full Court). In this case, which was decided pursuant to provisions of the Insurance [contd]

In New Zealand, the High Court held in *Quinby Enterprises (In Liquidation) v General Accident Fire & Life Assurance Corporation Public Ltd*[49] that the test since *Pan Atlantic* is 'whether the relevant information would have had an effect on the mind of a prudent insurer in weighing up the risk'.[50]

(d) Knowledge

It is frequently stated that the insured is under a duty to disclose all material facts which he in fact knows. This view was put most forcibly by Fletcher Moulton LJ in the leading case of *Joel v Law Union & Crown Insurance Co*:[51]

> The disclosure must be of all you ought to have realised to be material, not of that only which you did in fact realise to be so. But in my opinion there is a point here which often is not sufficiently kept in mind. The duty is a duty to disclose, and you cannot disclose what you do not know. The obligation to disclose, therefore, necessarily depends on the knowledge you possess ... [The] question always is, was the knowledge you possessed, such that you ought to have disclosed it?[52]

Nevertheless, as far as marine insurance is concerned, the law in the United Kingdom, Singapore, Australia and New Zealand requires the insured to disclose not only material facts which he or she knows but also those facts which he or she ought to know.[53] This is clearly the case where, although the fact in question was never within the insured's actual knowledge, ignorance was due to his or her intentional failure to make such inquiries as the insured might reasonably have been expected to make in the circumstances.[54] Similarly, where the insured's failure to make inquiries is unintentional a

48 [contd] Contracts Act (1984) (Australia) discussed below, the court expressly endorsed the view that there is no obligation upon the insured to disclose every circumstance in the past that might be of interest to the insurer; a distinction should be drawn between matters of general interest and determinative circumstances relevant to the critical decisions whether to accept the insurance and, if so, at what premium and on what conditions.

49 [1995] 1 NZLR 736.

50 *Ibid*, at 740. See also *Gooch v Switzerland Insurance Australia Ltd* (1995) 9 ANZ Insurance Cases 61-323; *Back v National Insurance Co of New Zealand Ltd* [1996] 3 NZLR 363; *Wayne Wilkinson Insurance Ltd v Kaialia Downs Ltd* (1995) 8 ANZ Insurance Cases 61-248.

51 [1908] 2 KB 863.

52 *Ibid*, at 884. See also *London General Omnibus Co Ltd v Holloway* [1912] 2 KB 72, at 85; *Dalgety & Co Ltd v Australian Mutual Provident Society* [1908] VLR 481, at 500; *Lee v British Law Insurance Co Ltd* [1972] 2 Lloyd's Rep 49, at 56; *Kathirvelu v Pacific & Orient Insurance Co Sdn Bhd* (1990) 3 MLJ 312; *Toh Kim Lian v Asia Insurance Co Ltd* (1996) 1 MLJ 149.

53 See the Marine Insurance Act 1906 (UK), s 18(1); Marine Insurance Act Cap 387, Singapore Statutes, rev ed, 1994, s 18(1); Marine Insurance Act 1909 (Australia), s 24(1); Marine Insurance Act 1908 (NZ), s 18(1). These sub-sections relevantly provide: '... the assured must disclose to the insurer, before the contract is concluded, every material circumstance which is known to the assured, and *the assured is deemed to know every circumstance which in the ordinary course of business, ought to be known by him.*' See, for example, *Economides v Commercial Union Assurance Co plc* [1997] 3 WLR 1066.

54 *Blackburn, Low & Co v Vigors* (1887) 12 App Cas 531, at 537.

marine policy is equally to be avoided where the insured should have made the enquiries in the ordinary course of business.[55] Therefore, it is clear that as far as marine policies are concerned the duty to disclose extends to all facts actually known and to all facts which the insured ought in the ordinary course of business to have known.

The position as far as non-marine policies are concerned is less clear cut.[56] The answer is best expressed by Clarke[57] when he observes:

> The law makes assumptions about what the proposer knew or should have known himself, simply as a human being in his position. Cockburn CJ talked of his being taken to know that of which he 'ought to have knowledge',[58] Lord Halsbury emphasises the appearances, looking to what the insurer was entitled to assume about the knowledge of the proposer.[59] It is likely that what the law expects of the commercial proposer is greater than what it expects of a consumer, otherwise the duty of knowledge is objectively assessed.

It is clear that insureds cannot reduce or extinguish their duty of disclosure through the strategem of delegation. A good example in this context is the case of *Lindsay v CIC Insurance Ltd*.[60] The insureds owned premises that were

55 *London General Insurance Co v General Marine Underwriters Association* [1921] 1 KB 104; *Australia & New Zealand Bank Ltd v Colonial & Eagle Wharves Ltd* [1960] 2 Lloyd's Rep 241.

56 See *Dalgety & Co Ltd v Australian Mutual Provident Society* [1908] VLR 481, at 500, where Cussen J observed that the extension of the obligation to disclose matters of which the proponent ought to have knowledge 'probably has little or no application to the case of a man effecting an insurance on his own life'. The matter was left open in *ANZ Bank v Colonial and Eagle Wharves Ltd; Boag (Third Party)* [1960] 2 Lloyd's Rep 241, where a Lloyd's all risks policy was involved; but in *Blackley v National Mutual Life Association of Australasia Ltd* [1970] NZLR 919, at 931 and *Avon House Ltd v Cornhill Insurance Co Ltd* (1980) 1 ANZ Insurance Cases 60-429, at 77-228, cases involving life and fire insurance respectively, the wider obligation to disclose is accepted; and see *Mutton v Insurance Corp of Ireland Ltd* (1985) 3 ANZ Insurance Cases 60-630, where Yeldham J (in a case involving motor vehicle insurance) held that the duty of disclosure extends to material facts which an insured ought, in the ordinary course of business, to have known. Similarly in *Edwards v AA Mutual Insurance Co* (1985) 3 ANZ Insurance Cases 60-668 (in a case involving fire insurance on a house), Tompkins J said 'it appears that the duty goes further to the extent that he is required to disclose not only what he knows but also what ought, in the ordinary course of affairs, to be known to a proponent'. Note that in *State Insurance General Manager v McHale* (1992) 7 ANZ Insurance Cases 61-102, Richardson and Hardie Boys JJ endorse the comment by McKenna J in *Lambert v Co-operative Insurance Society Ltd* [1975] 2 Lloyd's Rep 485, at 490: '... first, what does the application know or what can he be taken to know and, secondly what must he disclose. His knowledge, actual or presumed, will include such inferences as an ordinary person using reasonable care and judgment would draw from the facts known to him, for example, a headache. If the ordinary man would not have inferred a serious malady from a headache, knowledge of a malady cannot be proved.'

See also *Kathirvelu v Pacific and Orient Insurance Co Sdn Bhd* [1990] 3 MLJ 312; *Toh Kim Lian v Asia Insurance Co Ltd* [1996] 1 MLJ 149.

57 Clarke, 1997, p 611.

58 *Proudfoot v Montefiore* (1867) LR 2 QB 511, at 521.

59 *Blackburn, Low & Co v Vigors* (1887) 12 App Cas 531, at 537.

60 (1989) 16 NSWLR 673.

damaged by a fire. The insurer denied liability to provide an indemnity by reason of the insured's failure to disclose that part of the premises were at the relevant time being used as a brothel. The day to day management of the premises was left to a real estate agent and the insureds contended that they did not have any knowledge as to the usage of the premises. This argument was dismissed as Rogers CJ held that the law imputed to insureds the knowledge of appropriate agents. The managing agent of a block of shops and offices is such an agent. Accordingly, the agent's knowledge of matters relating to the property which impacted on the insurance risk was imputed to the owners. This conclusion precluded the owners through the expedient of delegation from avoiding knowledge of matters which might result in a proposal being refused or a higher premium being imposed.

Similarly, the alter ego doctrine in the general law of corporations ensures that the device of incorporation is not a 'bolthole'[61] for those who contract insurance without sufficient disclosure.[62] Knowledge is attributable to an insured corporation if it is within the scope of the employee's employment to receive such knowledge and he or she is therefore under a duty to communicate it to the employer.[63] Furthermore, there is clear authority[64] to the effect that a division of function among officers of a corporation does not relieve the corporation from responsibility determined by reference to the knowledge possessed by each of them. In other words, it is not possible to compartmentalise knowledge so as to limit obligations, including the duty of disclosure.

Conversely, there is no obligation to disclose information already known to the insurer.[65] The relevant matter must be known to an appropriate officer

61 Glanville Williams, 1983, p 970, states that one of the functions of the alter ego doctrine is to ensure that: 'the device of incorporation is not a bolthole for people who commit offences.'

62 *London General Insurance Co v General Marine Underwriters' Association* [1921] 1 KB 104; *Regina Fur Co Ltd v Bossom* [1957] 2 Lloyd's Rep 466; [1958] 2 Lloyd's Rep 425.

63 See *Tesco v Nattrass* [1972] AC 153; *South Australian Housing Trust v SGIO* (1989) 51 SASR 1, at 23; *VACC Insurance Ltd v BP Australia Ltd* (2000) 11 ANZ Insurance Cases 61-457.

64 See, for example, *London General Insurance Co v General Marine Underwriters' Association* [1921] 1 KB 104, at 110; *Hamilton v Whitehead* (1988) 166 CLR 121, at 127.

65 See, for example, the Marine Insurance Act 1906 (UK), s 18(3)(c); Marine Insurance Act Cap 387, Singapore Statutes, rev ed, 1994, s 18(3)(c); Marine Insurance Act 1909 (Australia), s 24(3)(c); Marine Insurance Act 1908 (NZ), s 18(3)(c). The relevant sub-section provides that in the absence of enquiry the insured does not have to disclose:

> ... any circumstances which are known or presumed to be known to the insurer. The insurer is presumed to know matters of common notoriety or knowledge, and matters which an insurer in the ordinary course of business, as such, ought to know.

See also *Carter v Boehm* (1766) 3 Burr 1905, at 1911; *St Margaret's Trust Ltd v Navigators & General Insurance Co Ltd* (1949) 82 LlL Rep 752; *Blackley v National Mutual Life Association of Australasia Ltd* [1972] NZLR 1038; *Macfie v SGIO (Qld)* (1985) 3 ANZ Insurance Cases 60-606.

or agent of the insurer or contained in current official records.[66] In the recent case of *Commercial Union Assurance Australia Ltd v Beard*[67] it was argued that an insurer had knowledge of certain facts by virtue of an extract from a newspaper article containing such facts located in the general files of the insurer. The New South Wales Court of Appeal rejected this argument holding that the newspaper extract did not amount to knowledge, it was merely a source from which knowledge could be gained. Furthermore, the extract was not contained in any relevant record of the insurer or file to which the insurer's officers could be expected to have recourse to for purposes of the relevant public liability policy. The decision in this case accords with Clarke's general view[68] that: '... there is little or no duty on the insurer to look in his desk; in his memory perhaps, but not his files.' This attitude that has its origins in marine insurance in the 18th and 19th centuries[69] is much less supportable in the modern context where most insurers have sophisticated information systems. These writers concur very strongly in the view expressed by Kirby P, as he then was, in *Antico v CE Heath Casualty & General Insurance Ltd*[70] where he states that: '... with many advances in information technology, persons dealing with large insurers are entitled to expect that information provided to them will be circulated to all relevant divisions.'[71] Cases such as *Malhi v Abbey Life Insurance*,[72] where the English Court of Appeal confirmed that an insurer cannot be expected to check earlier records of what an applicant did or did not disclose, involve paper records and the benefit of ignorance, it is suggested, will become increasingly rare as computerised records predominate.

Finally, on the topic of knowledge, there is no need for the insured to communicate to the insurer matters of general knowledge known to the business community at large, matters relating to the practice of the trade or industry that the insurer insures, and matters of public knowledge or notoriety.[73] As Tan Lee Meng[74] observes: '... an insurer ... cannot complain

66 See, for example, *Tate v Hyslop* (1885) 15 QBD 368, at 378; *Equitable Life Assurance Society v General Accident Assurance Corporation* 1904 12 SLT 348, at 351; *Pacific and Orient Insurance Co Sdn Bhd v Lim Sew Chong* [1985] 2 MLJ 60.

67 (2000) 11 ANZ Insurance Cases 61-458.

68 Clarke, 1997, p 622.

69 Park, *Marine Insurance* (5th edn, 1802), p 178; cited in Clarke, 1997, p 622.

70 (1996) 9 ANZ Insurance Cases 61-304.

71 *Ibid*, at 76-399.

72 [1996] LRLR 237.

73 See, for example, *Commercial Union Assurance Co v Niger Co Ltd* (1922) 13 LlL Rep 75; *The Moonacre* [1992] 2 Lloyd's Rep 501, at 517; *Anne Quinn v American Manufacturers* 369 F Supp 1312 (SDNY, 1973).

74 Tan Lee Meng, 1997, p 122. See, for example, *Tan Kang-Hua v Safety Insurance Co* (1973) 1 MLJ 6; *Pacific & Orient Insurance Co Sdn Bhd v Lim Sew Chong* (1985) 2 MLJ 60.

that he has not been told facts which he ought to be acquainted with.' The degree of knowledge that will be attributed to the insurer is not susceptible to any simple analysis. Relevant considerations include the currency of the information,[75] its notoriety,[76] knowledge of other reasonably competent underwriters insuring similar risks[77] and the particular expertise of the insurer.[78]

(e) Timing, proof and remedies

Disclosure is required before the contract of insurance is concluded[79] and the issue as to whether the duty is broken or not depends on the circumstances existing at the time the contract is made. With most types of insurance there is a new contract each year, as opposed to a continuing one (as with life insurance) and this reimposes a duty to disclose. The insured must with each renewal correct earlier representations that have become incorrect and disclose fresh material facts.[80] Disclosure is not required, in the absence of inquiry, of any circumstance which diminishes the risk,[81] or of any circumstances as to which information is waived by the insurer,[82] or of any circumstance which it is superfluous to disclose by reason of any express or implied warranty.[83]

The onus of establishing that there has been a breach of the duty of disclosure rests upon the insurer. The insurer must prove, on a balance of

75 See, for example, *Leen v Hall* (1923) 16 LlL Rep 100; cf *Bates v Hewitt* (1867) LR 2 QB 595.

76 See, for example, *George Cohen, Sons & Co v Standard Marine Insurance Co Ltd* (1925) 21 LlL Rep 30; *Roberts v Plaisted* [1989] 2 Lloyd's Rep 341.

77 *Canadian Indemnity Co v Canadian Johns-Manville Co* (1988) 54 DLR (4th) 468; (1990) 72 DLR (4th) 478, at 495, 506, 508.

78 See, for example, *Marc Rich Co AG v Portman* [1997] 1 Lloyd's Rep 225.

79 See, for example, the Marine Insurance Act 1906 (UK), s 18(1); Marine Insurance Act, Cap 387, Singapore Statutes, rev ed, 1994, s 18(1); Marine Insurance Act 1909 (Australia), s 24(1); Marine Insurance Act 1908 (NZ), s 18(1).

80 Generally as to the time for disclosure, see *Lishman v Northern Maritime Insurance Co Ltd* (1875) 10 LR CP 179; *Re Yager and Guardian Insurance Co Ltd* (1912) 108 LT 38; *Commercial Union Assurance Co v Niger Co Ltd* (1922) 13 LlL Rep 65; *Lambert v Co-operative Insurance Society* [1975] 2 Lloyd's Rep 485, at 487; *New South Wales Medical Defence Union Ltd v Transport Industries Insurance Co Ltd* [1985] 3 ANZ Insurance Cases 60-680; (1985) 4 NSWLR 107; compare *Black King Shipping Corp v Massie (The Litsion Pride)* [1985] 1 Lloyd's Rep 437; *Permanent Trustee Australia Ltd v FAI General Insurance Co Ltd* (1998) 44 NSWLR 186; *Housing Corporation of New Zealand v Hunt* (2001) 11 ANZ Insurance Cases 61-488.

81 See, for example, the Marine Insurance Act 1906 (UK), s 18(3)(a); *Carter v Boehm* (1766) 3 Burr 1905, at 1911; *St Paul Fire & Marine Insurance Co (UK) Ltd v McConnell Dowell Constructors Ltd* [1995] 2 Lloyd's Rep 116, at 124.

82 See, for example, the Marine Insurance Act 1906 (UK), s 18(3)(c); *Carter v Boehm* (1766) 3 Burr 1905, at 1911; *Hair v Prudential Assurance Co Ltd* [1983] 2 Lloyd's Rep 667, at 673; *Tat Hong Plant Leasing Pty Ltd v Asia Insurance Co Ltd* [1993] 3 SLR 563.

83 See, for example, the Marine Insurance Act 1906 (UK), s 18(3)(d); *De Maurier (Jewels) Ltd v Bastion Insurance Co Ltd* [1967] 2 Lloyd's Rep 550.

probabilities, that the insured knew or ought reasonably, in the ordinary course of business to have known, of the fact in question, but that he or she failed to disclose it and that it would have been material to a prudent insurer if disclosed.[84] Expert evidence of persons engaged in the insurance business may be led but such evidence must be directed to the general practice of insurers as a class.[85] Frequently, however, the materiality of an uncommunicated fact may be so obvious that it is unnecessary to call any expert evidence to establish this point.[86]

While the question as to whether a particular fact is material must be answered in the context of each individual case, certain broad categories of material circumstance are generally accepted. First, all facts that suggest that the subject matter of insurance is exposed to more than ordinary danger from the perils insured against; that is, facts affecting the physical hazard. For example, the nature, construction and use of an insured building, or whether it is particularly exposed to danger, would be material facts affecting the physical hazard in property insurance.[87] A proponent for life insurance must

84 *Joel v Law Union & Crown Insurance Co* [1908] 2 KB 863; *Roselodge Ltd v Castle* [1966] 2 Lloyd's Rep 113, at 127; *Babatsikos v Car Owners' Mutual Insurance Co Ltd* [1970] VR 297, at 301; *Pana Vana Letchumanan Chettiar v Jupiter General Insurance Co Ltd* [1939] MLJ 39; *Lee Bee Soon v Malaysia National Insurance Sdn Bhd* [1980] 2 MLJ 252.

85 *Horne v Poland* [1922] 2 KB 364, at 365; *Babatsikos v Car Owners' Mutual Insurance Co Ltd* [1970] VR 297, at 305; *Eagle Star Insurance Co Ltd v National Westminster Finance Australia Ltd* (1985) 58 ALR 165; (1985) 3 ANZ Insurance Cases 60-634; compare *Visscher Enterprises Pty Ltd v Pacific Insurance Co Ltd* (1980) 1 ANZ Insurance Cases 60-419. See Pickering (1991) 4 Insurance Law Journal 52.

86 *Glicksman v Lancashire and General Assurance Co* [1925] 2 KB 593, at 609; *Peters v National Insurance Co of New Zealand Ltd* (unreported, High Court, Wellington, 21 May 1982, A321/80, Quillam J); *Mutton v Insurance Corp of Ireland Ltd* (1985) 3 ANZ Insurance Cases 60-630, at 78-868.

87 See, for example, *Bufe v Turner* (1815) 6 Taunt 338; 128 ER 1065 (failure to disclose neighbouring fire on same evening insurance effected); *Franek v Manufacturers' Mutual Insurance Ltd* (1984) 3 ANZ Insurance Cases No 60-555 (fact that restaurant licensed material fact that should be disclosed); *Opossum Exports Ltd v Aviation & General (Underwriting Agents) Pty Ltd* (1985) 3 ANZ Insurance Cases 60-624 (failure to disclose insured helicopter to be flown by inexperienced pilot); *Athlone Pty Ltd v General Accident Fire & Life Assurance Corp and Challenor Insurance Pty Ltd* (1985) 3 ANZ Insurance Cases 60-648 (non-disclosure for purposes of hotel policy that part of premises used as a nightclub in breach of council development consent and the Liquor Act); *Randell v Atlantica Insurance Co Ltd* (1985) 3 ANZ Insurance Cases 60-672 (disclosure of entry of yacht into Sydney – Noumea 'blue water' race material); [1985] 80 FLR 253. Note *Holmes v GRE* (1989) 5 ANZ Insurance Cases 60-894, where the Supreme Court of Tasmania considered (*obiter*) that the mental health and behavioural problems of a proponent was not a material fact which should have been disclosed to the insurer when seeking house and content insurance – notwithstanding that the insured suffered from a condition which could cause its victims to commit dangerous and irrational acts such as setting a deliberate fire in a house; see also *Decorum Investments Ltd v Atkin (The Elena G)* [2001] 2 Lloyd's Rep 378 (insured not obliged to disclose mere speculations, vague rumours and unreasoned fears that a Russian enemy would seek to damage or destroy his insured yacht).

disclose facts relating to health and any occupation, leisure time pursuits, or intemperate habits that may affect the duration of his or her life.[88]

Secondly, those facts referable to the integrity of the insured such as character, qualities and reputation; that is, facts affecting the moral hazard. Under this head an insured is under an obligation to disclose, *inter alia*, previous convictions,[89] previous losses and claims,[90] whether insurance has ever before been declined or cancelled,[91] and her or his poor financial

88 See, for example, *Balckley v National Mutual Life Assn (Australasia) Ltd* [1972] NZLR 1038 (need to disclose fact of admission to hospital after completion of proposal); *Yorke v Yorkshire Insurance Co* [1918] KB 662 (taking of possibly harmful drugs); *Equitable Life Assurance Society v General Accident Assurance Corp* 1904 12 SLT 348 (failure to disclose occasional motor racing); *Payne v Mutual Life & Citizens Assurance Co Ltd* (1985) 3 ANZ Insurance Cases 60-617 (failure to disclose drug usage by life insured); *National & General Insurance Co Ltd v Chick* [1984] 2 NSWLR 86 (occupation as inquiry agent and gun licences should be disclosed).

89 *Lambert v Co-operative Insurance Society Ltd* [1975] 2 Lloyd's Rep 485; *Fanhaven Pty Ltd v Bain Dawes Northern Pty Ltd* (1982) 2 ANZ Insurance Cases 60-480; see also *Khoury v GIO (NSW)* (1982) 2 ANZ Insurance Cases 60-478, where the New South Wales Court of Appeal held that an insured must disclosure his beliefs as to the integrity of those living with him in insured premises; that is, his belief that a child or children had stolen from him a substantial sum of money. This decision was upheld on appeal by the Full High Court – see (1984) 58 ALJR 502, at 506; *Trimboli v Royal Insurance (Aust) Ltd* (1983) 2 ANZ Insurance Cases 60-500 where the insureds failed to disclose an earlier involvement in a business which a Royal Commission found was involved in drug trafficking; *Mutton v Insurance Corp (Ireland) Ltd* (1985) 3 ANZ Insurance Cases 60-630, where a truck driver failed to disclose when effecting insurance of his tipper truck that he had convictions for overloading and vehicle defects; *Inversiones Manria SA v Sphere Drake Insurance Co plc Malvern Insurance Co Ltd* and *Niagara Fire Insurance Co Inc (The Dora)* [1989] 1 Lloyd's Rep 69, where the insured failed to disclose criminal charges of smuggling goods; see also *Glover v Phoenix Assurance Co (NZ) Ltd* (1989) 5 ANZ Insurance Cases 60-698, where it was held that convictions involving dishonesty and judgments indicating a poor credit record would be material for any prudent insurer in assessing the risk. Generally, see Clarke (1984) LCMLQ 100. It should be noted that, by virtue of the new Crimes Legislation Amendment Act 1989 Pt VIIc which amends the Crimes Act 1914 (Australia), and subject to certain provisos, insureds are now not required to disclose records of their past criminal convictions which are more than 10 years old. Any individual affected by the new law may, as from 30 June 1990, complain to the Privacy Commissioner where he or she feels that his or her rights under the Act have been infringed. This new legislation applied to convictions for offences against Commonwealth laws. See also the Rehabilitation of Offenders Act 1986 (Qld) and the Spent Convictions Act 1988 (WA).

90 See *Engel v South British Insurance Co Ltd* (1983) 2 ANZ Insurance Cases 60-516; *Brooks v Sirius Insurance Co Ltd* (1985) 3 ANZ Insurance Cases 60-601; *Kyles Transport Pty Ltd v Zurich Australian Insurance Ltd* (1984) 3 ANZ Insurance Cases 60-600; *Gumodin Pty Ltd v Traders Prudent Insurance Co Ltd* (1985) 3 ANZ Insurance Cases 60-669; *Macfie v SGIO (Qld)* (1985) 3 ANZ Insurance Cases 60-606.

91 *Willcocks v New Zealand Insurance Co Ltd* [1926] NZLR 805; *Bazouni v Sun Alliance Insurance Ltd* (1981) 1 ANZ Insurance Cases 60-432; *Liga Knitting Mills v Lombard Insurance Co Ltd* (1984) 3 ANZ Insurance Cases 60-551; *Eagle Star Insurance Co Ltd v National Westminster Finance (Aust) Ltd* (1985) 58 ALR 165; (1985) 3 ANZ Insurance Cases 60-634; *Lissenden v Yorkville Nominees Pty Ltd (In Liq)* (1984) 3 ANZ Insurance Cases 60-597; (1986) 60 ALJR 218; *Ginns v Par Insurance Brokers* [1997] 1 Lloyd's Rep 173. Note, however, that a non-renewal of a policy on 'administrative' grounds was held not to be a material fact: *Barclay Holdings (Aust) Pty Ltd v British National Insurance Co Ltd* (1987) 4 ANZ Insurance Cases 60-770; (1987) 8 NSWLR 514.

state.[92] Prior losses may indicate that the risk to be insured is greater than normal 'either because of physical, facts unknown to the insurer, or because of the insured's lack of care in relation to his or her property'.[93] Similarly, prior cancellations or refusals of insurance may indicate a poor claims experience, a claims dispute with a prior insurer or other negative interaction such as a failure to co-operate in relation to a claim. As always though the question whether a fact is material must be answered in the context of the particular case. As Tompkins J observed in *Wayne Wilkinson Insurance Ltd v Kaialia Downs Ltd*[94] in relation to the materiality of a prior criminal conviction: '... such circumstances as the nature of the offence, the penalty imposed, the age and circumstance of the person at the time, the time which has elapsed ... the nature of the contract of insurance and the extent to which the potential liability of the insurer may depend on the integrity of the insured.'[95]

Thirdly, matters affecting the subrogation rights of an insurer may be material because if the insured has deprived himself or herself of the right to recover from third parties, the ultimate risk born by the insurer is increased.[96]

Fourthly, the insured must disclose gross over-insurance,[97] but it is not as a general rule bound to disclose that he or she is insured elsewhere unless such information is solicited in the proposal or elsewhere.[98]

The common law duty of disclosure may be varied by the parties; it may be limited or enlarged by the type of questions asked in the proposal form,[99] or altered by the language of the declaration made by the proponent or by the

---

92 *Gibbs v New Zealand Insurance Co Ltd* (unreported, High Court of Auckland, Chilwell J, 6 December 1983, A173/80 at 92); *Glover v Phoenix Assurance Co of New Zealand Ltd* (1988) 5 ANZ Insurance Cases 60-898. Cf *Marek v CGA Fire & Accident Insurance Co Ltd* (1985) 3 ANZ Insurance Cases 60-665.

93 Kelly and Ball, 2001, p 2437.

94 (1995) 8 ANZ Insurance Cases 61-248.

95 *Ibid*, at 75-787.

96 *Tate v Hyslop* (1885) 15 QBD 368; cf *Guthrie House Ltd v Cornhill Insurance Co Ltd* (1982) 2 ANZ Insurance Cases 60-466, where a clause affecting subrogation rights in a lease agreement was not disclosed by the insured (lessor); held immaterial by Hardie Boys J as the evidence disclosed that insurers did not generally vary the risk or the premium rate according to the contents of leases entered into by insureds as lessors. Moreover, it should be noted that s 68(2) of the Insurance Contracts Act 1984 (Australia) provides that the duty of disclosure does not require the insured to disclose the existence of a contract that limits subrogation rights.

97 *Tate v Hyslop* (1885) 15 QBD 368; *Pickersgill & Son v London and Provincial Marine & General Insurance Co Ltd* [1912] 3 KB 614; *Deaves v CML Fire & General Insurance Co Ltd* (1979) 53 ALJR 382; *Fruehauf Finance Corporation Pty Ltd v Zurich Australian Insurance Ltd* (1990) 20 NSWLR 359.

98 *McDonnell v Beacon Fire & Life Assurance Co* (1857) 7 UCCP 308.

99 See *Jester-Barnes v Licenses & General Insurance Co Ltd* (1934) 49 LlL Rep 231; *Glicksman v Lancashire and General Assurance Co* [1927] AC 139, at 143; *Edwards v AA Mutual Insurance Co* (1985) 3 ANZ Insurance Cases 60-668.

conditions of the policy.[100] In particular, the insured's duty to disclose material facts is supplemented by the duty to respond accurately to questions put by the insurer. There is, of course, a general duty in negotiating all kinds of contract not to misrepresent material facts, and contracts induced by material misrepresentation may be set aside at the instance of the innocent party. However, insurers have not been content to rely upon their rights at general law, and in many (if not, most) cases it is common for a proposal to contain a declaration that the answers to the various questions posed in the proposal are in every respect true, that the proposal and declaration shall be the basis of the contract, and that the insured agrees to accept the insurer's policy; the policy itself usually contains a recital incorporating the proposal and declaration.[101] The effect of this 'basis of the contract' clause is to incorporate the insured's answers into the policy and the insured is taken to have warranted the absolute accuracy of responses provided. The insurer, at common law, could repudiate liability for any breach, however immaterial. For example, in *Dawsons Ltd v Bonnin*[102] a lorry was destroyed by fire and the House of Lords held that the insurer could repudiate liability under a policy in respect of the vehicle, as the insured had inadvertently given the wrong address as the place where the vehicle would be garaged in answer to a question in the proposal; this error was immaterial in that it had no bearing on the premium payable nor on the decision to accept the risk. However, by making the answers in the proposal the basis of the contract of insurance the insurer was entitled to avoid liability, notwithstanding the immateriality of the incorrect response to the risk. As Viscount Haldane observed:

> If the [insurers] can show that they contracted to get an accurate answer to this question, and to make the validity of the policy conditional on that answer being accurate, whether the answer was of material importance or not, the fulfilment of this contract is a condition of the 'insured' being able to recover.[103]

The unrestrained operation of 'basis of the contract' clauses could, therefore, remove materiality as a limitation upon avoidance for misrepresentation.

---

100 *Jones v Provisional Insurance Co* (1857) 3 CBNS 65, at 86; 140 ER 662; *Darwen v Southern Cross Assurance Co Ltd* [1936] St R Qld 105; *National & General Insurance Co Ltd v Chick* [1984] 2 NSWLR 86; *State Insurance Ltd v Fry* (1991) 6 ANZ Insurance Cases 61-075.

101 See, for example, *Thomson v Weems* (1884) 9 App Cas 671; *Joel v Law Union & Crown Insurance Co* [1908] 2 KB 863; *Deaves v CML Fire & General Insurance Co Ltd* (1979) 23 ALR 539; *National & General Insurance Co Ltd v Chick* [1984] 2 NSWLR 86; (1984) 3 ANZ Insurance Cases 60-579. It is not essential that the proposal and the policy contain a 'basis' clause; if the policy contains a 'basis of the contract' clause but not the proposal, the clause if part of the contract and amounts to a warranty of the truth of particulars supplied (see *Dawsons Ltd v Bonnin* [1922] 2 AC 413). But if the proposal alone contains a basis clause, the clause is not part of the contract. See generally Hasson (1971) 34 MLR 29, and the cases there cited.

102 [1922] 2 AC 413.

103 *Ibid*, at 421. See also *Yorkville Nominees Pty Ltd v Lissenden* (1986) 60 ALJR 218, at 224.

A misstatement, however immaterial, would entitle the insurer to avoid the contract.[104]

The remedy for non-disclosure of material information at common law and pursuant to the Marine Insurance Acts in the United Kingdom, Singapore, Australia and New Zealand is rescission.[105] The non-disclosure does not automatically avoid the contract – the insurer is given an election to avoid the contract or to affirm it.[106] The effect of rescission or avoidance is that the contract is terminated and the parties are to be restored to the position in which they stood before the contract was entered into.[107] This retroactive effect means, in particular, that the insurer is not liable for claims arising between the making of the contract and the date of avoidance and the insurer must return the premium.[108]

3.2.3 Misrepresentation

The insured and the insurer are under a duty not to misrepresent material facts to each other. This duty, of course, applies to contracts in general. The misrepresentation may not be confined to the insured or insurer but may be made by their agents. An insurer, for example, may be liable for misrepresentation of its agent, usually as to the nature of the policy or the extent of the cover provided.[109] This can also amount to deceptive or misleading conduct under legislation such as s 52 of the Trade Practices Act 1974 (Australia).[110] Most commonly the issue of actionable misrepresentation arises in respect of a statement made in the course of negotiating a policy and the completion by an insured of a proposal form for such cover.

The basic elements of misrepresentation are: (a) the statement must have been made; (b) it must have been made by the insured or the insurer or their agent; (c) it must have been incorrect; and (d) the insured or insurer must have known or ought to have known that the statement was untrue.[111] At common

104 The operation of these clauses has been curtailed by statute in Australia and New Zealand: see the Insurance Contracts Act 1984 (Australia), s 24; the Insurance Law Reform Act 1977 (NZ), ss 4, 5.

105 See the Marine Insurance Act 1906 (UK), s 18(1); Marine Insurance Act, Cap 387, Singapore Statutes, rev ed, 1994, s 18(1); Marine Insurance Act 1909 (Australia), s 24(1); Marine Insurance Act 1908 (NZ), s 18(1).

106 *MacKender, Hill & White v Feldia AG* [1966] 2 Lloyd's Rep 449, at 455.

107 *Abram v Westville* [1923] AC 773, at 781; *Johnson v Agnew* [1980] AC 367.

108 See, for example, *Pan Atlantic Insurance Co Ltd v Pine Top Insurance Co Ltd* [1995] 1 AC 501.

109 *Holmes v Jones* (1907) 4 CLR 1692; *Toteff v Antonas* (1952) 87 CLR 647.

110 *SWF Hoists v SGIC* (1990) 6 ANZ Insurance Cases 61-002.

111 See, for example, *Derham & Derham v Amev Life Assurance Co Ltd* (1981) 56 FLR 34; *Deaves v CML Fire & General Insurance Co Ltd* (1979) 143 CLR 24.

law the innocent party is entitled to avoid the contract for misrepresentation.[112] Where a misrepresentation is of such a kind as to induce an insurer to enter into a contract of insurance, and particularly where it is intended to do so, it may be inferred in the absence of evidence to the contrary that the insurer did rely on it.[113]

All too often cases of misrepresentation of the *suppressio veri suggestio falsi* variety[114] are decided on the basis of non-disclosure by the insured of material facts.[115] This may be conceptually unsatisfactory[116] but, as might be expected, most of the legal questions that arise in the context of misrepresentation are the same as apply to non-disclosure. For example, the 'prudent insurer test' of materiality in relation to non-disclosure by the insured applies equally to misrepresentations at common law.[117]

There is no difference between marine and non-marine insurance in the law relating to material misrepresentation.[118] The common law position as stated in s 20(3) of the Marine Insurance Act 1906 (UK) provides that a misrepresentation may be as to a matter of fact or as to a matter of expectation or belief.[119] As to the former, it is true if it is substantially correct; that is, that the difference would not be considered material by a prudent insurer. In respect of the latter, it is true if it is made in good faith.[120]

An insurer who seeks to bind an insured to true answers to their questions contained in a proposal should state their questions clearly and unambiguously in addition to ensuring that they are sufficient to elicit the particularity that the insurer seeks.[121] As Derrington and Ashton[122] point out, there have been numerous cases in which it has been held that the answer is sufficient though the insurer has complained that the information sought has

112 *Broad & Montague Ltd v South East Lancashire Insurance Co Ltd* (1931) 40 LlL Rep 328.

113 *Gould v Vaggelas* (1985) 157 CLR 215, at 236, 250; *Orb Holdings Pty Ltd v Lombard Insurance Co (Aust) Ltd* (1994) 8 ANZ Insurance Cases 61-221.

114 That is, cases in which the statement complained of contains nothing actually false, but there is 'such a partial and fragmentary statement of fact, as the withholding of that which is not stated makes that which is stated absolutely false'; *Peek v Gurney* (1873) LR 6 HL 377, at 403, *per* Lord Cairns.

115 See Hasson (1975) 38 MLR 89, and the cases there cited.

116 *Ibid*; see also Birds, 1988, p 79.

117 See *Ionides v Pender* (1874) LR 9 QB 531.

118 *Highlands Insurance Co v Continental Insurance Co* [1987] 1 Lloyd's Rep 109.

119 See also Marine Insurance Act 1909 (Australia), s 26(3).

120 *Ibid*, s 26(4).

121 *Weston v Woollongong* (1975) 49 WCR (NSW) 221; *Corcos v De Rougemont* (1925) 23 LlL Rep 164; *Nairn v Royal Insurance Fire and General (No 2) Ltd* (1990) 6 ANZ Insurance Cases 61-010.

122 Derrington and Ashton, *The Law of Liability Insurance* (Draft 2nd edn, November 1999), Chapter 5, p 5.

not been provided. The proposal form must be read through the eyes of the lay proponent for the insurance cover.[123]

The question as to whether statements in issue are indeed untrue in an objective sense often depends upon the construction of the answers in the proposal in conjunction with the questions. The authorities have demonstrated that an answer may not be all it superficially seems and the effect of a proposal must be determined according to its precise terms.[124] Moreover, the construction placed upon one form of words may not be transported to a different form as the answers must be read in their literal and factual context; that is, in association with the respective questions and the proposal as a whole, and in the matrix of relevant circumstances as permitted by the ordinary rules of construction.[125]

A distinction often is drawn between a statement of fact and an expression of opinion or judgment. If a statement is advanced by an insured as an honest expression of opinion and there is a foundation for it, there is no deception – though others with a full knowledge of the facts may disagree. Expressed as such, as with any expression of expectation or belief, it cannot constitute a misrepresentation unless the opinion was not honestly held.[126] Subject to qualification where circumstances such as the position of the insured would indicate otherwise, the statement of an opinion does not imply that the basis of the belief is an objectively reasonable one.[127]

Difficulties arise where, in an answer to a question, an insured responds 'not applicable'. In *Deaves v CML Fire & General Insurance Co Ltd*[128] the High Court were unable to reach a unanimous conclusion on the effect of such an answer. The correct view, it is suggested, is that this response is an expression of opinion that the particulars sought are, for some unspecified reason, not applicable to the insured's proposal; it therefore could only constitute a misrepresentation if the opinion was not honestly held.[129]

---

123 See, for example, *Dixon v Royal Insurance Australia Ltd* (1999) 10 ANZ Insurance Cases 61-422; *Babatsikos v Car Owners Mutual Insurance Co Ltd* [1970] VR 297; *State Insurance General Manager v Hanham* (1990) 6 ANZ Insurance Cases 60-990; *McLeod v Simu Mutual Association* (1987) 4 ANZ Insurance Cases 60-784.

124 *National & General Insurance Co Ltd v Chick* (1984) 3 ANZ Insurance Cases 60-579; *McLeod v Simu Mutual Association* (1987) 4 ANZ Insurance Cases 60-784.

125 *Condogianis v Guardian Assurance Co Ltd* [1921] AC 125; *Kurban v Higgins* [1969] SASR 433; *Claude R Ogden v Reliance Fire Sprinkler Co* [1973] 2 NSWLR 7.

126 *Anderson v Pacific Fire & Marine Insurance Co* (1872) LR 7 CP 65, at 69; *Deaves v CML Fire & General Insurance Co Ltd* (1979) 143 CLR 24; *Timms v FAI Insurance Ltd* (1976) 12 ALR 506.

127 *Anderson v Pacific Fire & Marine Insurance Co* (1872) LR 7 CP 65, at 69; *Burns v MMI-CMI Insurance Ltd* (1995) 8 ANZ Insurance Cases 61-287.

128 (1979) 143 CLR 24, at 47 (Stephen J), 69 (Jacobs J), 62 (Mason J).

129 *Deaves v CML Fire & General Insurance Co Ltd* (1979) 143 CLR 24, at 47 (*per* Stephen J); *Burns v MMI-CMI Insurance Ltd* (1995) 8 ANZ Insurance Cases 61-287; *Protean Holdings Ltd v American Home Assurance Co* [1985] VR 187.

In general, a misrepresentation is not actionable unless it actually induces the party to whom it was made to enter into the contract. So far as insurers are concerned, inducement is analysed in terms of materiality; that is, the insured's misrepresentation must be a misrepresentation of a material fact, otherwise the insurer will be unable to discharge its onus of proof that it was induced to enter into the contract.[130] Materiality for these purposes is the same as for the purposes of the duty of disclosure.[131] However, insurers sought at common law to avoid questions of inducement and materiality through incorporation of 'basis' clauses in the proposal and in the policy. It is common for a proposal to contain a declaration that the answers to the various questions posed in the proposal are in every respect true, that the proposal and declaration shall be the basis of the contract, and that the insured agrees to accept the insurer's policy. The policy itself usually contains a recital incorporating the proposal and declaration and making it the basis of the contract.[132] The effect of this 'basis of the contract' clause is that the insured is taken to have warranted the absolute accuracy of his or her responses so that the contract depends on it.

At common law the insurer could repudiate liability for any breach regardless of its materiality and whether the matter actually contributed to the loss. For example, in *Dawsons Ltd v Bonnin*[133] a lorry was destroyed by fire and the House of Lords held that the insurer could repudiate liability under a policy in respect of the vehicle, as in answer to a question in the proposal the insured had inadvertently given the wrong address as the place where the vehicle would be garaged. This error was immaterial in that it had neither bearing on the premium payable nor on the decision to accept the risk. However, by making the answers in the proposal the basis of the contract of insurance the insurer was entitled to avoid liability. As Viscount Haldane observed:

> If the [insurers] can show that they contracted to get an accurate answer to this question, and to make the validity of the policy conditional on that answer

130 See *CCH Australian and New Zealand Insurance Reporter*, para 7-060; see, for example, *Smith v Chadwick* (1882) 20 Ch D 27, at 44; *Redgrave v Hurd* (1882) 20 Ch D 1, at 21; *National & General Insurance Co v Chick* (1984) 3 ANZ Insurance Cases 60-579; *Gould v Vaggelas* (1984) 157 CLR 215.

131 See *Mayne Nickless Ltd v Pegler* (1974) 1 NSWLR 228, at 239; *Dixon v Royal Insurance Australia Ltd* (1999) 135 FLR 183, at 197.

132 See, for example, *Thomson v Weems* (1884) 9 App Cas 661; *Joel v Law Union & Crown Insurance Co* [1908] 2 KB 863; *Deaves v CML Fire and General Insurance Co Ltd* (1979) 23 ALR 539; *National & General Insurance Co Ltd v Chick* [1984] 2 NSWLR 86; (1984) 3 ANZ Insurance Cases 60-579. It is not essential that the proposal and the policy contain a 'basis' clause; if the policy contains a 'basis of the contract' clause but not the proposal, the clause is part of the contract and amounts to a warranty of the truth of particulars supplied (see *Dawsons Ltd v Bonnin* [1922] 2 AC 413). But, if the proposal alone contains a basis clause the clause is not part of the contract. See Sutton, 1980, p 44, and generally see Hasson, 1971, and the cases there cited.

133 [1922] 2 AC 413.

being accurate, whether the answer was of material importance or not, the fulfilment of this contract is a condition of the 'insured' being able to recover.[134]

Avoidance is the appropriate remedy at common law for material misrepresentation in the answers in a proposal or in other oral misrepresentation.[135]

3.3 THE COMMON LAW MODIFIED: THE AUSTRALIAN PERSPECTIVE

Significant reform to the common law duty of disclosure and misrepresentation has occurred in Australia. This reform arises out of the report of the Australian Law Reform Commission, *Report on Insurance Contracts*, No 20, 1982. Detailed reform measures were effected by the Insurance Contracts Act 1984 (Australia) and a considerable volume of case law giving substance and clarity to this legislation has emerged in the period since its promulgation. The paragraphs below will outline the relevant provisions relating to disclosure as they represent one model for the reform of the common law.

First, the Insurance Contracts Act 1984 (Australia) does not apply to or in relation to contracts and proposed contracts covered by the Marine Insurance Act 1909 (Australia), although in 1998 the insurance of pleasure craft was excluded form the Marine Insurance Act and brought within the Insurance Contracts Act 1984 (Australia).[136]

Accordingly, while the common law is extensively modified by the Insurance Contracts Act 1984 (Australia), the Marine Insurance Act 1909 (Australia) remains firmly based upon the earlier United Kingdom legislation, and in conformity with the equivalent statutes in Singapore and New Zealand. Whether this status will continue is doubtful as the recently published Australian Law Reform Commission Report entitled *Review of the Marine Insurance Act 1909*[137] outlines proposals that would effect significant changes to the Act. Certain of these proposals relevant to the duty of disclosure are canvassed in the conclusions to this section.

Second, consistent with a perceived desirability of shifting the disclosure standard to that of the insured,[138] but recognising the undesirability of

134 *Ibid*, at 421. See also *Yorkville Nominees Pty Ltd v Lissenden* (1986) 60 ALJR 218, at 224.

135 *Highlands Insurance Co v Continental Insurance Co* [1987] 1 Lloyd's Rep 109.

136 Insurance Contracts Act 1984 (Australia), s 9(d); s 9A (as inserted by the Insurance Laws Amendment Act 1998 (Australia), s 3).

137 Report No 91, April 2001.

138 See the Australian Law Reform Commission, *Report on Insurance Contracts* (No 20, 1982), para 180.

limiting the duty of disclosure to the idiosyncratic standard of that party, s 21(1) of the Insurance Contracts Act 1984 (Australia) alters the focus from the expectation of a prudent insurer to the knowledge of both the insured and a reasonable person in those circumstances. The insured is therefore under an obligation to disclose every matter known to him or her which he or she knows to be relevant to the decisions of the insurer in deciding whether or not to effect the policy of insurance, or matters which a reasonable person in the circumstances of the insured would know to be so relevant. Section 21(1) provides:

> Subject to this Act, an insured has a duty to disclose to the insurer, before the relevant contract of insurance is entered into, every matter that is known to the insured, being a matter that –
>
> (a) the insured knows to be a matter relevant to the decision of the insurer whether to accept the risk and, if so, on what terms; or
>
> (b) a reasonable person in the circumstances could be expected to know to be a matter so relevant.

It should be noted that the obligation to disclose is limited to matters actually known to the insured and does not extend to constructive knowledge; that is, material facts which the insured ought, in the ordinary course, to have known. The drafting employed may give rise to complications. For example, in *Khoury v GIO (NSW)*,[139] the High Court of Australia held that a father's belief that one of his sons living in the family home was, or had been, systematically stealing money for gambling purposes from the father's business located in the same building as the family residence, was a matter which should have been disclosed to his houseowner's and householder's insurer. Whether a 'belief' – even reasonably held – would qualify for purposes of s 21(1) as a matter 'known to the insured' is doubtful, although there can be little question about the materiality of the information in question.[140] In *Advance (NSW) Insurance Agencies Pty Ltd v Matthews*[141] Young J took the view that 'the insured must have actual knowledge of the thing, the mere fact that he ought in the ordinary course of business to have known is insufficient'.[142] Similarly, in *CIC Insurance Ltd v Midaz Pty Ltd*,[143] the Queensland Court of Appeal held

139 (1984) 58 ALJR 502.

140 In *Permanent Trustee Aust Ltd v FAI General Insurance Co Ltd* (1998) 10 ANZ Insurance Cases 61-408, Hodgson CJ emphasised that: '... known in s 21(1) means more than suspected or believed. What is required is that the matter should be the subject of a true belief, held with sufficient assurance to justify the term "known".' (At 74-525.) See also *Australian Casualty and Life Ltd v Hall* [1999] 151 FLR 360, at 361; *Permanent Trustee Australia Co Ltd v FAI General Insurance Co Ltd* (2001) 11 ANZ Insurance Cases 61-491.

141 (1987) 4 ANZ Insurance Cases 60-813. See also Derrington and Ashton (1988) 1 Insurance Law Journal 1, at 4; also Derrington and Ashton, 1990, p 167.

142 (1987) 4 ANZ Insurance Cases 60-813, at 74-998.

143 (1998) 10 ANZ Insurance Cases 61-394; cf Rogers CJ in *Ayoub v Insurance Co Australia Ltd* (1989) 5 ANZ Insurance Cases 60-933, at 76-035, where the knowledge of the [contd]

that the duty of disclosure in s 21(1) does not extend to any matter unknown to the insured; the language does not suggest an intention to cover matters which should have been known but were not. The difficulty in defining the boundary between knowledge and belief and what significance to attach to beliefs, even those held with sufficient assurance, is well demonstrated in *Permanent Trustee Australia Co Ltd v FAI General Insurance Co Ltd*.[144] The insured through its broker sought and received a 30 day extension to its excess of loss cover. During this extension period the insured became aware of claims arising out of their trusteeship, which claims were subsequently settled, and the insured sought indemnity from the insurer under the excess of loss cover. The insurer rejected the claim on the ground of non-disclosure that the insured was seeking to place its cover elsewhere. The insured's brokers believed that if they had disclosed this fact to the insurer, it was likely that the 30 day extension would not have been granted. In upholding the trial judge's finding that this non-disclosure was within s 21(1) of the Insurance Contracts Act 1984, Handley JA, in the New South Wales Court of Appeal, observed:

> The belief of [the brokers] in the likely attitude of [the insurer] was held with sufficient assurance for [the brokers] to conduct themselves in a business transaction as if it were true. When a person, on the basis of some information, holds a belief on which that person is prepared to act in the world of practical affairs, he or she knows that fact for most legal purposes, and certainly for purposes of s 21.[145]

In reaching this conclusion the court accepted that a sharp distinction should not be drawn between matters relevant to the assessment of risk, and purely commercial considerations. Section 21 applied to matters that were relevant in a commercial sense to the terms on which an insurer was prepared to provide cover.

In the case of a joint policy of insurance, the words 'known to the insured' in s 21(1) have been interpreted to mean the collective knowledge of each co-insured. In *Advance (NSW) Insurance Agencies Pty Ltd v Matthews*[146] it was held

143 [contd] insured's broker was deemed to be the knowledge of the insured; see also *Lindsay v CIC Insurance Ltd* (1989) 5 ANZ Insurance Cases 60-913; (1989) 16 NSWLR 673, where Rogers CJ held that the knowledge of an agent was deemed the knowledge of the insured for the purposes of s 21(1). The Chief Justice further said that the knowledge of the agent is not confined to the agent charged with effecting the insurance. See, however, the comments by (the Honourable Mr Justice) Derrington (1990) Qld Law Soc Journal 5, at 8.

144 (2001) 11 ANZ Insurance Cases 61-491 (NSWCA); see also *Permanent Trustee Australia Co Ltd v FAI General Insurance Cases* 61-408 (Hodgson CJ).

145 (2001) 11 ANZ Insurance Cases 61-491, at 75-676 (Meagher and Powell JJA concurred).

146 *Advance (NSW) Insurance Agencies Pty Ltd v Matthews* (1989) 63 ALJR 365; (1989) 166 CLR 606; (1989) 5 ANZ Insurance Cases 60-910; see Ball (1988) 1 Insurance Law Journal 77; Nicholson (1989) 2 Insurance Law Journal 82 and (1989) 2 Insurance Law Journal 214.

that s 21(1) imposes a duty on each person who becomes insured to disclose material matters to the insurer. Deane J, who agreed with the overall conclusion of the joint judgment of Mason, CJ, Dawson, Toohey and Gaudron JJ but gave a separate judgment of his reasons for the decision, said:

> I do not agree with the view that the references to 'an insured' and 'the insured' in s 21(1) of the Insurance Contracts Act 1984 (Australia) ('the Act') should be read as distinct references to each of a number of joint insured with the consequence that the duty of disclosure of joint insured effectively becomes a number of separate duties rather than a joint one. It appears to me that, in the context of a statutory provisions defining the duty of disclosure of an insured and of the ordinary presumption that the statutory singular includes the plural, those references to 'an insured' and 'the insured' must, in the case of a joint policy of insurance, be read as collective references to the persons who constitute the insured under the policy.[147]

Accordingly, the argument that the knowledge of all the insureds was required before there was a duty to disclose was rejected by all members of the High Court.[148]

Under s 21(1) the insured's actual knowledge of the materiality is made relevant, though not essential, and the view of the hypothetical prudent insurer is discarded in favour of that of the particular insurer[149] as to the relevance of the fact. However, the very legitimate concern of the insurer that he or she should be appraised of sufficient material information in order that the risk be assessed, and the appropriate premium levied, is recognised in that objectivity has not been abandoned in favour of a totally subjective standard. The insured must disclose, as well, any matter that 'a reasonable person in the circumstances could be expected to know' is a relevant matter. This test is a 'far cry' from the formulation in the draft Bill of the legislation which required disclosure of what a person in the circumstances of the insured could reasonably be expected to know. This original formulation

147 *Ibid*, at 75-839. It may be noted that the Court of Appeal considered at length whether the policy was a composite or a joint policy. The majority in the High Court did not consider it necessary to decide the issue whilst Deane J decided that it was a joint policy of insurance. As to the effect of the classification, if any, see Courtenay (1989) 63 Australian Law Journal 587.

148 See, in particular, the majority judgment: (1989) 63 ALJR 365, at 369.

149 See Callaghan, 17 April 1985, p 13; see also the Insurance Act 1902 (NSW), s 18A; discussed by Sutton (1984) 12 Australian Business Law Review 215. Note also the comment by Brooking J in *Twenty-first Maylux Pty Ltd v Mercantile Mutual Insurance (Aust) Ltd* (1990) 6 ANZ Insurance Cases 60-954, at 76-304–05. Note that in *Henry Rae & Court v FAI General Insurance Co Ltd* (1992) 7 ANZ Insurance Cases 61-101, the Supreme Court of Western Australia emphasised that inducement of the particular insurer was essential before a misrepresentation could be material; *General Accident Insurance Co Australia Ltd v Kelaw Pty Ltd* (1997) 9 ANZ Insurance Cases 61-369. See also *Macquarie Bank Ltd v National Mutual Life Association Australia Ltd* (1996) 40 NSWLR 543, at 612–14; *Permanent Trustee Australia Co Ltd v FAI General Insurance Co Ltd* (2001) 11 ANZ Insurance Cases 61-491.

imported a high degree of subjectivity and in recognition of the extreme difficulties this could have occasioned insurers the legislature has in the Insurance Contracts Act 1984 (Australia) resiled from this position.[150]

The expression 'a reasonable person in the circumstances' has a certain ambiguity. It does not, it is argued, permit individual idiosyncrasies such as imperfect understanding of English, cultural background or unfamiliarity with business or insurance practice to be taken into account. These are intrinsic factors. Rather the expression permits a court to consider factors such as the general knowledge available to the proponent, the informality attendant upon negotiations where interim cover is arranged over the telephone, or the type of policy in issue, or the exposure to advertising and promotional material – in other words, to have regard to extrinsic factors.[151]

The contrary argument is expressed, in *EE Delphin v Lumley General Insurance Ltd*[152] where the District Court of Western Australia took the view that 'a reasonable person in the circumstances' referred to a reasonable person with the state of knowledge and educational background of the insured. The insurer had issued an insurance policy to the insured in respect of the contents of her house. Following renewal of the policy, the insured claimed to have suffered a burglary loss. Her claim for indemnity was denied on the basis of non-disclosure of her and her co-occupants' drug habits and convictions for the supply and use of drugs. The court found against the insurer on the ground that it had failed to prove its compliance with s 22 of the Act which requires an insurer, before a contract of insurance is entered into, to inform the insured of the duty of disclosure. The court said *obiter* that s 21 requires disclosure of matters which a reasonable person in the circumstances could be expected to know to be relevant to the insurer's decision whether to accept the risk. In this case, the question was whether a reasonable person in the circumstances of the insured, with her knowledge and educational background, could be expected to know that the intermittent use of drugs at the material date would be relevant to the insurer's decision regarding the issue of the policy. This test imports a high degree of subjectivity which the legislature had deliberately sought to avoid. It is suggested that the inclusion of the words 'a reasonable person in the circumstances' is designed to exclude the personal idiosyncratic traits of the insured concerned so as to avoid a finding against materiality in cases 'where the insured is somehow lacking in the capacity of a reasonable

150 See Sutton (1985) 13 ABLR 48, at 51.

151 See, generally, Tarr (1991) 4 Insurance Law Journal 227. See also *Twenty-first Maylux Ltd v Mercantile Mutual Insurance (Aust) Ltd* (1990) 6 ANZ Insurance Cases 60-954, at 76-304–05; *Ibrahim v Greater Pacific Life Insurance Co Ltd* (1996) 9 ANZ Insurance Cases 61-330.

152 (1989) 5 ANZ Insurance Cases 60-941. This case went on appeal to the Full Court of Western Australia; see (1990) 6 ANZ Insurance Cases 60-986. The Appeal Court did not disturb the trial judge's finding that no notice had been provided pursuant to s 22; s 21 was not considered on appeal.

person in respect of the necessary knowledge'.[153] It is therefore submitted that the better view is that the test embraced by the Insurance Contracts Act 1984 (Australia) may be perceived as an objective test modified by subjective criteria.[154]

While s 21(1) gives a positive general definition of what is to be disclosed this is modified by sub-s (2) which itemises specifically those matters that do not need to be disclosed; that is, a matter that diminishes the risk, that is of common knowledge, that the insurer knows, or in the ordinary course of business, ought to know, or as to which compliance with the duty of disclosure is waived by the insurer.[155] This provision covers the same ground as the Marine Insurance Act 1909 (Australia)[156] and does not add to, or vary, the position at common law. Of more interest is s 21(3) of the Insurance Contracts Act 1984 (Australia) which provides that:

> Where a person –
>
> (a) failed to answer; or
>
> (b) gave an obviously incomplete or irrelevant answer to, a question included in a proposal form about a matter,
>
> the insurer shall be deemed to have waived compliance with the duty of disclosure in relation to the matter.

Consequently, an insurer, having accepted an incomplete proposal without further inquiry, is precluded from later asserting non-disclosure in respect of a matter about which a question is asked in the proposal.[157] In a broad way, this conforms with the basic common law reasoning. For example, in *McLeod v SIMU Mutual Association*[158] the plaintiff had a business dealing in American cars and car parts. In 1983, he sought insurance cover from the defendant insurer. One of the questions in the proposal asked whether the plaintiff had any convictions for any offence (other than parking) in connection with a motor vehicle. The plaintiff answered that he had five previous speeding

153 See Derrington, 1990, at p 8; see also *Twenty-first Maylux Pty Ltd v Mercantile Mutual Insurance (Aust) Ltd* (1990) 6 ANZ 60-954; and Derrington and Ashton, 1988, at p 16.

154 Kelly, 30 May 1977, at p 5, is critical of this position. He asks: '[i]f I disclose everything I think is, or may be, relevant to the insurer, haven't I discharged that duty? What does it matter that someone else more intelligent or more knowledgeable or more thoughtful (the supposed reasonable person in my circumstances) would have done better? It's me you are insuring, not someone else! Let insurers ask questions specifically enough for them to get the information they need. After that, rely on concealment.'

155 In *Macfie v State Government Insurance Office (Qld)* (1985) 3 ANZ Insurance Cases 60-606, Derrington J held that the mere possession of information is not knowledge and there ought to be a connection between the acquisition of the information by the insurer (or its agents) and the particular application for insurance.

156 See s 24 of the Insurance Contracts Act 1984 (Australia).

157 This will not follow where an answer is incomplete, but not obviously so.

158 (1987) 4 ANZ Insurance Cases 60-784.

offences but did not disclose the fact that, three years prior, he was convicted for theft.[159] He gave evidence that when answering the question he had asked one of the insurer's employees the period to which the question related and whether it meant since 1981 when he owned the business. The insurer's employee did not indicate to the contrary. The High Court of New Zealand concluded:

> In this case, while I have no doubt that the concept of moral risk is important to a prudent insurer and that information as to a conviction may well have been significant in relation to motor vehicle insurance of this type in many cases, the circumstances here indicate that the risk was accepted on the day of the proposal and in the presence of the plaintiff so that, by virtue of the specific and limited question asked as to convictions, the specific explanation as to the extent of the question and the failure to enquire further, the insurer has indicated that it has no interest at that time in any further information and has effectively waived such information.[160]

While this largely turns on the estoppel of the insurer or its waiver of further disclosure by the representation of the insurer's agent as to the limited scope of the question, there is some parity in the reference to the insurer's failure to enquire further on knowing that the answer was limited so that it did not conform to the scope of the question. The court further said, *inter alia*, that the position may have differed if the questions in the proposal form had not been so specific and limited as to convictions. This conclusion seems logical in that it is difficult to see how a minor theft offence was 'a conviction in relation to a motor vehicle'.[161] In any event, his Honour held that, on the evidence given, he was not satisfied that a prudent insurer, having full knowledge of the circumstances of this conviction, namely that the insured had been convicted as a party to a minor theft of petrol in 1981, would have considered it material in determining whether he would have taken the risk on substantially the same terms.

The Insurance Law Amendment Act 1998 (Australia)[162] introduces a new s 21(A) into the Insurance Contracts Act 1984 (Australia). This section is expressed to apply to 'eligible contracts of insurance' entered into after 30 April 1998. The Insurance Council of Australia has agreed with the Australian Securities and Investments Commission that s 21A should apply to contracts that are prescribed contracts for purposes of the Insurance Contracts Act 1984 (Australia).[163] The legislature has acted in accordance with this

159 The plaintiff was fined $100 for being party to the offence.

160 (1978) 4 ANZ Insurance Cases 60-784, at 74-793.

161 *Ibid*. Technically, however, the conviction was in relation to the theft by the insured's brother-in-law of petrol from a boat to fill a motor vehicle's petrol tank. Therefore, construed widely, the question could cover this particular situation.

162 See s 3.

163 See Australian Securities and Investments Commission Circular No G1/98 *Insurance Law Amendment Act 1998 – New Duty of Disclosure Provisions and Other Changes.*

agreement as reg 2B[164] of the Insurance Contracts Regulations defines 'eligible contracts of insurance' as new contracts of motor vehicle insurance, home buildings and home contents insurance, sickness and accident insurance, consumer credit insurance and travel insurance.

The new section outlines what an insurer must do if a duty of disclosure is to apply to an insured in relation to a prescribed contract of insurance. Of central importance is the provision[165] that an insurer is taken to have waived compliance with the duty of disclosure in relation to the contract unless:

- before the contact is entered into, the insurer requests the insured to answer one or more specific questions that are relevant to the decision of the insurer whether to accept the risk and, if so, on what terms;[166] or
- before the contract is entered into, both: (a) the insurer requests the insured to answer one or more specific questions that are relevant to the decision of the insurer whether to accept the risk and, if so, on what terms; and (b) the insurer expressly requests the insured to disclose each exceptional circumstance that: (i) is known to the insured; and (ii) the insured knows, or a reasonable person in the circumstances could be expected to know, is a matter relevant to the decision of the insurer whether to accept the risk, and if so, on what terms; and (iii) is not a matter that the insurer could reasonably be expected to make the subject of a question under paragraph (a); and (iv) is not a matter covered by sub-s 21(2).[167]

These provisions constitute a challenge to comprehensibility standards, but in essence they require an insurer to do more than simply advise the insured of his or her duty of disclosure.[168] The insurer is obliged to pursue specific information relevant to the risk in order to enliven the duty of disclosure. The General Insurance Claims Review Panel[169] has given a cautious welcome to these new provisions as they consider that it will be easier for insureds to comply with the duty of disclosure on policy inception. An insurer who complies with (a) or (b) above, who asks the 'insured to disclose any other matters that would be covered by the duty of disclosure in relation to the contract', is taken to have waived compliance with the duty of disclosure in relation to those matters.[170] This is designed to prevent an insurer from asking a 'catch-all' question on top of specific ones.

Where an insurer complies with (a) above, the insured is taken to have complied with the duty of disclosure if he or she discloses each matter known

164 Regulation 2B inserted by SR No 191 of 1999, Sched 1, item 3.
165 Section 21A(2).
166 Section 21A(3).
167 Section 21A(4).
168 Insurance Contracts Act 1984 (Australia), s 22 (discussed below).
169 General Insurance Enquiries and Complaints Scheme Annual Report 1998, p 6.
170 Section 21A(5).

to him or her which a reasonable person in the circumstances could be expected to have disclosed in answer to that question.[171] In the case of the insurer's compliance with (b) above, the insured is taken to have complied with the duty of disclosure if he or she discloses each matter known to him or her which a reasonable person would disclose and complies with the request for information concerning exceptional circumstances.[172]

Section 22(1) of the Insurance Contracts Act 1984 (Australia) obliges an insurer to give pre-contract information to the insured in writing of the 'general nature and effect of the duty of disclosure';[173] and, if s 21A applies to the contract, also clearly to inform the insured in writing of the general nature and effect of s 21(A). Non-compliance with this requirement precludes an insurer from exercising 'a right in respect of a failure to comply with the duty of disclosure unless that failure was fraudulent'.[174] This requirement of notice applies to cover notes and all interim insurance and to renewals of general insurance contracts, as each such renewal constitutes a separate contract.[175] For example, in *Lumley General Insurance Ltd v Delphin*,[176] the court held against the insurer on the ground that the insurer had failed to prove that it had informed the insured, as required by s 22, of her duty of disclosure. The insurer sought to prove compliance by adducing evidence of its system of sending a renewal notice containing information about the duty of disclosure to customers. The court held that although the evidence of the system could lead to a favourable inference of compliance (especially as the insured had paid the premium) it was insufficient to prove a compliance of s 22 in the case before the court because the evidence was ambiguous. Indeed, the trial judge, Keall J, took the view that a computerised system whereby notices were printed and dispatched to policy holders fell 'a great deal short of establishing that a particular notice was in fact posted and received'.[177]

171 Section 21A(6).

172 Section 21A(7).

173 A prescribed form of writing is given in Scheds 1 and 2 to the Insurance Contracts Regulations SR No 162 of 1985; see reg 3 and s 22(2) of the Act. The Australian Law Reform Commission's *Report on Multiculturalism and the Law* (1992) recommends clearer advice to consumers of the general nature and effect of the duty of disclosure under the Insurance Law Amendment Act. The disclosure requirement in relation to s 21A was added by the Insurance Laws Amendment Act 1998 (Australia), s 3. Similarly, in Singapore, the Insurance Act Cap 142, rev ed, 1994, s 24, makes it mandatory for the insurer to warn the insured in the proposal form for insurance that non-disclosure or misrepresentation of a material fact could lead to loss of benefits under the policy.

174 Insurance Contracts Act 1984 (Australia), s 22(3).

175 *Ibid*, ss 11(2), 11(9). See *Breville Appliances Pty Ltd v Ducrou* (1992) 7 ANZ Insurance Cases 61-125; *Alexander Stenhouse Ltd v Austcan Investments Pty Ltd* (1993) 7 ANZ Insurance Cases 61-166; cf *Austcan Investments Pty Ltd v Sun Alliance Insurance Ltd* (1992) 7 ANZ Insurance Cases 61-116.

176 (1990) 6 ANZ Insurance Cases 60-986.

177 (1989) 5 ANZ Insurance Cases 60-941, at 76-130. Thus, Keall J held that the insurer had neither orally nor in writing informed the insured of her duty of disclosure. [contd]

Insurers are therefore required to keep careful records of notification to an insured under s 22 (for example, proof of actual posting of renewal notice to the insured concerned or receipt forms from the insured acknowledging notices) to avoid a defeat of its defence of non-disclosure under s 21(1), assuming the latter can be established. The required notification may be given orally and later confirmed in writing in the special circumstances set forth in s 69 of the Insurance Contracts Act 1984 (Australia).

The recent New South Wales Court of Appeal decision in *Suncorp General Insurance Ltd v Cheihk*[178] has emphasised that the general nature and effect of the duty of disclosure must be 'clearly' made known to the insured in writing. Giles JA observes that:

> It will always be a question of fact and degree, but the purpose of s 22 is to ensure that the insured is informed of the significant and important matters of his duty of disclosure and the consequences of failure to comply with the duty of disclosure, so that his insurance cover will not be imperilled by ignorance of those matters. The insured is to be informed clearly. Both the purpose of s 22 and its terms call for insistence on a proper standard of information giving.

Consequently, a statement on the reverse side of a certificate of insurance that was not highlighted in any way was inadequate and the insurer was held not to have clearly informed the insured of his duty of disclosure. Given that many a non-disclosure may be attributed to ignorance or forgetfulness on the face of it, the remedy provided by s 22 represents a satisfactory compromise. An innocent non-disclosure will not attract any legal consequences in the absence of the requisite statutory warning whereas an insurer's rights in respect of a fraudulent non-disclosure are preserved notwithstanding failure to give the statutory warning. Not only does fraudulent non-disclosure involve the deliberate withholding of information in informed circumstances but the need to deter fraud justifies harsher consequences.

Unfortunately, the intent behind s 22 has been significantly 'watered down' by s 11(10) of the Insurance Contracts Act 1984 (Australia). This section, introduced by the Statute Law (Miscellaneous Provisions) Act (No 2) 1986 (Australia), provides that:

> ... where ... at or before the original entering into, or renewal, extension or reinstatement, of a contract of insurance, the insurer has given information to the insured as required by s 22 ... the requirement ... to give information to the insured shall be deemed to be satisfied at or before any subsequent renewal, extension or reinstatement of the contract.

177 [contd] This decision was affirmed by the Full Court of the Supreme Court in *Lumley General Insurance Ltd v Delphin* (1990) 6 ANZ Insurance Cases 60-986. See also *Breville Appliances Pty Ltd v Ducrou* (1992) 7 ANZ Insurance Cases 61-125. The Full Court did not consider s 21 of the Insurance Contracts Act 1984 (Australia) as the trial judge's finding, that the insurer did not give notice pursuant to s 22, was not disturbed.

178 (1999) 10 ANZ Insurance Cases 61-442, at 75-024.

This amendment has been strongly criticised as creating an imbalance between the insured's duty of disclosure and that of the insurer. Moreover, the means whereby the change has been effected has been described by Kelly[179] as a misuse of the omnibus bill procedure:

> Translated, this Delphic utterance indicates that an insurer only has to give the insured a disclosure notice once. Having done that, the insurer has no duty to warn an insured about his or her duty of disclosure when the relevant contract is being renewed. Now, that is directly contrary to the principle of utmost good faith; and also to the principle that insureds should be given the information necessary to protect themselves against nasty surprises. The insured's duty to warn the insured about the existence of that duty is discharged once and for all!
>
> Anyone who knows anything about the communication of legal duties knows full well that a warning a year ago about something that is barely understood even at that time is most unlikely to be in the insured's mind when renewing a contract of insurance. The amendment of the Act restored the previous, quite unacceptable, inequality between insurer and insured. It relieved the insurer of its duty of utmost good faith in relation to giving a warning about the duty of disclosure on each relevant occasion. Section 11(10) is a blemish on the Act. Parliament should never have passed the amendment. It is inconsistent with the Act's underlying principles.

Conversely, it could be asserted that s 11(10) does no more than reduce a burden placed upon insurers. Prior to the promulgation of the Insurance Contracts Act 1984 (Australia) there was no obligation upon an insurer to provide pre-contract information as to the duty of disclosure – in the absence of knowledge that the insured was labouring under a misapprehension or in similar circumstances. The supporters of s 11(10) simply assert that this provision restores the pre-Act position in circumstances where the insured has already received clear information about his or her disclosure obligations.

The Insurance Contracts Act 1984 (Australia) effects significant changes to the remedies available for non-disclosure and misrepresentation. In relation to general insurance the remedies are not available to the insurer if 'the insurer would have entered into the contract, for the same premium and on the same terms and conditions, even if the insured had not failed to comply with the duty of disclosure'.[180] It is, it is argued, desirable that an imprudent insurer should not be entitled to recourse for non-disclosure or misrepresentation if its underwriting decision would have been the same if the true facts had been

179 Kelly (1987) 15 Australian Business Law Review 275.

180 Insurance Contracts Act (Australia), s 28(1). See, for example, *General Accident Insurance Co Australia Ltd v Kelaw Pty Ltd* (1997) 10 ANZ Insurance Cases 61-369. Compare Kerr J in *Berger & Light Diffusers Pty Ltd v Pollock* [1973] Lloyd's Rep 442, at 463; Somers J in *Avon House Ltd v Cornhill Insurance Co Ltd* (1980) 1 ANZ Insurance Cases 60-429; see discussion above, and see also *Itobar Pty Ltd v Mackinnon & Commercial Union Assurance Co* (1985) 3 ANZ Insurance Cases 60-610; *Pan Atlantic Insurance Co Ltd v Pine Top Insurance Co Ltd* [1995] 1 AC 501.

disclosed. The insurer may avoid a contract of general insurance *ab initio* if the non-disclosure or misrepresentation is fraudulent.[181] In the case of a joint policy of insurance where there is fraud on the part of one joint insured but not on the part of the other, such fraud on the part of the one joint insured is sufficient to characterise the failure to disclose or the misrepresentation as 'fraudulent'.[182] The interpretation given to the words 'an insured' in s 21(1) and in s 28(1) is that, where there is more than one insured, the duty of disclosure applies to 'each and every insured'. Thus a failure by one would affect the entitlement to claim of another.[183]

Pursuant to s 28(3), the insurer cannot avoid a contract for innocent non-disclosure or innocent misrepresentation.[184] Instead, the liability of the insurer in respect of a claim is reduced to the amount that would place it in a position which would have resulted if the failure to disclose or misrepresentation had not occurred. It was intended, it is suggested, that unless fraud is involved, an insurer cannot avoid the insurance contract for innocent non-disclosure or innocent misrepresentation. This prevents an insurer from escaping liability altogether in cases where the non-disclosure or misrepresentation of the material fact would have had no, or only a limited, effect on its decision with respect to the issue of the policy. At the same time, however, Parliament considered it necessary to balance the interests of both the insurer and the insured. Section 28(3) therefore permits the insurer, in cases of innocent non-disclosure and misrepresentation, to reduce the amount of liability in order to restore it to the position it would have been in had the material fact been disclosed or the misrepresentation not been made. If the circumstances are such that the insurer would have issued the policy nevertheless but would have charged a higher premium then it would be entitled under s 28(3) to reduce the claim by the amount of the additional premium. If the insurer would not have entered into the contract at all, then it would be entitled to pay nothing in respect of the claim except to refund the premium paid by the insurer.[185]

181 Insurance Contracts Act 1984 (Australia), s 28(2). For a recent detailed analysis of fraud, see *FAI General Insurance Co Ltd v McSweeney* (1998) 10 ANZ Insurance Cases 61-400, at 74, 348–74, 354.

182 *Advance (NSW) Insurance Agencies Pty Ltd v Matthews* (1989) 5 ANZ Insurance Cases 60-910; (1989) 166 CLR 606.

183 *Ibid*, at 75-837; at 617.

184 Insurance Contracts Act 1984 (Australia), s 28(3). Generally, see Ball (1992) 5 Insurance Law Journal 1.

185 See *Advance (NSW) Insurance Agencies Pty Ltd v Matthews* (1989) CLR 606, in particular, the judgment of Deane J at 622 where he rejects (*obiter*) the analysis of this point in *Advance (NSW) Insurance Agencies Pty Ltd v Matthews* (1987) 4 ANZ Insurance Cases 60-813; *Ferrcom Pty Ltd v Commercial Union Insurance Co of Australia Ltd* (1993) 176 CLR 332 affirming *Commercial Union Assurance Co of Australia Ltd v Ferrcom* (1991) 22 NSWLR 389; *Zurich Australian Insurance Ltd v Contour Mobel Pty Ltd* (1990) 6 ANZ Insurance Cases 60-984, at 76-559; *Duthie v Rolf H Wick & Association (Aust) Pty Ltd* (1994) 8 ANZ Insurance Cases 61-223. See Australian Law Reform Commission, *Report on* [contd]

Problems of proof arise regarding whether the insurer would have entered into the contract, and, if so, what the position would have been in the absence of the non-disclosure or misrepresentation. As these matters are peculiarly within the knowledge of the particular insurer, and the onus of establishing that position rests with it,[186] difficulties in accurately ascertaining this information are inevitable. Any insurer endeavouring to avoid liability on the basis that it would not have entered into the contract at all had it known the true facts, must lead detailed evidence as to office practice and produce underwriting guidelines designed to optimise its notional position.

The insurer's right to avoid a contract of general insurance *ab initio* for fraudulent non-disclosure or fraudulent misrepresentation is placed on a different footing largely because of the need to deter fraudulent conduct by the insuring public.[187] Moreover, given that fraud constitutes a flagrant breach of the duty of utmost good faith, avoidance of the contract would seem to be the only appropriate remedy. 'Fraud' under s 28(2) is established by showing: (1) that the insured gave information knowing it to be false; or (2) that the non-disclosure was made recklessly without regard to its veracity. As far as the insurer's entitlement to avoid the contact of insurance for fraudulent non-disclosure under s 28(2) is concerned, it is clear that evidence that the insured either gave the information knowing it to be false or that the non-disclosure was made recklessly without care as to its truth, is sufficient to establish 'fraud' for the purposes of s 28(2).[188] The standard of proof required is that usually applicable to fraud.[189] The purpose and seemingly the result of these provisions is to strike a reasonable balance between the interests of the parties.

Similar remedies are provided for in the case of life insurance in ss 29 and 30 of the Insurance Contracts Act 1984 (Australia). As for general insurance,

185 [contd] *Insurance Contracts* (No 20, 1982), paras 192, 194. Also see notes to draft Bill in Appendix A of the Commission's Report, p 184, and Derrington, 1990, at p 11; see also the comments of Brookings J in *Twenty-first Maylux Pty Ltd v Mercantile Mutual Insurance (Aust) Ltd* (1990) 6 ANZ Insurance Cases 60-954, at 76-306–07; and Derrington and Ashton, 1990, pp 172–73. See also *dicta* of Hanson J in *Burns v MMI-CMI Insurance Ltd* (1994) 8 ANZ Insurance Cases 61-228, *Permanent Trustee Australia Co Ltd v FAI General Insurance Co Ltd* (2001) 11 ANZ Insurance Cases 61-491, and Sutton (1995) 23 Australian Business Law Review 225.

186 For example, in *Ayoub v Lombard Insurance Co (Aust) Pty Ltd* [1989] 97 FLR 285, Rogers CJ was not prepared to conclude, on the whole of the evidence, that the insurer would not have issued the cover note had the misrepresentation not been made by the insured. His Honour found that 'the practice of the [insurer] was not sufficiently uniform' (at 287). See also *Bauer Tonkin Insurance Brokers v CIC* (1996) 9 ANZ Insurance Cases 61-298.

187 Australian Law Reform Commission, *Report on Insurance Contracts* (No 20, 1982), para 196.

188 *Plasteel Windows (Aust) Pty Ltd v CE Heath Underwriting Agencies Pty Ltd* (1989) 5 ANZ Insurance Cases 60-926, at 75-970 and 75-971, *per* Cole J.

189 See, for example, *Von Braun v Australian Associated Motor Insurers Ltd* (1999) 10 ANZ Insurance Cases 61-419.

the insurer does not have a remedy if he would have entered into the contract of life insurance even if the insured had not failed to comply with the duty of disclosure or had not made the misrepresentation.[190] Section 29 does not apply where the failure was in respect of the date of birth of one or more of the insureds as this receives special attention in s 30.[191] Save for these two cases, non-reliance or misstatements of age, s 29 provides for the remedies in the life insurance area. If the failure was fraudulent, the insurer has an option to avoid the contract.[192] As far as innocent non-disclosure is concerned the insurer is given a three year period after the contract was entered into to discover the non-disclosure or misrepresentation; if he would not have entered into the contract at all had the true facts been known to him at that time he may avoid the contract within that three year time period; conversely, if the insurer elects not to avoid the contract,[193] he may vary the sum insured in the proportion that the premiums payable under the contract bear to the premiums payable if there had been no breach by the insured, and any such variation has effect from the time when the contract was entered into.[194] As with general insurance, if the insurer can discharge the heavy onus of proving fraud he may avoid the policy; not only does this accord with the *uberrimae fidei* principle but the significance of such misconduct in the insurance field cannot be underestimated; for example, the insurer may be lulled into a state of mind where he does not pursue inquiries into matters which may turn out to be very material.[195] As for innocent non-disclosure, the principle of proportionality adopted by the statute will transfer the cost of any additional risk and the loss attributable to such additional risk to the insured,[196] and if the insurer would not have taken the risk at all he may avoid the contract. With innocent non-disclosure the sword of Damocles does not hang over the insured's head indefinitely as the insurer must exercise his rights under s 29 within three years of entry into the agreement.

With respect to misstatements of age, s 30 provides that there is to be no avoidance of the contract even if they are fraudulent. Instead, the sum insured is adjusted in accordance with a formula provided in the Act and the adjustment has retrospective effect. The effect of this provision, and its

190 Insurance Contracts Act 1984 (Australia), s 29(1)(c).

191 *Ibid*, s 29(1)(d). See also the Life Insurance Act 1945 (Australia), s 83 which gives special treatment to misstatements of the age of the life insured. By virtue of s 86A of the Life Insurance Act 1945 (Australia), s 83 does not apply to or in relation to a policy to which the Insurance Contracts Act 1984 (Australia) applies.

192 Insurance Contracts Act 1984 (Australia), s 29(2).

193 Whether under s 29(2) or s 29(3) or otherwise.

194 See the Insurance Contracts Act 1984 (Australia), s 29(2), (3), (4), (5), (6).

195 See, for example, *Carter Bros v Renouf* (1962) 111 CLR 140.

196 For a discussion of proportionality, see the English Law Commission, *Report on Insurance Law, Non-Disclosure and Breach of Warranty* (Law Com No 104, 1980), para 4.7; Australian Law Reform Commission, *Report on Insurance Contracts* (No 20, 1982), paras 188–90.

forerunner, s 83 of the Life Insurance Act 1945 (Australia),[197] is to substitute for the benefits provided under the contract benefits which are reasonable having regard to the true age of the life insured. No time limit is imposed for such variation to be made. It is difficult to reconcile the avowed intention of the Insurance Contracts Act 1984 (Australia)[198] that utmost good faith should be the paramount duty, with the position that fraud in the context of misstatement of age does not entitle an insurer to avoid the policy in question. For the sake of consistency and in the interests of the preservation of the good faith principle it is submitted that the insurer should be entitled to avoid the policy if he or she proves a fraudulent misstatement of age.

Stipulations in a proposal form to the effect that a failure to answer a particular question will be deemed to be an answer in the negative are rendered ineffective.[199] Not only do such stipulations lead to uncertainty and confusion,[200] but the insured may be deemed to have provided a false answer. The section also provides that a person does not make a misrepresentation merely by failing to answer a question in the proposal form or by giving an obviously incomplete or irrelevant answer to such question. This section requires the insurer to pursue a full and proper answer if it may later wish to rely on a misrepresentation from these sources. However, it only applies where the question is unanswered or is obvious. It is a misrepresentation if the statement is only a half-truth which appears to be complete, and an insurer should not be expected to check on every answer which is, on its face, relevant and complete. Moreover, s 24 of the Insurance Contracts Act 1984 (Australia), which is headed 'warranties of existing facts to be representations', provides that a statement made in or in connection with a contract of insurance, being a statement made by or attributable to the insured, with respect to the existence of a state of affairs does not have effect as a warranty. It instead takes effect as though it was a statement made to the insurer by the insured during the negotiations for the contract but before it was entered into. This has a dramatic impact upon the common law. It 'sounds the death knell to the "basis of the contract clause" in a proposal'[201] and such clauses 'are tossed into the dust-bin of history'.[202] That is, the

197 Section 83 will continue to regulate the position as far as contracts not covered by the Insurance Contracts Act (Australia) are concerned – essentially, contracts of life insurance entered into before 1 January 1986. See the Life Insurance Act 1945 (Australia), s 86A.

198 As enshrined in ss 12 and 13 of the Act.

199 Insurance Contracts Act 1984 (Australia), s 27.

200 See the Australian Law Reform Commission, *Report on Insurance Contracts* (No 20, 1982), para 184. Uncertainty and confusion arise particularly in relation to questions not obviously susceptible to a negative answer.

201 Sutton (1985) 13 ABLR 48, at 52.

202 Callaghan, 17 April 1985, p 13.

insurer is precluded from elevating statements or promises to the status of warranties by inserting a 'basis of the contract clause' in the proposal and policy.

The expression 'a state of affairs' could logically include a statement of past or existing or future fact but it is unlikely that a construction of this expression will be held to embrace continuing or promissory warranties.[203]

Section 26 of the Insurance Contracts Act 1984 (Australia) also excludes certain statements from the category of misrepresentations. First, an untrue statement does not constitute a misrepresentation where it was made on the basis of a belief honestly and reasonably held; that is, not only must the proponent hold such a belief at the relevant time but it must also be a belief that a reasonable person in the circumstances would have held.[204] Accuracy is no longer required, only honest and objectively reasonable belief. This successfully counters the practice of many insurers to require from an insured a guarantee of accuracy as to the existence of facts in circumstances where the actual knowledge, recollection or judgment of the insured[205] in question makes such requirement grossly unfair. Secondly, an untrue statement will amount to a misrepresentation only if the person who made it knew, or a reasonable person in the circumstances could be expected to have known, that the statement would have been relevant to the decision of the insurer as to whether to accept the risk and, if so, on what terms.[206] This re-introduces the requirement of materiality which had applied to misrepresentation in ordinary policies but had been rendered irrelevant in cases such as *Dawsons Ltd v Bonnin*[207] through 'basis of the contract' clauses and warranties. As with non-disclosure, the reasonable insured again supplants the prudent insurer as the arbitrator of materiality. Further, the result of s 28 is that materiality is essential for avoidance of misrepresentation in respect of all insurance contracts covered by the Act and the assessment of this question is by reference to the particular insurer – not the hypothetical reasonable or prudent insurer. The onus is on the insurer to establish that a reasonable person could have been expected to have known of the materiality of the representation to the insurer.[208]

Further to this, Derrington and Ashton comment:

> It should be noted that the standard is not what the insured may claim to have understood by the question but rather the meaning apparently understood, and this would seem to be a deduction from the words of the answer in the total relevant context. The insured will probably not be allowed to give evidence of any subjective belief. The remaining question is whether

203 *Ibid*, pp 13–14.

204 Insurance Contracts Act 1984 (Australia), s 26(1).

205 For example, as to medical condition or history.

206 Insurance Contract Act 1984 (Australia), s 26(2). See, for example, *Australian Mutual Provident Society v Lose* (1997) 9 ANZ Insurance Cases 61-381.

207 [1922] 2 AC 413.

208 Insurance Contracts Act 1984 (Australia), s 26(1).

> circumstances personal to the insured, such as reduced intellect, should be taken as part of the 'circumstances' mentioned in the section. The answer again is probably in the negative, because of the requirement of reasonableness. The purpose of referring to that is to apply an objective standard.[209]

Finally, even in those circumstances where an insurer is entitled to avoid a contract of general insurance for fraudulent non-disclosure or fraudulent misrepresentation, the fraudulent customer is not necessarily lost. Pursuant to s 31, a court is given an overriding power to disregard avoidance if it would be harsh and unfair not to do so and the insurer has not been significantly prejudiced by the failure.[210] Both criteria must be met. This relief, according to *Plasteel Windows (Aust) Pty Ltd v CE Heath Underwriting Agencies Pty Ltd*[211] is confined to a consideration of the position of the insured but not that of third parties. In the exercise of this discretion, the judge must 'juggle and weigh [these] hairy coconuts'[212] having regard to the need to deter fraudulent conduct in relation to insurance and must weigh the extent of the culpability of the insured in the fraudulent conduct against the magnitude of the loss that would be suffered by the insured if the avoidance were not disregarded.[213] Moreover, the court may consider any other relevant matters.[214] If a court decides to exercise its discretion in favour of an insured, the effect is to preserve the claim only in respect of the loss and the contract is not resuscitated or reinstated.[215] As well, it should be noted, the amount recoverable lies within the court's discretion. Instead of allowing recovery of the whole amount, it may give judgment for such part of the amount as it thinks just and equitable in the circumstances.[216]

3.4 THE COMMON LAW MODIFIED: THE NEW ZEALAND PERSPECTIVE

(a) Contractual Remedies Act 1979

A false or misleading statement may render the maker of the statement liable in damages and/or entitle the innocent party to cancel the contract that he or

209 Derrington and Ashton, *The Law of Liability Insurance* (Draft 2nd edn, November 1999), Chapter 5, p 48.

210 Insurance Contracts Act 1984 (Australia), s 31(1), (2). See *Von Braun v Australian Associated Motor Insurers Ltd* (1999) 10 ANZ Insurance Cases 61-419.

211 (1989) 5 ANZ Insurance Cases 60-925.

212 The expression is that of Callaghan, 17 April 1985, p 18.

213 Insurance Contracts Act 1984 (Australia), s 31(3).

214 *Ibid.*

215 Insurance Contracts Act 1984 (Australia), s 31(4).

216 *Ibid*, s 31(1). See, for example, *Von Braun v Australian Associated Motor Insurers Ltd* (1999) 10 ANZ Insurance Cases 61-419.

she entered into in reliance upon the misstatement. The general position in New Zealand as between parties to a contract is succinctly stated in the Contractual Remedies Act 1979. Section 6(1) of the Act provides as follows:

> (1) If a party to a contract has been induced to enter into it by a misrepresentation, whether innocent or fraudulent, made to him by or on behalf of another party to that contract –
>
> (a) he shall be entitled to damages from that other party in the same manner and to the same extent as if the misrepresentation were a term of the contract that has been broken; and
>
> (b) he shall not, in the case of a fraudulent misrepresentation, or of an innocent misrepresentation made negligently, be entitled to damages from that other party for deceit or negligence in respect of that misrepresentation.

Furthermore, a contracting party is entitled to cancel a contract[217] where it has been induced by a misrepresentation but only if the parties have expressly or impliedly agreed that the truth of the representation is essential to the representee, or it is shown that the misrepresentation has a profound effect upon the benefit or burden of the contract.[218]

This Act effected significant changes to the law in a number of ways, in that:

1 At common law, a person who was induced to enter into a contract due to the fraudulent misrepresentation of the other party, could rescind the contract[219] and/or institute an action in the tort of deceit for damages.[220]

  Section 6 of the Contractual Remedies Act 1979 abolishes the action for pre-contract fraudulent misrepresentation and provides that it is no longer possible to bring tort actions.

2 At common law, if the misrepresentation was innocent or negligent the remedy of rescission was initially the only remedy available.[221] However, by virtue of the decision of the House of Lords in *Hedly Byrne & Co v Heller & Partners Ltd*[222] an action in damages in the tort of negligence could lie

---

217 Generally, see the Contractual Remedies Act 1979, s 7. See Dawson [1991] NZ Recent Law at 20–26.

218 Contractual Remedies Act 1979, s 7(4).

219 See Cheshire and Fifoot, 1984, p 228 *et seq*.

220 See *Derry v Peek* (1889) 14 App Cas 337. The representee had to prove that the representor knew that the statement was false, or had no belief in its truth, or made it recklessly, not caring whether it was true or false. See also *Archer v Brown* [1984] 2 All ER 267 (misrepresentation and deceit contrasted). The Contractual Remedies Act 1979, s 6(1), does not preclude the possibility of a tort action being brought against an *agent* for misrepresentation.

221 The reference to the 'common law' in this context includes equitable principles, for the common law, as opposed to equity, which gave no remedy for innocent misrepresentation. See *Anson's Law of Contract*, 1979, p 248; compare *Riddiford v Warren* (1901) 20 NZLR 572.

222 [1964] AC 465.

where the representation was made negligently. However, in respect of innocent misrepresentations, the representee was 'faced with a "take it or leave it" choice of proceeding with the contract uncompensated or taking the drastic step of rescinding'.[223] The Contractual Remedies Act 1979 abolishes the action for pre-contract negligent misrepresentation, eliminates the possibility of bringing a tort action, and makes it possible to claim damages in respect of an innocent misrepresentation.[224] As Dawson and McLauchlan[225] explain: 'The philosophy behind [s 6] is that where a person has made a representation which induces another to contract with him, he should be responsible for the accuracy of the representation irrespective of fault.' An actionable misrepresentation *per se* gives a right to damages and these damages are assessed 'as if the representation were a term of the contract that has been broken'.[226]

3 While the right to terminate the contract where it has been induced by misrepresentation is retained, this right is severely restricted. At common law the right to rescind did not depend on a finding that the misrepresentation complained of related to a matter of fundamental importance or had serious consequences.[227]

4 Cancellation differs from rescission in that it operates *de futuro* only; at common law a party was entitled to rescind the contract *ab initio* and seek restitution of benefits conferred; under the Contractual Remedies Act 1979 a wide discretion is arrogated to the court in terms of restoration of benefits, and cancellation does not automatically result in certain consequences such as recovery of money paid over or property transferred pursuant to the contract.[228]

The term 'misrepresentation' is not defined in the Act with the result that reference must be made to the common law where the term has been defined as a 'false statement of existing or past fact'.[229] Generally speaking, statements as to intention or law, or of opinion, are not actionable. Whereas a misstatement by an insurer's agent as to the nature of a life insurance policy

---

223 Dawson and McLauchlan, *The Contractual Remedies Act 1979*, 1981, p 12.

224 Section 6.

225 Dawson and McLauchlan, 1981, p 12.

226 Section 6(1)(a).

227 Dawson and McLauchlan, 1981, p 45. These writers point out, however, that '[w]here the misrepresentation was very trivial, the representee could be denied rescission on the ground that the representation was immaterial, that is, it did not induce the contract'.

228 Contractual Remedies Act 1979, s 9: *Giles v Edwards* (1797) 7 TR 181; *Le Seur v Morang & Co Ltd* (1910) 20 OR 594.

229 See Contracts and Commercial Law Reform Committee, *Misrepresentation and Breach of Contract* (1967), para 13.3; see also Cheshire and Fifoot, 1984, p 220 *et seq*. A detailed analysis of the meaning of misrepresentation is outside the scope of this book. See Burrows (1986) 6 Otago LR 220, at 221–22; *Ware v Johnson* [1984] 2 NZLR 518.

was a misrepresentation of fact, 'a statement the inaccuracy of which could have been shown at once',[230] a mere estimate as to the return to be derived from taking out a life insurance policy is not a misrepresentation of fact.[231] A statement of valuation or as to good health is clearly a statement of opinion and even if the opinion turns out to be unfounded or incorrect, no liability attaches to the maker of the statement, so long as the statement was given *bona fide*.[232] However, if the proclaimed opinion is not entertained at the time when it is expressed, it is a misrepresentation as to the present state of the maker's mind, that is, of fact.

While a misrepresentation as to a matter of law is generally not actionable,[233] there are exceptions; for example, it has been held that wilful misstatements of the law are actionable.[234] Where a statement amounts to an objective statement of fact which is demonstrably false, no difficulty arises in establishing an actionable misrepresentation.[235] However, it is clear that an incomplete statement which creates a misleading impression may amount to an actionable misrepresentation.[236]

Finally, there may be a misstatement without any false statement having been made in plain terms; for example, if a number of statements taken together and reasonably interpreted convey a misleading impression of the facts.[237]

Where a misrepresentation has been made by, or on behalf of, another party to the contract thereby inducing the aggrieved party to enter into the contract, the remedy of damages and/or the remedy of cancellation may be available.[238] Where the false or misleading statement emanates from the other contracting party no difficulty arises. However, most insurers are corporate entities and necessarily must act through agents, and the question as to whether statements made by an agent are binding upon his or her principal must be resolved by the application of normal agency principles.[239] As far as inducement is concerned, a representation has no effect if the person to whom

230 *Equitable Life Assurance Society of the United States v Bertie* (1890) 8 NZLR 579, at 591.

231 *Boyd v Colonial Mutual Life Assurance Society* (1910) 29 NZLR 41; *Horncastle v Equitable Life Assurance Society of the United States* (1906) 22 TLR 735.

232 *Joel v Law Union & Crown Insurance Co* [1908] 2 KB 863; MacGillivray and Parkington, 1988, p 234.

233 *Rashdall v Ford* (1866) LR 2 Eq 750, at 754; Cheshire and Fifoot, 1984, p 222.

234 *West London Commercial Bank v Kitson* (1884) 13 QBD 360, at 362; *Harse v Pearl Life Assurance Co* [1904] 1 KB 558; MacGillivray and Parkington, 1988, p 236.

235 *Equitable Life Assurance Society of the United States v Bertie* (1890) 8 NZLR 579.

236 See *Ware v Johnson* [1984] 2 NZLR 518; Burrows, 1986, at 223–24.

237 *Aarons Reefs Ltd v Twiss* [1896] AC 273, at 281.

238 Contractual Remedies Act 1979, ss 6, 7.

239 See below.

it is made does not rely upon it.[240] However, a representee is assisted in that it is presumed as a reasonable inference of fact, that where a material misrepresentation is made, and a contract is entered into, that the representee must have acted in reliance upon the misrepresentation.[241] Finally, on the question of inducement, it is clear that s 6 of the Contractual Remedies Act 1979 does not require that the representation be shown to be *material*.[242] The question of inducement is a matter dependent upon the representee's state of mind, as opposed to 'materiality' which is referable to the state of mind of a 'reasonable man of business'.[243] Of course, if the representation is shown to be material, in the sense that a reasonable person may have been induced to enter the contract in question, the representee may more easily discharge the onus of demonstrating inducement.

Therefore, if a party to a contract can establish that he or she was induced to enter the contract by a misrepresentation made by or on behalf of another party to the contract, that party is entitled to damages as if the representation were a term of the contract; that is, he or she is entitled to be put in as good a position as if the representation had been true.[244] A party to a contract can cancel the contract where it has been induced by a misrepresentation but only if the contracting parties have expressly or impliedly agreed that the truth of the representation is essential to him or her,[245] or it is shown that the representation has a substantial effect upon the benefit or burden of the contract to the cancelling party.[246] Clearly, the effect of this legislation is to restrict the circumstances in which the remedy of cancellation may be granted to those cases where the misrepresentation has a substantial impact upon the party wishing to cancel.[247]

240 Cheshire and Fifoot, 1984, p 225.

241 MacGillivray and Parkington, 1988, p 248.

242 See Dawson and McLauchlan, 1981, pp 24–25.

243 *Nicholas v Thompson* [1924] VLR 554. See *Perring v VR Wood Ltd* (unreported, High Court, Nelson, 30 July 1984, A31/83, Eichelbaum J).

244 See *Doyle v Olby (Ironmongers) Ltd* [1969] 2 QB 158, at 167; Stoljar (1975) 91 LQR 68. Generally, see *ME Torbett Ltd v Keirlor Motels Ltd* (unreported, High Court, Auckland, 30 March 1984, A539/83, Casey J); *New Zealand Motor Bodies Ltd v Emslie* (unreported, High Court, Dunedin, 6 June 1984, A93/82, Barker J). See Burrows (1986) 6 Otago LR 220, at 227–30 and the cases there cited.

245 Contractual Remedies Act 1979, s 7(4)(a).

246 *Ibid*, s 7(4)(b). Generally, see *Worsdale v Polglase* [1981] 1 NZLR 722; *Gallagher v Young* [1981] 1 NZLR 734; *Young v Hunt* [1984] 2 NZLR 80; *Ware v Johnson* [1984] 2 NZLR 518; *Ansell v New Zealand Insurance Finance Ltd* (unreported, High Court, Wellington, 6 June 1984, A434/83, Quilliam J); *Hughes v Guardian Royal Exchange Assurance Co of New Zealand* (1988) 5 ANZ Insurance Cases 60-879.

247 See *New Zealand Tenancy Bonds Ltd v Mooney* [1986] 1 NZLR 280; *Bird v Bickness* [1987] 2 NZLR 543; *Broadbank Corp Ltd v Martin* [1988] 1 NZLR 446; *Progeni Systems Ltd v Hampton Studios Ltd* (unreported, High Court, Christchurch, 11 August 1987, CP 105/86, Tipping J); *Sharplin v Henderson* [1990] 2 NZLR 134. Generally, see Dawson [1991] NZ Recent Law Review 19, at 20–23.

Certain types of contractual terms which seek directly to exclude liability for pre-contract statements are regulated by the Contractual Remedies Act 1979.[248] It is by no means uncommon to find a clause to the following, or like, effect in contracts: 'This document contains the whole of the contract between the parties thereto.'[249] Notwithstanding the presence of such a clause, a New Zealand court is not precluded from ascertaining the true state of affairs 'unless the court considers that it is fair and reasonable that the provision should be conclusive between the parties'.[250] Where an insured has been induced to enter into a contract of insurance by a misrepresentation by an agent in discussions preceding the conclusion of the transaction, it is unlikely that the court will regard any such 'merger' clause as being conclusive.[251] The disparity in bargaining power between the average insured and insurer and the unlikelihood of the insured having received independent legal advice prior to commencement are significant factors to be weighed in the balance. However, every case will turn on its own facts and the court may have regard to all the circumstances of the case in deciding whether it is fair and reasonable that the clause should be conclusive. Where a clause in a contract simply denies the existence of any agency or authority to make representations, the court does not have to apply a 'fair and reasonable test' but may inquire directly into what the true position is.[252]

It must, however, be emphasised that s 4 of the Contractual Remedies Act 1979 does not empower the court 'to disregard true exemption clauses – clauses which exclude or limit liability, or the availability of any remedy, for misrepresentation or breach of contract'.[253] Section 5 of the Contractual Remedies Act 1979 provides that:

> If a contract expressly provides for a remedy in respect of misrepresentation or repudiation or breach of contract or makes express provision for any of the other matters to which ss 6–10 of this Act relate, those sections shall have effect subject to that provision.

The rationale behind the inclusion of s 5 is that the parties should be free to determine the extent of their rights *and* obligations and to outline the

248 Section 4.

249 Cited in Dawson and McLauchlan, 1981, p 36.

250 Contractual Remedies Act 1979, s 4(1). In deciding whether a clause should be treated as conclusive or not, the court shall have regard 'to all the circumstances of the case, including the subject matter and value of the transaction, the respective bargaining strengths of the parties, and the question whether any party was represented or advised by a solicitor at the time of the negotiations or at any other relevant time'.

251 Such as the clause given above.

252 Contractual Remedies Act 1979, s 4(2).

253 Dawson and McLauchlan, 1981, p 38. These writers make the pertinent comment that 'it is anomalous that s 4 enables a court to disregard a clause saying "there are no representations" but *not* one saying "no liability for representations"'.

consequences to be visited upon any breach of those obligations.[254] Therefore, where a policy of insurance contains a provision that specified what consequences are to ensue where there has been a misrepresentation, this clause will effectively exclude the application of ss 6–10 of the Act, that is, those sections providing for the remedies of damages and cancellation. Of course, where an insurance contract is silent on the matter of remedies in respect of misrepresentation, repudiation or breach, the rights and obligations of insurer and insured are determined by reference to the Contractual Remedies Act 1979.

However, it is usual for insurers to address their attention fully, or in part, to the question of misstatement. An insured is under a duty to disclose all material facts relating to the insurance sought, and the insurer usually solicits information from the insured by asking a number of questions in a proposal form for such insurance.[255] The insured is usually required to warrant that his or her answers are true and that they shall form the basis of the contract of insurance.[256] Where the insured has warranted the accuracy of his or her statement and such warranty has become part of the contract by being incorporated (usually by reference), an incorrect answer to any question in the proposal, no matter how apparently trivial, however innocently made, and however immaterial to the risk, entitles the insured *at common law* to avoid the contract.[257] The Contractual Remedies Act 1979 does not affect this situation as s 5 of that Act permits the parties to make express provision in their contract for such a contingency; it is only where the insurance contract fails to provide a remedy in respect of misrepresentation that recourse must be had to the more restrictive circumstances in which cancellation may be granted under the Act. However, this is not to suggest that the insurer has a carte blanche to avoid contracts of insurance for any misstatement, however innocent or immaterial, if the insurer takes the trouble to insert an appropriate clause in his or her policy to cover such misstatements. There are other major statutory provisions which are designed to regulate the situation.[258]

---

254 See the Contracts and Commercial Law Reform Committee, *Misrepresentation and Breach of Contract* (1967), para 20; [1979] 77 New Zealand Parliamentary Debates 624.

255 A proposal form is an application form for insurance; this form customarily constitutes the offer which is open for acceptance by the insurer. See below.

256 See discussion below.

257 See Hasson, 1971; Sutton (1972) 5 NZULR 123; and the discussion below.

258 It should be noted that it is stipulated in s 15(h) of the Contractual Remedies Act that nothing in the Act shall affect 'any other enactment so far as it prescribes or governs terms of contracts or remedies available in respect of contracts, or governs the enforcement of contracts'. Accordingly, insofar as cancellation is governed by the Insurance Law Reform Act 1977, the Contractual Remedies Act will not apply; save for the case of verbal representations and oral contracts. See Borrowdale [1987] NZLJ 30, at 30–31.

(b) *Insurance Law Reform Act 1977*

The Contracts and Commercial Law Reform Committee in their Report entitled *Aspects of Insurance Law*[259] advocated that the latitude afforded insurers to avoid policies for misstatement should be curtailed. The legislature accepted the Committee's recommendations and the Insurance Law Reform Act 1977 contains a number of provisions pertaining to misstatement.

Section 4 of the Insurance Law Reform Act 1977 provides as follows:

(1) A life policy shall not be avoided by reason only of any statement (other than a statement as to the age of the life insured) made in any proposal or other document on the faith of which the policy was issued, reinstated, or renewed by the company unless the statement –

- (a) was substantially incorrect; and
- (b) was material; and
- (c) was made either –
  - (i) fraudulently; or
  - (ii) within the period of three years immediately preceding the date on which the policy is sought to be avoided or the date of the death of the life insured, whichever is the earlier.

(2) For the purposes of sub-paragraph (i) of paragraph (c) of sub-section (1) of this section, a statement is made fraudulently if the person making it makes it –

- (a) knowing it is incorrect; or
- (b) without belief in its correctness; or
- (c) recklessly, without caring whether it is correct or not.

A statement is substantially incorrect only if the difference between what is stated and what is actually correct would have been considered material by a prudent insurer.[260]

A statement is material only if that statement would have influenced the judgment of a prudent insurer in fixing the premium or in determining whether he or she would have taken or continued to risk upon substantially the same terms.[261] Therefore, s 4 of the Insurance Law Reform Act 1977 severely restricts the insurer's ability to avoid a life insurance policy for misstatements. Before an insurer can avoid such a policy he or she must show that the misstatement was substantially incorrect, was material, and was made fraudulently or within a period of three years prior to death or avoidance. It was contended on behalf of the insurance industry that any fraudulent misstatement should be grounds for avoidance, but there is no logical reason why an immaterial misstatement, whether fraudulent or not, should give the

259 First Report, April 1975.

260 Insurance Law Reform Act 1977, s 6(1).

261 *Ibid*, s 6(2).

insurer the right to avoid the policy.[262] It is important to bear in mind that s 4 applies only to *written* statements contained in a document which induced the issuance, reinstatement or renewal of a life policy. As far as misstatements of age are concerned, special provision is made in s 7 to the effect that a life policy is not to be avoided by reason only of a misstatement of age. A simple adjustment in the amount recoverable or the premium payable under the policy is all that is required.[263]

Section 5 of the Insurance Law Reform Act 1977 provides that:

> (1) A contract of insurance shall be not avoided by reason only of any statement made in any proposal or other document on the faith of which the contract was entered into, reinstated, or renewed by the insurer unless the statement –
>
> (a) was substantially incorrect; and
>
> (b) was material.
>
> (2) Nothing in this section shall –
>
> (a) apply in respect of any contract of insurance embodied in a life policy; or
>
> (b) limit the provisions of ss 4 and 7 of this Act.

This section has been subjected to extensive judicial scrutiny. In *Preece v State Insurance General Manager*[264] the respondent insurer had issued a motor vehicle policy to the appellant insured. A question in the proposal for the policy had read: 'Has the vehicle or its engine been modified in any way since manufacture?' The insured's response was: 'Yes. Replace and install standard 2000cc.' In fact, in addition to the installation of this engine, he had installed a new gearbox and a new exhaust manifold and had fitted 'wide rear rims with radial tyres'. Following an accident the insured claimed under the policy, but the insurer asserted that it was not bound to indemnify the insured on the ground that, by failing to disclose the additional modifications to the vehicle, the policy was avoided for a substantial and material misstatement. This argument was upheld in the District Court and the insured appealed.

Thorp J observed that ss 5 and 6 of the Insurance Law Reform Act 1977 were designed to alleviate:

> ... the harshness and artificiality resulting from the common practice of insurers requiring proponents to warrant the complete accuracy of all answers to questions put by insurers, with the result that any inaccuracy, whether by way of positive misstatement or omission, and whether major or trivial, material or immaterial to risk or loss, voided the policy.[265]

---

262 The Contracts and Commercial Law Reform Committee, *Aspects of Insurance Law* (April 1975), para 10.

263 Insurance Law Reform Act 1977, s 7(2), (3).

264 (1982) 2 ANZ Insurance Cases 60-493.

265 *Ibid*, at 77-807.

The combined effect of these sections meant that an insurer could only avoid a policy when the difference between what was stated in the proposal and what was actually correct would have been considered material by a prudent insurer and would have influenced that insurer's judgment in fixing the premium or determining whether he or she would have taken or continued the risk upon substantially the same terms. Thorp J held that the installation of the new gearbox and exhaust manifold was necessarily incidental to the installation of the larger engine, and that the omission of this additional information was insignificant and did not make the answer substantially incorrect. As far as the radial tyres were concerned, it was held that the installation of such tyres on all four wheels in normal standard sizes would not call for special consideration by an insurer and the omission of that information was not material, nor did it render the answer that was given substantially incorrect. Consequently, the appeal was allowed.

This case may be contrasted with *Peters v National Insurance Co of New Zealand Ltd*.[266] The plaintiff antique dealer effected a policy of insurance against loss by burglary with the defendant insurer. Antique jewellery was taken from the plaintiff's shop and a claim in respect of this loss was rejected by the insurer on the ground that there had been non-disclosure by the plaintiff in her answers to questions in the proposal. Two of the questions and answers given were as follows:

> 7 Have thieves ever entered or attempted to enter any of your premises? If so, what precautions have been taken to prevent a recurrence? 'No.'
>
> 13 (a) Have you ever sustained loss by burglary or house-breaking?
>
> (b) If so, give details and, if insured, state name of company claimed on.
>
> (a) 'Burglary at home.'
>
> (b) 'Gen Accident didn't pay.'
>
> (c) The defendant insurer contended that these answers were untrue in that they failed to disclose prior thefts and other burglaries which ought to have been disclosed. As regards the negative answer to question 7 in the proposal, Quillam J observed: 'To have answered "No" to that question if there had been, for example, a single theft of a small amount, may well not have been substantially incorrect, but to do so when there had been four thefts of a total value of $6,790, two of which had occurred barely two months previously, must certainly be regarded as substantially incorrect.'

Moreover, the learned judge had no difficulty in categorising the answer to question 13 as being substantially incorrect, in that four other burglaries and an attempted burglary had taken place and a substantial loss had been sustained. On the issue of materiality, Quillam J held that the proponent's history of losses from burglary and theft are certainly matters which would

266 Unreported, High Court, Wellington, 21 May 1982, A321/80, Quillam J.

affect the rate of premium and, indeed, the decision whether to accept the risk in the first place. Therefore, in terms of s 5, the misstatements in the proposal were substantially incorrect and material and the insurer was accordingly entitled to decline liability. Similarly, in *Opossum Exports Ltd v Aviation & General (Underwriting Agents) Pty Ltd*[267] the insurer was entitled to repudiate liability under a policy insuring a helicopter (to be used for deer recovery) against accidental damage where the insured had stated that the nominated pilot had 700 hours of flying experience in helicopters and that he had two years experience in deer recovery. These statements were substantially incorrect and material in terms of s 5 in that the pilot had only 120 hours flying experience in helicopters and none of these hours had been on deer recovery work.[268]

A number of cases[269] have considered the failure on the part of the insured to disclose previous criminal convictions. Consider the case of *McFarlane (t/a Grove Contractors) v State Insurance Office General Manager*.[270] The insured arranged motor vehicle insurance with the defendant insurer. In a proposal form for the insurance, the insured expressly denied any previous convictions. In fact, the insured had accumulated a very extensive criminal record. The insurer denied a claim under the policy, alleging material non-disclosure. Eichelbaum J quoted with approval from the judgment of Richardson J in the Court of Appeal in *Misirlakis v New Zealand Insurance Co Ltd*[271] where his Honour held:

> Whether criminal convictions are material to the particular risk can only be determined in the light of all the circumstances existing at the time the proposal is completed or the insurance is otherwise proposed for. That must include in the case of the convictions themselves, the nature of the offending,

267 (1985) 3 ANZ Insurance Cases 60-624.

268 See also *Charles v South British Insurance Co Ltd* (unreported, Court of Appeal, 9 July 1986, CA 72/82, Cooke P, Richardson and McMullin JJ) (failure by insured to disclose existence of other disablement cover in respect of illness, was material non-disclosure at common law or pursuant to s 6 of the Insurance Law Reform Act 1977); *Nathan Finance Ltd v The National Insurance Co of New Zealand* (1991) 6 ANZ Insurance Cases 61-080 (failure by insured to debt position and correct name of registered owner of a vehicle material); *Snake Enterprises Ltd v Guardian Royal Exchange Assurance* (1993) 7 ANZ Insurance Cases 61-174 (failure to disclose pre-existing back abnormality on entering disability insurance contract was material); *Countrywide Finance Ltd v State Insurance Ltd* (1973) 7 ANZ Insurance Cases 61-168 (incorrect statement that a vessel had an externalised alarm system was a material misrepresentation).

269 See, for example, *Trimboli v Royal Insurance Australia Ltd* (1983) 2 ANZ Insurance Cases 60-500; *Misirlakis v New Zealand Insurance Co Ltd* (1985) 3 ANZ Insurance Cases 60-633; *McLeod v SIMU Mutual Association* (1987) 4 ANZ Insurance Cases 60-784; *McFarlane v State Insurance General Manager* (1989) 5 ANZ Insurance Cases 60-807; *Glover v Phoenix Assurance Co of New Zealand Ltd* (1989) 5 ANZ Insurance Cases 60-698; *State Insurance General Manager v Hanham* (1990) 6 ANZ Insurance Cases 60-990; *Nairn v Royal Insurance Fire & General (NZ) Ltd* (1990) 6 ANZ Insurance Cases 60-010; *State Insurance Ltd v Fry* (1991) 6 ANZ Insurance Cases 61-075.

270 (1989) 5 ANZ Insurance Cases 60-887.

271 (1985) 3 ANZ Insurance Cases 60-633, at 78-897.

> the penalty, the age and circumstances of the person concerned at the time, and the time which has elapsed since the offending, and those matters must be assessed against all other relevant risk factors.

In holding that the convictions in this case were material to the risk and should have been disclosed, Eichelbaum J observed that while many were of a minor nature, the cumulative effect of some 38 convictions for assault, threatening behaviour, obstructing and assaulting law enforcement officers, and so on, over a nine year period was really serious. He said:

> I consider that their nature and proximity in time should fairly be taken as indicating to a reasonable prudent insurer that there was a likelihood of continuing irresponsibility on the part of the assured. Or ... they were referable to the integrity of the insured; the moral hazard.[272]

Accordingly the judge held that the insurer was entitled to deny the claim on the basis of a material misstatement within the meaning of s 5 of the Insurance Law Reform Act 1977.

The courts will come to the assistance of the insured where a waiver can be established, or where on a true construction of the proposal form the insurer has narrowed the duty of disclosure. For example, in *State Insurance General Manager v Hanham*[273] an insured was held to be relieved from the duty to disclose previous criminal convictions. In that case a motor vehicle policy was in issue, and the proposal contained a specific question in relation to motor vehicle offences, but none in relation to any other offences. It was held that the duty of disclosure was modified, because the specific question indicated that convictions for other offences were not material to the particular risk.[274]

In *McFarlane (t/a Grove Contractors) v State Insurance General Manager*[275] the insured argued that the insurer in fact set a trap by asking ambiguous questions about criminal convictions in its proposal form; this, the insured asserted, was in breach of the duty of good faith imposed on both parties to an insurance contract. Eichelbaum J commented as follows:

> I have little doubt that insurers deliberately refrain from asking about a proponent's general criminal record, for marketing reasons. This notwithstanding, when it suits they maintain such a record should have been disclosed. There is a lot to be said for the view that insurers should not be able to have it both ways. However, the issue must be decided according to well established legal principles.[276]

---

272 (1989) 5 ANZ Insurance Cases 60-887, at 75-663.

273 (1990) 6 ANZ Insurance Cases 60-990.

274 See also *State Insurance General Manager v Peake* [1991] 2 NZLR 287.

275 (1989) 5 ANZ Insurance Cases 60-887.

276 *Ibid*, at 75-663.

In other words, if there is ambiguity it will be resolved against the insurer in accordance with the *contra proferentem* principle, but if not the insurer will be entitled to avoid the policy if it discharges the onus of providing that there has been a non-disclosure of a material matter.

Strictly speaking, the terminology employed in ss 5 and 6 of the Insurance Law Reform Act 1977 does not encompass promissory warranties without 'uncomfortable linguistic contortions'.[277] However, the Court of Appeal has not hesitated in applying these sections in relation to a promissory warranty. Consider the case of *Hing v Security & General Insurance Co (NZ) Ltd*.[278] The insured proposed to move a house from one site to another and completed a proposal form with the insurer to cover this removal. The proposal identified a haulage contractor and a declaration in the proposal stated that the statements in the proposal were complete and true to the best of the insured's knowledge, and that the proposal shall form the basis of the policy. Instead of using the nominated haulage contractor, the insured substituted another contractor and himself took a supervisory role at a crucial stage of the haulage. The house fell off the trailer transporting it, down a steep bank. The insured claimed under the Contractors' All Risks Policy. The Court of Appeal held that the insurer was not liable, in that: (a) the risk the insurer undertook was materially different from the risk in fact run; and (b) the statement in the proposal as to who was to undertake the haulage was 'substantially incorrect' and material within the meaning of ss 5 and 6 of the Insurance Law Reform Act 1977.

In conclusion, ss 4–7 of this Act introduce useful flexibility in the adjudication of disputes between insurer and insured. The courts may come to the assistance of an innocent insured where an insurer is endeavouring to avoid liability for breach of a non-material statement in a proposal or other document on the faith of which the policy was issued, but the legitimate interests of the insurer are protected in that material misstatements entitle the insurer to avoid liability. Finally, it should be noted that the issue of materiality is resolved in much the same way as under the Marine Insurance Act 1908,[279] and at common law.

277 See Borrowdale, 1987, at 31. The point is made that: 'it is difficult to bring a promissory warranty within the notion of a "misstatement" which is "substantially incorrect". An affirmative warranty is breached in the making if the facts to which it relates are untrue or inaccurate. The warranty is breached because the insured's answers are incorrect. But by definition there can be no breach of a promissory warranty at the time of making the warranty; breach consists of the insured's failure during the currency of the policy to act in accordance with the warranty.'

278 (1989) 5 ANZ Insurance Cases 60-886.

279 Section 20(4).

3.5 CONCLUSIONS

Limited reform of the common law relating to non-disclosure and misrepresentation has occurred in England and Singapore. Under s 2(2) of the Misrepresentation Act 1967 (UK) and s 2(2) of the Misrepresentation Act (Cap 360, Singapore Statutes, rev ed, 1994), the court is given a discretion, in cases of negligent or innocent misrepresentation, to award damages in lieu of rescission. In exercising this discretion the court is directed by the sub-section to have regard to the nature of the misrepresentation and the loss that would be caused if the contract was upheld, as well as the loss that rescission of the contract would cause to the other party.[280] Additionally, but only in Singapore, a warning must be displayed on the face of proposal forms advising the insured that non-disclosure and misrepresentation of material facts can lead to a loss of benefits under the policy.[281] These legislative changes to the common law relating to misrepresentation and non-disclosure are in stark contrast to the more wide reaching reforms in New Zealand and, especially, Australia. The debate as to what should be done is a continuing and long standing one.

The prudent insurer test of materiality imposes a heavy and often unjustifiable burden on the insured or proponent. As the English Law Reform Committee in their Fifth Report, *Conditions and Exceptions in Insurance Policies*[282] observed, many facts which are material to insurers would not appear to even an honest and careful proponent to be facts which he or she ought to disclose. The Committee therefore recommended 'that for the purpose of any contract of insurance no fact should be deemed material unless it would be considered material by the reasonable insured'.[283] Unfortunately, this recommendation has not yet been implemented in the United Kingdom. For example, in *Lambert v Co-operative Insurance Society*,[284] the insurer refused to indemnify Mrs Lambert who had insured her husband's and her own jewellery against all risks on the ground that she had not disclosed: (i) that some years before entering into the policy her husband was convicted and fined for stealing cigarettes; and (ii) that eight years after entering into the policy her husband was imprisoned for further offences

280 See, for example, *The Lucy* [1983] 1 Lloyd's Rep 188; *Highlands Insurance Co v Continental Insurance Co* [1987] 1 Lloyd's Rep 109.

281 *Insurance Act* (Cap 142, rev ed, 1994), s 24.

282 1957; Cmnd 62.

283 *Ibid*, para 14. See also English Law Commission, *Report on Insurance Law, Non-Disclosure and Breach of Warranty* (Law Com No 104, 1980), para 4.58; NSW Law Reform Commission, *Insurance Contracts: Non-Disclosure and Misrepresentation* (No 34, 1983).

284 [1975] 2 Lloyd's Rep 465; see also *Kelsall v Allstate Insurance Co Ltd* (1987) *The Times*, 20 March (CA).

involving dishonesty – a fact which Mrs Lambert did not disclose when renewing the policy. Although it was found that Mrs Lambert had acted in good faith throughout, the Court of Appeal unanimously gave judgment for the insurers holding that both convictions would be considered material by prudent insurers. McKenna J in delivering the leading judgment said: 'I would only add to this long judgment the expression of my personal regret that the Committee's recommendation has not been implemented. The present case shows the unsatisfactory state of the law.'[285] The English Law Commission[286] noted again in 1980 that reforms were greatly needed and similar views have been expressed in Singapore[287] and New Zealand.[288]

The prudent insurer test means that an insured or proponent may exercise both care and complete good faith in entering into a contract of insurance, believing that security has been effected, and yet much later find that this protection is in fact worthless because he or she failed to mention a fact which a prudent insurer might consider material to the risk. It is suggested that the doctrine of disclosure as it presently exists goes beyond the scope of the principle of *uberrimae fidei* on which it is supposed to depend. The adoption of a 'reasonable insured' or 'reasonable proponent' test of materiality in relation to the duty of disclosure would redress the imbalance that currently exists to a significant extent. It is argued that the test of the reasonable insured might be difficult to apply in practice because it 'could be an extremely nebulous

285 [1975] 2 Lloyd's Rep 465, at 491. A similar lament is expressed in the joint judgment of Richardson and Hardie Boys JJ in *State Insurance General Manager v McHale* (1992) 7 ANZ Insurance Cases 61-103, at 77-439 where they state: 'the law in New Zealand as to materiality and the duty of disclosure is not satisfactory. It can lead to uncertainty and injustice. It is unfortunate that it was not addressed when the 1977 reforms were enacted. The test of the reasonable assured has much to commend it.' See also the comments of Cooke P in this case: (1992) 7 ANZ Insurance Cases 61-103, at 77-433.

286 *Insurance Law, Non-Disclosure and Breach of Warranty* (Law Com No 104, 1980). The Commission notes at para 9.1 that: 'The English law concerning non-disclosure and warranties has been strongly criticised by our courts and by academic writers. The fact that its full application is capable of causing hardship to persons who insure in their private capacity is already recognised by the measures of self-regulation adopted by the insurance industry in the Statements of Insurance Practice. However, we have no doubt that these do not provide any adequate substitute for the reform of the law which is clearly needed, particularly since they leave the insurer in the position of judge and jury as to whether or not the full rigour of the law should be applied in individual cases.'

287 Tan Lee Meng, 1997, at 150–51, observes that: 'While it is accepted that disclosure of material facts by the insured is necessary to protect the insurer's interests, the law has leaned too much in favour of insurers on many occasions.'

288 The Contracts and Commercial Law Reform Committee in New Zealand delivered two major reports on insurance law; namely, *Aspects of Insurance Law* (1975) and *Aspects of Insurance Law* (2) (1983). Extensive reforms to the law of insurance were enacted in the Insurance Law Reform Act 1977 (NZ) and in the Insurance Law Reform Act 1985 (NZ). These reforms are discussed in detail in Tarr and Kennedy, 1992. While written statements in proposals and other documents are the subject of express controls (see, for example, Insurance Law Reform Act 1977 (NZ), ss 4, 5), general duty of disclosure reform has not been promulgated.

one'.[289] The short answer to this is that this test is no more nebulous than the test of materiality currently applied. While it may be argued that under the prudent insurer test the court has ready reference to the yardstick of the prudent insurer, the identification of this person is not an easy task. Is the person, for example, Mr Archer, an expert witness for Lloyd's underwriters, who gave evidence to the effect that a man who had stolen apples when he was 17, after which time he had lived a blameless life for 50 years, was too big a risk to insure against the risk of loss of valuables?[290] Therefore, a danger with the 'prudent insurer' test, aside from the heavy obligation as to disclosure on the insured or proponent, is that idiosyncrasies of individual insurers may replace the objective standard of the reasonable insurer. While it is recognised that the acceptance of a reasonable insured test may lead to similar problems in relation to the identification of the reasonable insured, the courts are well acquainted with the notion of the reasonable person test, and this test has already been applied in a number of insurance cases.[291]

However, while such a change in the test of materiality would assist many insureds, the reasonable insured test is not free from difficulty. As the Australian Law Reform Commission observes,[292] such a test is not justified by the principle *uberrimae fidei* because a 'severe loss is no less severe merely because it is suffered by one who, acting in the utmost good faith, falls short of the suggested standard'. Moreover, not all insureds can meet the standard of the hypothetical reasonable insured; a person's capacity to measure up to such a standard will depend upon factors such as education, culture, language, social and commercial experience.[293] However, notwithstanding the undoubted truth of this assertion, it must not be forgotten that the insurer has a very legitimate concern that he or she should be appraised with sufficient material information in order that the risk be assessed, and the appropriate premium levied; to abandon objectivity in favour of a totally subjective standard, such as what the particular insured regarded as being material, would expose the insurer to undue risk. Therefore, it is suggested that a reform of the test of materiality by adopting a reasonable insured test would represent a significant step forward for the general body of insureds.

An alternative strategy for reform would be to give the courts a general power to exercise a discretion where the existing rules result in injustice. The New Zealand legislature has already provided in s 11 of the Insurance Law

289 See Sutton, 1980, p 104.

290 *Roselodge Ltd v Castle* [1966] 2 Lloyd's Rep 113, at 132.

291 *Joel v Law Union & Crown Insurance Co* [1908] 2 KB 863, at 864; *Guardian Assurance Co Ltd v Condogianis* (1919) 26 CLR 231, at 245; *Horne v Poland* [1922] 2 KB 364, at 367; *Roome NO v Southern Life Association of Africa* (1959) 3 SA 638; *Anglo-African Merchants Ltd v Bayley* [1970] 1 QB 311, at 319.

292 *Report on Insurance Contracts* (No 20, 1982), para 180. Generally, see the Insurance (Amendment) Act 1983 (NSW); noted by Sutton (1984) 12 ABLR 215.

293 *Ibid*.

Reform Act 1977 that if the terms of an insurance contract limit or exclude the liability of the insurer in certain circumstances and in the view of the court or arbitrator determining the claim such limitation or exclusion was inserted because the existence of the circumstances was in the view of the insurer likely to increase the risk of the loss, the terms of the contract will not prevent the insured from being indemnified if he or she proves on a balance of probability that the loss was not *caused or contributed to* by the circumstances. The underlying rationale for this provision is to be found in the Report of the Contracts and Commercial Law Reform Committee, *Aspects of Insurance Law*, where it is stated that: '[I]t is unreasonable for insurers to avoid liability on the grounds that the risk is increased where the loss results from some cause other than the circumstances relied on as increasing the risk.'[294] Thus, if the insured proves that the breach of the exclusionary clause was not causative of the loss, indemnity shall not be denied.[295]

However, where an insurer is seeking to bar recovery because of non-disclosure of a material fact the actual cause of the loss is not relevant in deciding whether the uncommunicated fact is material.[296] It is submitted that this is totally inequitable and illogical given the approach adopted with exclusionary clauses. Instead of the 'all or nothing' approach that exists at present, the courts could be empowered to adjust the rights and obligations of the parties to a contract of insurance where there has been non-disclosure. The circumstances in which avoidance would be the appropriate remedy could be restricted in much the same way that cancellation is restricted under the Contractual Remedies Act 1979 (New Zealand).[297] The court could be empowered to make such order as it thinks just, for example, declare the contract to be valid and subsisting, cancel the contract, grant relief by way of damages.[298] The court could be directed to have regard to the nature of the non-disclosure, whether it was fraudulent or innocent, whether the particular insurer would have been influenced in the decision to accept risk if he or she were acquainted with the undisclosed circumstance, and the existence or non-existence of a causal link between the uncommunicated fact and the loss. It is submitted that the flexibility inherent in such an approach would not only permit justice to be done between the parties, but would accord with the

294 First Report, April 1975, para 29.

295 See *Sampson v Gold Star Insurance Co Ltd* [1980] 2 NZLR 742; *Barnaby v South British Insurance Co Ltd* (1980) 1 ANZ Insurance Cases 60-401.

296 See, for example, *Woolcott v Sun Alliance and London Insurance* [1978] 1 WLR 493.

297 Section 7(4).

298 Damages could be assessed along the lines advocated by the Australian Law Reform Commission in their *Report on Insurance Contracts* (No 20, 1982), para 188; that is, by notionally treating the non-disclosure as a term of the contract, damages would be the difference between the cost to the insurer of bearing the risk it has *agreed* to bear and the cost to the insurer of bearing the *actual* risk.

statutory discretion to be found in some modern contract statutes.[299] As Tan Lee Meng[300] observes, the present 'all or nothing' approach to avoid the contract altogether or to affirm it, ought to be made more flexible. He states:

> Where a prudent insurer would not have taken the risk at all had he been aware of the fact which has been misrepresented or not disclosed, the insurer should be allowed to avoid liability. However, where the misrepresentation or non-disclosure is not the result of a deliberate act on the insured's part and a prudent insurer would have taken the risk but at a slightly higher premium, there is room for the 'proportionality principle' and the insurer ought to provide cover in accordance with the ratio between the premium which has actually been paid and the premium which ought to have been paid by the insured had the risk been correctly declared.[301]

Where a proposal form is used the insurer should not be allowed to later claim that a fact outside the scope of the proposal form is material, and to avoid the policy because of non-disclosure of that fact. Failure to ask a question on a particular matter in the proposal should be conclusive in deciding that the insurer regarded the matter as immaterial and should absolve the proponent from the duty of full disclosure. Alternatively, if the duty of disclosure is not confined to answering questions set out in the proposal form it is suggested that the proposal form should contain a clear notice to the proponent to this effect. In addition, it is submitted that the insured should receive notification that the duty of disclosure is reimposed each time a policy is renewed.[302] It is at least arguable that it is unreasonable for the duty of disclosure to extend to periodic renewals *in the absence of notice*, as it appears questionable whether a reasonable insured would realise that the duty of disclosure arose on each renewal.

It is interesting to note that the National Consumer Council in the United Kingdom[303] advocates reforms that correspond with those contained in the Insurance Contracts Act 1984 (Australia); namely, a duty of disclosure, notice

---

299 For example, the Minors Contracts Act 1969; the Illegal Contracts Act 1970; the Contractual Mistakes Act 1977; the Contractual Remedies Act 1979; the Credit Contracts Act 1981 and the Contracts (Privity) Act 1982. See also the Insurance Contracts Act (1984) (Australia), ss 21, 22.

300 Tan Lee Meng, 1997, p 151.

301 *Ibid*, p 152.

302 As discussed above, pursuant to s 22 of the Insurance Contracts Act 1984 (Australia) an insurer is required before a contract of insurance is entered to clearly inform the insured in writing of the general nature and effect of the duty of disclosure, and non-compliance with this provision would relieve an insured from liability for non-disclosure, except where that failure to disclose was fraudulent. Similarly, in Singapore, the Insurance Act Cap 142, rev ed, 1994, s 24, makes it mandatory for the insurer to warn the insured in the proposal form for insurance that non-disclosure or misrepresentation of a material fact could lead to loss of benefits under the policy.

303 *Report of Insurance Law Reform* (1997, London).

of that duty and remedies that have now been tested over a 15 year period.[304] Contrary to various insurance industry submissions received by the Australian Law Reform Commission[305] the 'sky did not fall' with the introduction of these sweeping changes to the common law. In fact, the insurance industry in Australia is extremely healthy with numerous insurers conducting business in a very competitive market.[306] The response of the Association of British Insurers[307] to the National Consumer Council Report was, predictably, very negative. The Association argues that self-regulatory arrangements already in place are sufficient and that the overall case for comprehensive legislative reform of insurance law had not been made out.[308]

If reform to this area of the law is proceeded with, it would be worthwhile considering simply abrogating a general duty of disclosure in relation to certain classes of insurance contract. This is, in effect, the outcome achieved by the new s 21A in the Insurance Contracts Act 1984 (Cth) Australia in relation to 'consumer' insurance contracts. Certainly, reform is needed. There can be little doubt that a duty of utmost good faith cannot continue to be invoked to sustain the present test of materiality and the scope of the duty of disclosure in England – a situation where insureds must provide information assessable by reference to the judgment of the prudent insurer and where an honest or innocent failure to comply with the duty can still have disastrous consequences for the insured.

Finally, mention should also be made of the Australian Law Reform Commission Report, *Review of the Marine Insurance Act 1909*.[309] This Report advocates significant amendments to the duty of utmost good faith, the duty of disclosure and the misrepresentation provisions under the Act. The Australian Law Reform Commission recommends that:

- Section 23 of the Marine Insurance Act 1909 should be amended to provide that there is implied in a contract of marine insurance a provision requiring each party to act towards the other party with utmost good faith in terms of ss 13 and 14 of the Insurance Contracts Act 1984 (Australia).[310] The adoption of this recommendation will cure the 'all or nothing' problem that the remedy of avoidance or rescission has presented to the English courts in cases like *Manifest Shipping Co Ltd v Uni-Polaris Insurance Co Ltd (The Star Sea)*[311] and *K/S Merc-Skandia XXXXII v Certain Lloyd's*

304 See *Recommendations 4, 5* and *6*.

305 See the Australian Law Reform Commission, *Report on Insurance Contracts* (No 20, 1982), paras 177, 183, 193.

306 See, for example, KPMG *1999 Insurance Industry Survey*.

307 *Insurance Law Reform, The Response of the Association of British Insurers to the National Consumer Council Report* 1997 (London: ABI).

308 See, for example, paras 2.1, 2.2, 9.1, 9.2.

309 Report No 91, April 2001.

310 *Ibid, Recommendation 20*, paras 10.121–30, 10.137–38.

311 [2001] 1 Lloyd's Rep 389, at 400.

Underwriters (The Mercandian Continent). With the adoption of the duty of utmost good faith as a statutory implied term, the broader range of contractual remedies becomes available in relation to all breaches of the duty of utmost good faith and the 'anomalous and disproportionate' outcomes contemplated by Lord Hobhouse in *Manifest Shipping Co Ltd v Uni-Polaris Co Ltd (The Star Sea)* may be circumvented. Also inherent in the regime established by ss 12–14 of the Insurance Contracts Act 1984 (Cth) is the flexibility given to the courts to modify contractual obligations and their performance, having regard to this statutory implied utmost good faith provision.

- The Marine Insurance Act 1909 should be amended to provide that the duties of utmost good faith extend for the life of the relationship between the parties to any contract of marine insurance, except in relation to any claim or other aspect of that relationship which is the subject of litigation between the parties. In such cases the duties of utmost good faith cease when one party commences litigation against the other but only in relation to the claim or other aspect of the relationship which is the subject of that litigation.[312]
- Sections 24(1) and 26(1) of the Marine Insurance Act 1909 should be amended to provide that an insured must disclose accurately all circumstances that it knows, or a reasonable person in its position would know, to be material.[313]
- Sections 24(1) and 26(1) of the Marine Insurance Act 1909 should be further amended by deleting the references to the insurer's right to avoid and a new provision should be inserted to set out the insurer's modified rights covering both non-disclosure and misrepresentation:[314]
  (1) to provide that an agent must disclose all circumstances that it knows, or a reasonable person in its position would know, to be material, to reflect the amended obligation owed by the insured; and
  (2) by deleting 'or to have been communicated to', removing the insured's agent's obligation to disclose what ought to have been communicated to it.[315]
- The Marine Insurance Act 1909 should be amended to insert provisions which provide that if the insured has breached its duties relating to non-disclosure and misrepresentation:
  (1) if the breach is fraudulent, the insurer is entitled to avoid the policy from its outset with no return of premium;

312 Report No 91, April 2001, *Recommendation 21*.

313 *Ibid*, *Recommendation 22*.

314 *Ibid*, *Recommendation 23*.

315 *Ibid*, *Recommendation 24*.

(2) if the breach is not fraudulent:

(a) where the insurer would not have entered into the contract if it had known of the undisclosed circumstance or the truth of the misrepresented circumstance, the insurer is entitled to avoid the policy from its outset but with a return of premium;

(b) where the insurer would have entered into the contract but on other conditions, the insurer is not entitled to avoid the policy; but

(i) is not liable to indemnify the insured for a loss proximately caused by the undisclosed or misrepresented circumstance;

(ii) is entitled to vary its liability to the insured to reflect the amount of any variation in premium, deductible or excess that would have been imposed if it had known of the undisclosed circumstance or the truth of the misrepresented circumstance; and

(iii) is entitled to cancel the policy in accordance with the other provisions of the Marine Insurance Act 1909 on cancellation which are the subject of Recommendation 18.[316]

- The Marine Insurance Act 1909 should be amended to include a provision based on s 12 of the Insurance Contracts Act that the only duty of pre-contractual disclosure is that provided by ss 24–26 of the Marine Insurance Act 1909 and that a contract of marine insurance may not impose a greater duty, or provide for remedies more favourable to the insurer, than those stipulated by the Marine Insurance Act 1909 as amended in accordance with these recommendations. The Marine Insurance Act 1909 should also be amended to permit express terms in contracts of marine insurance which provide for the insured's post-contractual duty of disclosure.[317]
- The Marine Insurance Act 1909 should be amended to provide that following insurers are deemed to have been induced to enter into a contract if all leading insurers were induced.[318]

While there is little doubt that reform of marine insurance legislation is overdue,[319] caution should, it is suggested, be exercised in effecting change in

316 *Ibid, Recommendation 25.*

317 *Ibid, Recommendation 26.*

318 *Ibid, Recommendation 27.*

319 See, for example, Clarke, 4–6 June 1998; Schoenbaum (1999) 23 Tulane Maritime Law Journal 1; Luxford, 5–8 November 1995; Derrington, PhD thesis, 1998.

one jurisdiction in an area of law and practice that is so interdependent with other jurisdictions.[320] However, the reforms proposed are selective and as a consequence may not impact too adversely upon the benefits of uniform maritime insurance practice.

320 This is recognised by the Australian Law Reform Commission, particularly in the light of possible moves towards harmonisation of international marine insurance regimes: see *Review of the Marine Insurance Act 1909* (Report No 91, April 2001), paras 3.63–78.

CHAPTER 4

CONCEALMENT: THE USA APPROACH

4.1 INTRODUCTION

The non-disclosure of relevant information by an individual who is applying for insurance is generally referred to in the United States as concealment. Unlike the Anglo-Commonwealth position where the insured's duty of disclosure is of major significance even in the area of consumer information contracts, concealment does not occupy the same central position in the United States. The principal rationale for this difference is that in most jurisdictions in the United States the insurer must show that the applicant intentionally concealed material information[1] – the burden of proving fraudulent withholding of information is clearly a very difficult burden to discharge. This task is made even more onerous by specialised legislation requiring the insurer to establish not only the materiality of information concealed but also the inducement,[2] and legislation that prohibits challenges to policies for fraudulent misrepresentation or fraudulent concealment after two years.[3]

This divergence in approach is particularly interesting as the United States courts, like their Anglo-Commonwealth counterparts, recognise the 18th century case of *Carter v Boehm*[4] as laying the foundation for their position. In this case, the insurer had set up as a defence against the insured, the argument that the insured had not disclosed (in a marine policy) a highly material fact, namely, the weakness of Fort Marlborough on the island of Sumatra and the probability that the Fort would be attacked by the French. Lord Mansfield, in

---

1 See, for example: *General Reinsurance v Southern Surety* 27 F 2d 265, 273 (8 Cir, 1928); *Blair v National Security Insurance Co* 126 F 2d 955 (3 Cir, 1942); *Transcontinental Insurance Co v Minning* 135 F 2d 479 (6 Cir, 1943); *Harris v State Farm Mutual* 232 F 2d 532 (6 Cir, 1956); *National Aviation Underwriters Inc v Fischer* 386 F 2d 582 (8 Cir, 1967); *The Home Insurance Co of Illinois (New Hampshire) v Spectrum Information Technologies Inc* 930 F Supp 825 (EDNY, 1996).

2 See, for example, Alabama Code 1977, tit 27, s 12 and s 14; Massachusetts General Laws Ann c 172 s 186 (1977); Wisconsin Statutes Ann s 631.11(1) (1979); *Davis-Scofield v Agricultural Insurance Co* 109 Conn 673, 678 (1929); *Aetna Casualty and Surety Co v Retail Local 906 of AFL-CIO Welfare Fund* 921 F Supp 122, 131 (EDNY, 1996).

3 See, for example, *McKinney's New York Insurance Law* 155(1)(b) (1966); Keeton and Widiss, 1999, at pp 689–95; *Sutton v American Health & Life Insurance Co* 683 F 2d 92 (Va, 1982).

4 (1766) Burr 1905.

rendering judgment, included what was to become the widely quoted observation that:

> The special facts, upon which the contingent chance is to be computed, lie most commonly in the knowledge of the insured only; the underwriter trusts to his representation, and proceeds upon confidence, that he does not keep back any circumstances within his knowledge, to mislead the underwriter into a belief that the circumstances does not exist, and to induce him to estimate the risk, as if it did not exist.[5]

As has been discussed earlier, the English position on utmost good faith subsequently devolved from this statement with the result that an insured in that jurisdiction is at this time, affirmatively required, under penalty of avoidance of the insurance contract, to disclose all information likely to be material to an insured affecting the risk. By contrast, the United States courts have, while giving recognition to this quote, focused additionally on Lord Mansfield's subsequent directive in *Carter* that an insured's duty to disclose should generally only arise in relation to facts that the insured 'privately knows, and *the* [*insurer*] is ignorant of, *and has no reason to suspect*'.[6] This qualification effectively reduces an insured's duty to being *only* that of disclosing circumstances so unique as to be undiscoverable by an insurer exercising due diligence. The significantly more passive role insurers are entitled to play in relation to information gathering in English jurisdictions therefore is unsupportable in most jurisdictions in the United States.

Given how entrenched the respective rules are in each jurisdiction at this time, the relative merits of each position are largely irrelevant. It is probable, however, that the narrower reading adopted in the United States sits more comfortably with the actual outcome of *Carter v Boehm*. After all, it was the insured – not the insurer – who ultimately prevailed – on the grounds that disclosure was unnecessary given the insurer's ability, if it had exercised due diligence, to ascertain the true situation for itself.[7] With the inclusion of this directive, the duty of the insured to affirmatively provide all information

5 *Ibid*, at 1909.

6 *Ibid*, at 1911.

7 Hasson (1969) 32 MLR 615, at 632–34, goes further in this respect stating that: 'the classical doctrine on this subject as stated in *Carter v Boehm* has been misunderstood and misapplied by English courts. By way of sharp contrast, American courts in the 19th century correctly understood and interpreted the case.' Hasson goes on to argue that the UK interpretation of the case actually 'reflects only very recent judicial doctrine and not a rule of great antiquity. Indeed, the alleged principle, so far from being a correct statement of law in all types of insurance, does not even accurately describe the law with regard to marine insurance in the 18th century'. Hasson subsequently concludes that '[no one] to my knowledge, has been able to find a case where the defense of *uberrimae fidei* succeeded before Lord Mansfield'. See Hasson (1984) 47 MLR 505, at 508.

material to an insurer's decision – or that he should reasonably have known in this respect – while the insurer remains largely passive in this process is less sustainable.

In part this divergence arises out of the historical attitude in the United States towards regulation of the insurance industry. As the Canadian academic, Hasson, notes, insurance contracts in the United States have traditionally been 'treated by the courts and legislature with special reverence'.[8] In contradistinction to their Anglo-Commonwealth counterparts, United States policy makers have generally ensured that regulation in this field produces insurance contracts that are significantly more favourable to an insured than are the ordinary rules of the law of contract.[9] The English rules of insurance law, on the other hand, constitute a reversal of this approach: ordinary rules governing the law of contract, such as, for example, the purchase of goods and services, are generally more favourable to a consumer than are insurance provisions that have been left largely unregulated.[10]

The impetus for this divergence may be partially traceable to socio-historical influences present at the start of the 20th century in these jurisdictions. Historically, United Kingdom and United States perceptions of the integrity of their insurance industries has varied substantially. Unlike the United Kingdom where, until the last decade, the insurance industry has generally been held in high esteem for its fair dealing and probity, the United States insurance industry has traditionally attracted substantial criticism and distrust and had been subject to a number of consumer-oriented reform regimes.[11]

Similarly, the contrast in levels of state welfare available in each country during the first three decades of the last century can be seen to have contributed significantly to the nature of public concern/activism directed at their relative insurance industries. In this respect, Hasson[12] argues that the presence in the United Kingdom by the 1930s of an 'embryo welfare state' had the fundamental effect of weakening the movement for insurance law reform that was being played out at that time in the United States. As a result of this, he contends that: 'private insurance has come to be seen as the icing on the

8 Hasson (1984) 47 MLR 505, at 508.

9 See, for example, Woodruff, 1924, where Professor Woodruff observes at p v: 'What do they know of the law of insurance who only the law of contract know.' Quoted in Hasson (1984) 47 MLR 505. See also Kessler (1943) 43 Columbia Law Review 629.

10 See Hasson (1984) 47 MLR 505, at 507.

11 See Kimball, 1960; Roger Grant, 1979.

12 Hasson (1984) 47 MLR 505.

welfare cake and social reformers have concentrated their energies on trying to improve the social – rather than the private – insurance scheme.'[13]

In the United States, however, without the parallel presence of welfare provisions, regulation of private insurance was more of a necessity and, consequently, reform of any perceived injustices of more pressing impetus. Not until the 1940s when welfare provisions were sufficiently in place in the United States to alleviate this condition is there an abatement in legislative reform initiatives. As Hasson[14] points out, this timing is not coincidental in that 'the reform of private insurance lost a great deal of its momentum since then'.[15]

Aside from the above, however, the possibility presents itself that United States judicial interpretation of 19th century English case law, particularly as reflected in the cornerstone judgment by Circuit Judge (subsequently Chief Justice and President) Taft in *Penn Mutual Life Insurance Co v Mechanics Savings Bank & Trust Co*,[16] is responsible for the dilution of the *uberrimae fidei* standard from general insurance law practice. Although Lord Mansfield's judgment in *Carter v Boehm* in generally cited as the standard precedent for Anglo-Commonwealth jurisdictions' use of utmost good faith, and the imposition of a wide general duty of disclosure, an actual reading of the case itself potentially lends significantly less authority to its use in this context. Indeed, closer analysis of Lord Mansfield's work cumulatively in relation to this subject is arguably much closer to the United States formulation of the role of disclosure in insurance contracts than that now observed in the United Kingdom.

Setting aside the jurisprudential issues raised by such arguments, however, the reality remains that the doctrine of *uberrimae fidei* and the principal duty of disclosure is, at present, very much the core of most jurisdictions' insurance regulatory schemes outside the United States. That its usefulness is, in contemporary contexts, increasingly under fire is born out by the series of law reform initiatives cited earlier and by resultant legislative amendments; for example, the Insurance Contracts Act 1984 (Australia).[17] It seems unlikely that with growing pressures towards uniformity arising out of the increasingly borderless nature of the insurance industry that there will not be some movement towards a common approach to non-disclosure/concealment at least in relation to consumer contracts.

---

13 *Ibid*, at 521.

14 *Ibid*.

15 *Ibid*, at 522.

16 72 Fed 413 (6 Cir, 1896).

17 See, in particular, s 21A of the Insurance Contracts Act 1984 (Australia) whereby the insured's duty of disclosure is restricted to answering specific questions asked by the insurer; and to responding to an additional general request by the insurer, specified in the section, if the insurer asks at least one specific question. The duty of disclosure is waived in respect of all other matters. See discussion in Chapter 3.

Against this background the remainder of this chapter fleshes out the current state of the doctrine of concealment as it functions in the United States context.

4.2 CONCEALMENT

In the leading case of *Penn Mutual Life Insurance Co v Mechanics' Savings Bank & Trust Co*,[18] Taft CJ, of the Sixth Circuit Court of Appeals distinguished marine insurance, on the one hand, from fire and life insurance on the other. The learned judge stated:

> ... in cases of fire and life insurance, the parties stand much more nearly on an equality. The subject of the fire insurance is usually where the insurer can send its agents to give it a thorough examination, and determine the extent to which it is exposed to danger of fire from surrounding buildings, or because of the plan of material of its own structure. The subject of life insurance is always present for physical examination by medical experts of the insurer, who often acquire, by lung and heart tests, and by chemical analysis of bodily excretions, a more intimate knowledge of the bodily condition of the applicant than he has himself. Then, too, the practice has been grown of requiring the applicant for both fire and life insurance to answer a great many questions carefully adapted to elicit facts which the insurer deems of importance in estimating the risk. In life insurance, not only is the applicant required to answer many general questions concerning himself and his ancestors, but he is also subjected to an extended examination concerning his bodily history. This was true in the case at bar. When the applicant has fully and truthfully answered all these questions, he may rightfully assume that the range of examination has covered all matters within ordinary human experience deemed material by the insurer, and that he is not required to rack his memory for circumstances of possible materiality, not inquired about, and to volunteer them. He can only be said to fail in his duty to the insurer when he withholds from him some fact which, though not made the subject of inquiry, he nevertheless believes to be material, to the risk, and actually is so, for fear it would induce a rejection of the risk, or, what is the same thing, with fraudulent intent. A strong reason why the rule as to concealment should not be so stringent in cases of life insurance as in marine insurance is that the question of concealment rarely, if ever, arises until after the death of the applicant, and then the mouth of him whose silence and whose knowledge is generally claimed avoid the policy is closed. The application is generally prepared, and the questions are generally answered, under the supervision of an eager life insurance solicitor. Only the barest outlines of the conversations between the applicant and the solicitor are reduced to writing. The applicant is likely to trust the judgment of the solicitor as to the materiality of everything not made the subject of express inquiry, and, with the solicitor's strong motive for securing the business, there is danger that

18 72 F 413 (6 Cir, 1896).

> facts communicated to him may not find their way into the application. With respect to a contract thus made, it is clearly just to require that nothing but a fraudulent non-disclosure shall avoid the policy. Nor does this rule result in practical hardship to the insurer, for in every case where the undisclosed fact is palpably material to the risk the mere non-disclosure is itself strong evidence of a fraudulent intent. Thus, if a man, about to fight a duel, should obtain life insurance without disclosing his intentions, it would seem that no argument or additional evidence would be needed to show the fraudulent character of the non-disclosure. On the other hand, where men may reasonably differ as to the materiality of a fact concerning which the insurer might have elicited full information, and did not do so, the insurer occupies no such position of disadvantage in judging of the risk as to make it unjust to require that before the policy is avoided it shall appear, not only that the undisclosed fact was material, but also that it was withheld in bad faith. To hold that good faith is immaterial in such a case is to apply the harsh and rigorous rule of marine insurance to a class of insurance contracts differing so materially from marine policies in the circumstances under which the contracting parties agree that the reason for the rule ceases.[19]

In accordance with this reasoning, United States courts have concluded consistently that an intentional concealment of a material fact by an applicant for insurance may provide an insurer with either a valid defence to a claim or the basis for the rescission of the insurance contract.[20] Fraudulent concealment has been defined as 'where the insured, having actual knowledge of material facts, has intentionally failed to disclose them truthfully' and 'where the insured, though not having actual knowledge of material facts, yet has intentionally, and in bad faith, refused to become acquainted with the facts'.[21] This definition is very close to that adopted in Anglo-Commonwealth jurisprudence.[22]

Conversely, where the applicants' failure to reveal information is not a matter of intentional concealment then, for most types of insurance, such omission does not constitute a sufficient basis for a defense by an insurer in a majority of states.[23] However, a wider duty in relation to concealment remains in the case of marine insurance contracts and reinsurance contracts and where

19 *Ibid*, at 434–36.

20 See, for example, *Holtzclaw v Bankers Mutual Insurance Company* 448 NE 2d 55, at 58 (Ind App, 3d Dist, 1983) and cases cited at footnote 1 above.

21 *General Reinsurance v Southern Surety* 27 F 2d 265, at 273 (8 Cir, 1928); see also *Sutton v American Health & Life Insurance Co* 683 F 2d 92 (Va, 1982); *International Ship Repair & Marine Services Inc v St Paul Fire & Marine Insurance Co* 922 F Supp 577 (MD Fla, 1996); *Compagnie de Reassurance d'Ile de France v New England Reinsurance Corp* 944 F Supp 986, 995–96 (1996).

22 See, for example, *Derry v Peek* (1889) 14 App Cas 337 (England); *Taylor v London Assurance Corporation* [1935] SCR 422 (Canada); and *Advance (NSW) Insurance Agencies Pty Ltd v Matthews* (1988) 12 NSWLR 250, at 256.

23 See, for example, *Sebring v Fidelity-Phoenix Fire Insurance Company* 255 NY 382, 174 NE 761 (1931); *Pinette v Assurance Co of America* 52 F 3d 407, 409 (2 Cir, 1995).

legislative intervention expressly permits rescission for negligence or inadvertent concealment.[24] Notwithstanding improvements in communication, availability of data or ships and shipping and greater means and resources to investigate losses, the principle of *uberrimae fidei* applies unabridged in the marine insurance context. As a consequence the insured is obliged to disclose to the insurer at the time of making a contract of marine insurance all material information affecting the risk and this duty may be broken even by innocent/inadvertent concealment.[25] The role of *uberrimae fidei* in the reinsurance area is not as well explored as litigation involving reinsurance contracts was a rarity until more recent times. However, recent decisions in the United States[26] confirm the applicability of the *uberrimae fidei* doctrine to reinsurance transactions with the corresponding obligation to disclose material facts attaching to the insured. The trend in these modern cases as noted, for example, in *Compagnie de Reassurance d'Ile de France v New England Reinsurance Corp*[27] has been: 'to recognise *uberrimae fidei* as the traditional operative standard, but to interpret it so as to require rescission of reinsurance contracts only where the reinsured acted in bad faith or where the reinsurers suffered prejudice form a failure to disclose.'[28]

In general, the insured must disclose to the insurer all facts materially affecting the risk and this duty extends up until the point in time when the insurer accepts the application for insurance.[29] As the purpose of disclosure and the provision of information through application forms is to enable the insurer to decide whether to provide cover and, if so, on what terms, the duty

24 See, for example, *Dinkins v American National Insurance Co* 92 Cal App 3d 222, 232; 154 Cal Rptr 775, 781 (1979); Keeton and Widiss, 1999, at p 573.

25 See, for example, *Chester v Assinibioia Corp* 355 A 3d 880, 882 (Del, 1976); *King v Allstate Insurance Co* 906 F 2d 1537, 1544 (11 Cir, CA, 1990). Accordingly, the rule for disclosure/concealment in marine insurance is similar to the Anglo-Commonwealth approach.

26 See, for example, *Security Mutual Casualty Co v Affiliated FM Ins Co* 471 F 2d 238, 241 (8th Cir, 1972); *Carlingford Australia General Ins Ltd v St Paul Fire & Marine Ins Co* 722 F Supp 48 (SDNY, 1989); *Sumitomo Marine & Fire Ins Co v Cologne Reinsurance Co* 75 Ny 2d 295, 552 NE 3d 139, 143; 552 NYS 2d 891 (NY, 1990); *Christiania General Ins Corp of New York v Great American Ins Co* 979 F 2d 268, 278–81 (2d Cir, 1992); *North River Ins Co v CIGNA Reinsurance Co* 52 F 3d 1194, 1212–13 (3d Cir, 1995); *Unigard Security Ins Co Inc v North River Ins Co* 4 F 3d 1049, 1054 (2d Cir, 1993).

27 944 F Supp 986 (Dist Ct Mass, 1996).

28 *Ibid*, at 994.

29 See, for example, *Stipcich v Metropolitan Life Insurance Co* 277 US 311; 48 S Ct 512; 72 L Ed 895 (1928); *Mackenzie v Prudential Insurance Co of America* 411 F 2d 781 (6 Cir, 1969); *United Savings Life Insurance Co v Coulson* 560 SW 2d 211 (Tex Civ App, 1977); *State Farm Life Insurance Co v Lawless* 586 SW 2d 468 (Tenn App, 1979); *Affiliated FM Insurance Company v The Kushner Companies and Bruckner Plaza Associates* 265 NJ Super 454; 627 A 2d 710 (NJ, 1993). Unless the contract of insurance stipulates otherwise, there is no duty to notify changes of risk during the insurance period. Note also that the parties may contract exclusively on the basis of conditions and circumstances as they exist at the date of the application, in which case a failure to disclose any facts or changes arising later will not avoid the policy: see *Stipcich v Metropolitan Life Insurance Co*, 277 US 311; 48 S Ct 512; 72 L Ed, 895 (1928).

to disclose information arises whenever the insurer has to make such a decision; namely, on entry into a new contract, renewal of a policy, and in respect of any change to current insurance.[30] Accordingly, where events or facts are discovered or arise between the making of an application and the issuance of a policy that increase the risk, the applicant has a duty to inform the insurer of these events or facts. An intentional concealment of such a material fact will provide a defence to the insured's subsequent claim, if the insurer was unaware of the information.[31]

The requirement, in the preponderance of cases, that fraud be demonstrated before an insurer can rescind a non-marine insurance contract for concealment imposes a very significant break upon litigation for non-disclosure. In addition, concealment ordinarily implies an intentional withholding of information of which the insurer has or should have had knowledge, and the insured cannot be held to have concealed a fact of which he had no knowledge or which he had no reason or duty to know.[32] This is, of course, true even under the stricter rule of marine insurance.[33] Moreover, concealment to avoid a policy of insurance must involve the non-disclosure of a matter material to the risk.[34] The insurer bears the burden of proving materiality in determining whether a concealment or misrepresentation was material and, therefore, whether rescission of an insurance contract is allowed on that basis; evidence of the insurer's practices with regard to the acceptance or rejection of similar risks and underwriting guidelines is acceptable.[35] Finally, it is clear that the particular insurer must show reliance.[36] Whether this reliance must also be reasonable is a matter of some disagreement.[37]

30 See authorities in footnote above, and see also Clarke, 1999, at Chapters 23–24.

31 See, for example, *Lennon v John Hancock Mutual Life Insurance* 339 Mass 37; 157 NE 2d 518 (Mass, 1959); *Carroll v Preferred Risk Insurance Co* 215 NE 2d 801 (Ill, 1966).

32 See, for example, *Citizens' Trust & Guaranty Co v Globe & Rutgers Fire Insurance Co* 229 F 326 (US App, 1915); *Equitable Life Assurance Society v Paterson* 41 Ga 338 (Ga, 1870); *McDaniel v Insurance Co of Oregon* 243 Ore 1; 410 P 2d 814 (Ore, 1966); *March v Metropolitan Life Insurance Co* 186 Pa 629; 40 A 1100 (Pa, 1898); *Koch v Transcontinental Insurance Co* 223 Wisc 105; 269 NW 539 (Wisc, 1936).

33 See, for example, *General Interest Insurance Co v Ruggles* 25 US 408; 6 L Ed 674 (US, 1827).

34 See, for example, *Columbia Insurance Co v Lawrence* 35 US 507; 9 L Ed 512 (US, 1836); *Olson v Standard Marine Insurance Co* 109 Cal App 2d 130; 240 P 2d 379 (Cal App, 1952); *Martin v Mutual Benefits Health & Accident Association* 71 Cal App 2d 557; 162 P 2d 980 (Cal App, 1945); *Hughes v Millers' Mutual Fire Insurance Co* 147 Tenn 164; 246 SW 23 (Tenn, 1922).

35 See, for example, *Zulcosky v Farm Bureau Life Insurance Co* 206 Mich App 95; 520 NW 2d 366 (App den 448 Mich 927 (1994)).

36 See, for example, *Holtzclaw v Bankers Mutual Insurance Company* 448 NE 2d 55 (Ind App, 3d Dist, 1983); *Wiedmayer v Midland Mutual Life Insurance Company* 108 Mich App 96; 310 NW 2d 285 (1981); *Tedder v Union Fidelity Life Insurance Co* 436 F Supp 847 (EDNC, 1977); *Woodall Industries Inc v Massachusetts Life Insurance Co* 483 F 2d 986 (6 Cir, CA, 1973).

37 See, for example, *State Farm Mutual Automobile Insurance Co v Price* 181 Ind App 258; 396 NE 2d 134, 136 (1979); see also Keeton and Widiss, 1999, at p 571.

The elements of fraud, materiality and reliance impose, individually and collectively, significant obstacles in the path of an insurer seeking rescission of an insurance contract on the basis of concealment of information.

4.3 MISREPRESENTATION AND WARRANTIES

In the United States, as in the Anglo-Commonwealth environment, the application form or proposal for insurance is the most important document upon which the insurer relies in evaluating the risk and in reaching a decision as to whether cover should be provided, and if so, at what premium. Where the insured provides incorrect information the insurer is entitled to relief when it is proved: (a) that the information was not correct; (b) that the information was material or important either to the insurer's decision to insure or to the terms of the insurance contract; and (c) that the insurer in fact relied upon the incorrect information.[38] As Keeton and Widiss[39] assert, when these three elements are satisfied: 'there is a clear basis for a court to grant a request for either rescission of the insurance contract or an affirmative defense to an insured claim without requiring proof of any additional facts in support of the requested remedy or defense.'[40]

Insurers, however, have not been content to rely upon remedies or defences founded upon concealment or misrepresentation *per se*. They have sought in the United States, as in England, Australia, New Zealand and elsewhere in the world to enhance their position through the incorporation of various warranties into their policies. Of particular relevance here are warranties as to the accuracy of information provided to the insurer. For example, an application form or proposal for insurance may contain a declaration that the answers in the proposal are in every respect true, that the proposal and the declaration shall be the basis of the contract, and that the insured agrees to accept the insurer's policy on these terms; the policy itself usually contains a recital incorporating the proposal and the declaration. The effect of this is to incorporate the insured's answers into the policy and the insured is taken to have warranted the absolute accuracy of his or her responses. This 'warranty' rule provides the insurer with an absolute defence to any claim for insurance benefits if it is proved that the applicant submitted incorrect information to the insurer which was incorporated into the policy as

38 See, for example, *Crawford v Standard Insurance Co* 49 Or App 731; 621 P 2d 583 (1980); *State Farm Mutual Automobile Insurance Co v Price* 181 Ind App 258; 396 NE 2d 1345; 136 (3d Dist, 1979).

39 Keeton and Widiss, 1999.

40 *Ibid*, at 570.

a warranty.[41] This corresponds with the position in the United Kingdom and is exemplified by the judgment of the House of Lords in *Dawsons Ltd v Bonnin*.[42]

The unrestrained operation of this 'warranty' rule could therefore occasion great hardship as any misstatement, however immaterial, would entitle the insurer to avoid the contract. Not surprisingly, therefore, the courts and the various state legislatures have sought to constrain the operation of these warranties. In every state there are now statutory provisions that to some extent modify the common law rules as to whether information submitted to an insurer may achieve the status of a warranty. In general, most states have legislated to preclude insurers from elevating statements or information submitted in an insurance application to the status of warranties.[43] Instead, these statements and other information are deemed or considered to be representations. This approach, which is analogous to that adopted in Australia,[44] reasserts the requirements of materiality and reliance which the warranty 'rule' abandons. The courts' antipathy to these warranties is evident in their reluctance to construe stipulations as warranties in the absence of clear, unmistakable and unequivocal language.[45]

It should be noted that where, upon the face of an application for a policy, a question appears not to be answered at all, or to be imperfectly answered, the issue of a policy without further inquiry is a waiver of the want or imperfection, which renders immaterial the omission to answer more fully.[46] Similarly, where an applicant for life insurance gives sufficient information to alert an insurer to his or her medical condition or history, the insurer is bound to make such further inquiry as is reasonable under the circumstances in order

41 See *Hay v Utica Mutual Insurance Company* 551 SW 2d 954, 958 (Mo App, Springfield District, 1977).

42 [1922] 2 AC 413.

43 See, for example, Iowa Code Annotated Charter 509.2 (1949); Marine Revised Statutes Annotated Tit 24-A, s 2616 (1974); Michigan Compiled Laws Annotated s 500.4016 (1983); Vernon's Annotated Texas Statutes Insurance Code, Art 3.44(4) (1981). Accordingly, the Michigan Law provides in s 4016 that: 'There shall be a provision that all statements made by the insured, shall, in the absence of fraud, be deemed representations and not warranties ...'

44 The Insurance Contracts Act 1984 (Australian), s 24, provides that: 'A statement made in or in connection with a contract of insurance, being a statement made by or attributed to the insured, with respect to the existence of a state of affairs does not have effect as a warranty but has effect as though it were a statement made to the insurer by the insured during the negotiations for the contract but before it was entered into.' See the High Court of Australia decision in *Advance (NSW) Insurance Agencies Pty Ltd v Matthews* (1989) 166 CLR 606, at 614, where the majority said: 'Section 24 is important because it has the effect of converting into representations what would otherwise be warranties on the part of the insured with respect to the existence of a state of affairs.'

45 See, for example, *Franklin Life Insurance Co v William Champion and Company* 350 F 2d 115, 120–21 (6 Cir, 1965); *Lane v Travelers Indemnity Company* 391 SW 2d 300, 402 (Tex, 1965); *Lumbermans Mutual Casualty Company v Myrick* 596 F 2d 1313 (5 Cir, 1979).

46 See, for example, *Phoenix Life Insurance Company v Raddin* 120 US 183; 7 S Ct 500 (Dist Ct, Mass, 1887).

to ascertain facts surrounding information given. If the insurer fails to investigate records of that condition or history made available by the insured, the insurer is charged with information in those records.[47] There are, of course, limitations to the inquiries that an insurer may reasonably be expected to undertake. For example, where a manufacturer of asbestos products sought an excess insurance policy it had a duty to disclose all material facts which might affect the risk it sought to cover. This duty was not limited by the fact that the insurer had an opportunity to inspect the insured's premises because the insured was negotiating to provide coverage for a vast array of risks, including coverage for asbestos related injuries, and the risks were not of the nature that an insurer could assess through the simple expedient of a site visit.[48] However, a failure by an insured to supply information concerning his health, when an inquiry was made by an insurer or its agent and neither the certificate nor the master policy of insurance informed the insured that certain illnesses were not covered by a credit life policy, does not raise a defence of fraud or material misrepresentation in an action on the policy.[49] It is therefore incumbent upon insurers to be careful in posing any questions pertinent to risk assessment, to follow up in relation to incomplete answers or matters partially disclosed and make such further inquiries as are reasonable in light of the disclosures made. Failure to act with care may result in the insurer being debarred from relying upon concealment or misrepresentation in any defence to a claim.

4.4 CONCLUSIONS

The doctrine of *uberrimae fidei* was originally grounded in the supposition that in any insurance relationship, the insured is in a far better position than the insurer to be aware of the risks associated with a contract of insurance, and should therefore be obliged to reveal such risks to the insurer. However, while this assumption may have been accurate in the area of marine insurance (from whence the doctrine of *uberrimae fidei* originated), where historically the insurer had no practical ability to inspect an insured vessel located in a foreign port or at sea, it does not necessarily hold true today or for other types of primary insurance, such as fire insurance or life insurance. In the latter cases,

47 See *Ellingwood v NN Investors Life Insurance Co* 111 NM 301; 805 P 2d 70 (1991).

48 See *Owens-Corning Fiberglass Corp v American Centennial Insurance Co* 74 Ohio Misc 2d 263; 660 NE 2d 823 (CP Ct, 1995).

49 See *Block v Voyage Life Insurance Co* 303 SE 2d 742 (Ga, 1983) where no health questions were asked of an insured and the credit life policy issued contained no disqualification or exclusion for pre-existing health problems – the policy was not valid notwithstanding the insured's failure to inform the insurer that he had a terminal illness. See also *Mulvihill v American Annuity Life Insurance Co* 328 NW 2d 402 (Mich App, 1982).

it is feasible for the insurer to inspect insured property or examine the insured individual before issuing a policy.[50] Accordingly, it was not unreasonable that the courts in the United States recognised that in the ordinary case, primary insurers in the non-marine areas did not need the level of protection that *uberrimae fidei* provided.[51] This is reflected in the much reduced burden upon the insured to volunteer information in negotiating a non-marine insurance contract.

In consequence there is a greater responsibility vested in the insurer to seek out information with the insured retaining the obligation to respond truthfully to any inquiries made. As a general rule if the insurer makes no inquiry and the insured makes no representations as to the facts in question, concealment not amounting to actual fraud in relation to such facts is not a ground for avoidance of the insurance contract, since the insured may assume that the insurer has satisfied itself as to the risk.[52] This position does achieve an appropriate balance between the parties, especially in relation to consumer insurance contracts.

50 See *Compagnie de Reassurance d'Ile de France v New England Reinsurance Corporation* 944 F Supp 986, 993 (US District Ct, Mass, 1996).

51 See, for example, *Penn Mutual Life Insurance Co v Mechanics' Savings Bank & Trust Co* 72 F 413 (6 Cir, 1896); *Stipcich v Metropolitan Life Insurance Co* 277 US 311, 316; 72 L Ed 895; 48 S Ct 512 (1928).

52 See, for example, *Phoenix Insurance Co v Hamilton* 81 US 504; L Ed 729 (US, 1871); *Hartford Protection Insurance Co v Harmer* 2 Ohio St 452 (Ohio, 1853); *Southard v Occidental Life Insurance Co* 31 Wis 2d 351; 142 NW 2d 844 (Wisc, 1966); *Kludt v German Mutual Fire Insurance Co* 152 Wis 637; 140 NW 321 (Wisc, 1913). Note that notwithstanding the difference between marine and other types of insurance, the insured may not withhold information of such unusual and extraordinary circumstances of peril to property, person or liability as could not, with reasonable diligence be discovered by the insurer or reasonably be anticipated by it as a foundation for specific inquiries. See, for example, *Bebee v Hartford County Mutual Fire Insurance Co* 25 Conn 51 (Conn, 1856); *Curry v Commonwealth Insurance Co* 27 Mass 535 (Mass, 1830); *North American Fire Insurance Co v Throop* 22 Mich 146 (Mich, 1871).

CHAPTER 5

STANDARD COVER AND THE INSURED'S EXPECTATIONS

5.1 INTRODUCTION

As is clear from the economic literature canvassed in Chapter 2 and from the marketplace data considered in Chapter 6, insureds commonly do not have the time, inclination or capacity to understand the nature and extent of their insurance contracts.

These problems are compounded by obscure drafting and readability problems. Not only is the allegation made that policies are drafted in terms which are only intelligible to experts, but the information relevant to an issue may be contained in a combination of any two or more of the proposal form, the preamble, the definition section, clauses dealing with exclusions or conditions, and the schedule.[1] Compounding such problems are 'fine print' legibility difficulties which led one American judge to observe that '[s]eldom has the art of typography been so successfully diverted from the diffusion of knowledge to the suppression of it'.[2]

Of course, not all insurance policies and documents suffer from poor readability and strenuous efforts have been made by many insurers to express their forms in 'plain English'.[3] Moreover, legislative and judicial intervention have in most jurisdictions provided relief for consumers from at least the legibility issues attaching to fine print clauses by specifying print size requirements and even, in some instances, typesetting and colour specifications. Similarly, issues attaching to contracts containing abnormally onerous clauses from the perspective of the average consumer, particularly

1 See, for example, *Guardian Assurance Co Ltd v Underwood Constructions Pty Ltd* (1974) 48 ALJR 307, 308, where Mason J described a policy as a 'jumble of ill-assorted documents expressed in that distinctive style which insurance companies have made their own'. Cited in Australian Law Reform Commission, *Report on Insurance Contracts* (No 20, 1982), para 39. More recently, in *Forsikringsaktieselskapet Vesta v Butcher* (1989) 5 ANZ Insurance Cases 60-904; [1989] 1 Lloyd's Rep 331. Lord Bridge of Harwich on Lloyd's reinsurance policy noted that: 'the only people who can expect to profit from the obscurities of the present form ... are the lawyers.'

2 *Delancey v Insurance Co* 52 NH 581, 587–88 (1873); *per* Doe CJ cited by Procaccia (1979) 14 Israel Law Review 74, at 75.

3 See, for example, *Hajjar v NRMA Insurance Ltd* (1985) 3 ANZ Insurance Cases 60-647; *Legal and General Insurance Australia Ltd v Eather* (1986) 4 ANZ Insurance Cases 60-749; 6 NSWLR 390; *Nitschke v Rossair Pty Ltd; Australian Underwriting Pool Pty Ltd (Third Party)* (1989) 5 ANZ Insurance Cases 60-921; *Ross v NRMA Ltd* (1993) 7 ANZ Insurance Cases 61-170. See Sutton (1985) 13 ABLR 298; Kelly (1994) 9 Insurance Law Bulletin 48.

those found in the context of contracts of adhesion, predicate enforceability on whether adequate notification of their inclusion is presented in the document itself under judicial decisions such as Lord Denning's famous comments in *Thornton v Shoe Lane Parking*[4] and the Court of Appeal judgment in *Interfoto Picture Library v Stiletto Visual Programs Ltd*. Recently instituted provisions in the Unfair Terms in Consumer Contracts Regulations 1999[5] have now given regulatory effect to these requirements. Similar results have been achieved in most US states through a matrix of 'plain English' and good faith requirement provisions.[6] A minority of US courts have additionally – albeit controversially, as discussed below – recognised requirements that, despite literal wording of clauses which might otherwise deprive an insured of recourse under the contract, in certain circumstances, the 'reasonable expectations' of the insured in entering the arrangement in the first place are to be protected.

Within this context, however, it must be recognised that the pursuit of simplification is not without its pitfalls and complications. Legalese may have the virtue of brevity and the benefit of precedent and precision.[7] Both insurer and insured may be prejudiced by the abandonment of technical wordings which have been subject, in many instances, to a considerable history of judicial interpretation.[8] The adoption of 'plain English' is not, therefore, a panacea for all problems. Indeed, clarity may be eroded through the substitution of colloquial expressions and terms for the technical counterparts. Lawyers are very good at finding ambiguity in broad, simple expressions. As Young J observed in *Ross v NRMA Life Ltd*,[9] the alteration of standard wording through adoption of 'plain English' may present problems as to what the policy means. Construction of the policy may require the insured:

> ... to go back to all the ancient old law that was applicable in the mumbo jumbo legalese that the parties have deliberately decided to avoid. It would be strange indeed if inelegant plain English was held to have the same effect of the old time mumbo jumbo.[10]

Plain English may also cause any attempt at precision to have a structure so complicated that a party is lost in the resulting maze of related provisions.

This chapter looks at the rules in Australia prescribing standard cover in six areas of consumer insurance. Minimum terms and conditions are prescribed for home buildings and home contents insurance, motor vehicle, consumer credit, travel and personal accident insurance. The Australian Law

4 [1971] 2 QB 163.

5 See, in specific, sections 5, 6, 7.

6 See, for example, Washington Act.

7 Procaccia (1979) 14 Israel Law Review 74, at 80.

8 Australian Law Reform Commission, *Report on Insurance Contracts* (No 20, 1982), para 43.

9 (1993) 7 ANZ Insurance Cases 61-170, at 77-963.

10 *Ibid*.

Reform Commission[11] was of the opinion that the imposition of standard cover in these key consumer areas would simplify insurance for insureds and would protect them against unexpected exclusions and obligations. Under the standard cover regime, the insurer can derogate from the standard for the policy in question provided the insurer clearly informs the insured in writing of the limitations or departures from the standard inherent in the insurer's policy.[12]

The standard cover provisions are isolated for separate consideration as they represent an endeavour to deliver peace of mind that certain minimum terms and conditions and coverage are offered by the insurer in the absence of notice to the contrary. This chapter examines the means whereby such notice may be provided and the efficacy of that process.

Regulatory intervention aside, an insured's understanding of his or her cover as gleaned through pre-contractual vetting may still vary significantly from the policy's actual contents. Outside the ambit of the standard cover provisions, however, other processes or mechanisms have been developed, or are emerging, that serve to regulate or correlate more closely this information or understanding conveyed to the insured. Before turning to standard cover, therefore, this chapter will consider the common law *contra proferentem* rule of construction, the nature and commercial purpose of the policy and its business efficacy as an influence on its construction and the need to deliver a policy consistent with the terms indicated by the proposal form. In addition, brief consideration is given to the United States doctrine of reasonable expectations and to the potential afforded by the enactment of the good faith provisions in the Insurance Contracts Act 1984 (Australia)[13] for courts to rewrite or reconstrue parties' obligations.

5.2 THE INSURED'S EXPECTATIONS

5.2.1 *Contra proferentem*

The Australian Law Reform Commission[14] described the common law *contra proferentem* rule[15] as 'the main protection for the insured under the existing law' against his or her understandable ignorance of many insurance provisions. The rule is based on the principle that a person is responsible for

11 *Report on Insurance Contracts* (No 20, 1982), para 55.

12 Insurance Contracts Act 1984 (Australia), s 35(2).

13 Sections 13, 14.

14 *Report on Insurance Contracts* (No 20, 1982), para 49.

15 The full expression is *verba chartarum fortius accipiuntur contra proferentem*; that is, an ambiguous provision is construed most strongly against the person who selected the language: *Black's Law Dictionary*, p 296.

ambiguities in his or her own expression in a document that is proffered to another, and may not induce another into a contract on the supposition that the selected words may mean one thing, while at the same time hoping that a court which has to construe them will give them another meaning, more to his or her advantage.[16] As the insurers themselves generally, though not always, draft policies and other documentation such as cover notes and proposals, it is evident they are best placed to monitor and control the precision and clarity achieved in the material produced. When ambiguity issues arise out of such documentation therefore, resolving such dilemmas in this manner seems the eminently more reasonable approach.[17] The same principle applies in reverse where, for example, the insured's broker proffers the policy or special terms to be added to a standard policy.

Accordingly, the *contra proferentem* rule is a useful constructional device that may offer a means of protecting an insured, or indeed an insurer, in an individual case where the justice of the principle warrants it. Its principal limitations are that it may only be invoked for true ambiguity, and it may only be deployed in the process of litigation, though it must be considered by the parties' advisers. It does not serve to address the imbalance in information and understanding in a pre-contractual setting, but may be of assistance in the

16 *Anderson v Fitzgerald* (1853) 4 HLC 484, 510–11; *Voet, Commentarius ad Pandectas*, 18.1.27, in describing the Roman origins of the rule put the matter thus: 'Dubious pacts are to be construed against the party by whom they are imposed, as everyone must impute it to his own imprudence that he has not expressed himself more plainly.'

17 See, for example, *Griffiths v Fleming* [1909] 1 KB 805 (extrinsic evidence may be adduced to show that there was a mistake, so that the written contract does not express what was clearly agreed between the parties); *Eskine v Adeane* (1873) 8 Ch App 756 (that a collateral contract exists not varying the terms of the written agreement but containing a separate undertaking); *Scragg v United Kingdom Temperance & General Provident Institutions* [1976] 2 Lloyd's Rep 227 (parol evidence may be received to show that a word or clause is used in a particular sense); *Codelfa Construction Pty Ltd v State Rail Authority of NSW* (1982) 149 CLR 337 (that a custom or usage in a particular trade or business must be imported into the agreement); *Jervis v Berridge* (1873) 8 Ch App 351 (where the written contract is only part of the whole contract evidence may be adduced); *Manufacturers' Mutual Insurance Ltd v Stargift Pty Ltd* (1985) 3 ANZ Insurance Cases 60-615 (the juxtaposition of the phrases may create ambiguity and 'that doubt should be resolved adversely to the insurer who had proffered the document'); *Dickinson v Motor Vehicle Insurance Trust* (1987) 74 ALR 197 (the word 'use' in relation to an auto extends to everything that fairly falls within the conception of the use of a motor vehicle and may include a use not involving locomotion); *Carr v Guardian Assurance Co Ltd and Cracknell and Crimp* [1928] NZLR 108 ('In a case on the line, in a case of real doubt, the policy ought to be construed most strongly against the insurers; they frame the policy and insert the exception' at 112); *Houghton v Trafalgar Insurance Co Ltd* [1945] 1 QB 247; *Cameron v Commercial Union General Insurance Co Ltd* (1983) 2 ANZ Insurance Cases 60-542 (before the *contra proferentem* maxim may be invoked there must be a genuine ambiguity, and the ambiguity should not be 'created' so as to permit the maxim's application, as *per* Roper J); *Belcher v Southern Insurance Co Ltd* (1872) 2 NZCA 59 (where printed and written words cannot be reconciled, written takes precedent). See generally, MacGillivray and Parkington, 1988, p 454; Sutton, 1991; Tarr and Kennedy, 1992, pp 165–69. Procaccia (1979) 14 Israel Law Review 74, at 102. See also Liederman (1986) LMCLQ 79, at 83–85.

fair resolution of ambiguities in a post-contractual dispute.[18] To the extent that it operates, it is fair, which is its *raison d'être*; and insofar as it provides a remedy to whichever party may be unfairly disadvantaged, its application is also fair.

5.2.2 Policy in accordance with proposal

The terms of consumer insurance contracts are not specially arranged between the parties. The insurer's standard form policies incorporate a multitude of terms and conditions and it is on the basis of these terms and conditions that an insurer is prepared to do business. To this end, proposals drafted by the insurer commonly contain a clause whereby the prospective insured agrees to accept the insurer's policy 'subject to the terms and conditions contained therein'.

Generally, the effect of such a clause is that such terms and conditions of the insurer's usual policy are binding regardless of whether the insured has previously sighted or otherwise become acquainted with them.[19] Insurers do not, however, retain 'carte blanche to deliver a policy inconsistent with the terms indicated by the proposal form'.[20] In *Phoenix Assurance Co of New Zealand Ltd v Campbell*, the High Court upheld a magistrate's striking out of a $300 deductible clause in a motorcycle policy that had not been mentioned in the proposal. Wilson J concluded:

> I do not think that that agreement by the proposer enables the company to insert any term or condition contrary to the terms shown in the proposal itself, and a term limiting liability to $1,425, when the policy is for $1,725, and the premium is paid on that amount, is a term contrary to the terms of the proposal. The attempt by the insurance company to so limit its liability must therefore fail.

Similarly, rectification of policies introducing clauses at odds with the proposals received by the insureds were granted in *Braund v Mutual Life & Citizens' Assurance Co Ltd*[21] and *Randell v Atlantica Insurance Co Ltd*.[22] In *Braund*, the New Zealand Supreme Court rejected provisions exempting the

18 See generally ALRC *Report on Insurance Contracts* (No 20, 1982), para 49.

19 *Steadfast Insurance Co Ltd v F & B Trading Co Ltd* (1971) 125 CLR 578, at 586. See also *Southern Cross Assurance Co Ltd v Australian Provincial Assurance Association Ltd* (1939) 39 SR (NSW) 174, at 189; *Tasmanian Government Insurance Office v Morando Bros Pty Ltd* [1970] Tas LR 147. Notice of unusual terms must be given to an insured pursuant to the Insurance Contracts Act 1984 (Australia), s 37.

20 *Phoenix Assurance Co of New Zealand Ltd v Campbell* (unreported, High Court, Auckland, 3 February 1976, M314/75, Wilson J). Noted in [1976] 2 NZRL 83 and in Tarr and Kennedy, 1992.

21 [1926] NZLR 529.

22 [1985] 80 FLR 253.

insurer from a variety of accidents as constituting material variations from the proposal. The court emphasised that the insurer is under a duty to ensure that the policy issued accords with the terms of the proposal form. When the policy issued departs from the proposal the insurer is bound to give the insured reasonable notice of the introduction of new terms. In the absence of such notification, the insured is entitled to assume that the policy is substantially in accordance with the proposal, and the court may rectify the policy to conform with the proposal.

Building on this, it was held in *Randell* that where there is prior agreement between the insurer and insured, the policy should not be inconsistent with that prior agreement. Therefore, a policy provision was to be disregarded to the extent that it was inconsistent with the oral contract[23] that formed the basis for the policy's being issued.[24] Subsequent precedent clarifies that where the insured has requested and obtained cover on certain terms, the insurer cannot later, in the absence of clear evidence, argue that the policy should include certain of its 'usual or standard terms and conditions';[25] or that because the insurance was arranged by a broker, that the broker was to be deemed to have requested cover on the insurer's usual or standard terms and conditions.[26]

In Chapter 6 below, it is recorded that the General Insurance Enquiries and Complaints Scheme is commonly confronted with cases where promotional literature or brochures describing consumer insurance contracts are at variance with policy documentation – mostly because the promotional material does not fully reflect the exclusions from, or limitations upon, the promised cover. The Claims Review Panels frequently resolve to rectify these policies to accord with the insured's expectations.

5.2.3 Business efficacy, nature and commercial purpose of the policy

The business efficacy, nature and commercial purpose of the policy are further considerations that a court may take into account in reconciling an insured's legitimate expectations and the actual policy delivered as part of its construction of the words used in the policy. As Vautier J observed in *Tru-Line*

23 In *Randell*, the insured arranged insurance over a yacht through a broker. The cover was to include both charter and private use. The yacht was lost during the period of interim cover and the policy, which exempted private use, was issued after the loss. The court held the terms of the interim cover were set by oral agreements between the broker and insurer, followed by confirmation of cover.

24 See also *Re Bradley and Essex and Suffolk Accident Indemnity Society* [1912] 1 KB 415, at 430; *Inn Cor International Ltd v American Home Assurance Co* (1947) 42 DLR (3d) 46; *Calder v Batavia Sea and Fire Insurance Co Ltd* [1932] SASR 46.

25 CCH Australia Ltd, *Australian Law and New Zealand Insurance Reporter*, para 4-405.

26 *L'Union des Assurances de Paris IARD v Dynamic Satellite Surveys Pty Ltd* (1996) 9 ANZ Insurance Cases 61-331.

Plumbers Ltd v CML Fire & General Insurance Co Ltd:[27] '... it is essential ... to have regard to the nature of the policy in question and what it was intended to cover.' In this regard, the commercial purpose is an essential consideration.[28]

A good illustration is afforded by *Alex Kay Pty Ltd v General Motors Acceptance Corp and Hartford Fire Insurance Co*.[29] The insured, a car hire firm, effected an insurance policy which provided an indemnity in respect of losses sustained by the insured in the course of its operations, unless that loss arose from 'a breach of contract, agreement or obligation'. The insured claimed for losses sustained when a customer failed, in violation of the rental agreement, to return a car. The claim was resisted on the ground that the loss arose from a breach of contract. Sholl J rejected this argument as undermining the commercial objective of the contract, noting that:

> This is a commercial contract. One of its professed objects is to indemnify the insured with respect to loss of, or damage to, one of its vehicles, which was ... to the knowledge of the parties to be used in the insured's business of letting out cars for hire, and indeed a larger premium was attached on that account. From a commercial point of view, it would be the merest common sense for the insurer to assume that any hirer of one of their cars would be under a contractual obligation, express or implied, to return it in good order and condition, and not to damage or lose it by negligence.[30]

As a matter of business common sense and having regard to the nature of the policy and what it was intended to cover, he limited the operation of the clause to losses arising out of the insured's breach of contract with another party; for example, where the insured incurred liability through supplying a defective vehicle pursuant to a hire agreement.[31]

More recently, in *Legal & General Insurance Australia Ltd v Eather*[32] the court was required to give commercial effect to the interpretation of 'all reasonable precautions'. This question arose in the context of the insured's multi-risk policy over his investment jewellery collection that required him 'to take all reasonable precaution to avoid or minimise injury, loss or damage'. The insured, in transporting the jewels from home (where he had been storing them in an unlocked cupboard for the eight years prior) to his bank, placed the jewels in a calico bag on the back seat of his car, next to a radio which he

27 Unreported, High Court, Auckland, New Zealand, 26 February 1982, M191/81.

28 See *Fraser v BN Furman (Productions) Ltd* [1967] 1 WLR 898; *Tru-Line Plumbers Ltd v CML Fire & General Insurance Co Ltd* (unreported, High Court, Auckland, New Zealand, 26 February 1982, M191/81, p 7).

29 [1963] VR 458.

30 *Ibid*, at 462.

31 See also *Cornish v Accident Insurance Co* (1889) 23 QBD 453; *Re Sun Alliance Insurance Ltd ex p Bonastre* [1974] Qld R 128; *State Government Insurance Commission v Steven Bros Pty Ltd* (1984) 58 ALJR 346, at 349; *Transport Industries Insurance Co Ltd v New South Wales Medical Defence Union Ltd* (1986) 4 ANZ Insurance Cases 60-736, at 74-410, *per* Kirby P.

32 (1986) 4 ANZ Insurance Cases 60-749; 6 NSWLR 390.

was taking for repair. On the way, he stopped at a side street near a shop where he had business to transact. Despite covering the bag and radio with a beach towel and locking the car he returned to find both stolen. The insurer refused the claim as failing to constitute proper care in light of the requisite that the insured 'take all reasonable precautions to avoid or minimise injury, loss or damage'. The insurer contended that actions in accordance with the policy provision would have included going directly to the bank, taking the jewels with him, or placing the jewels in the trunk or glove box.

The court (Kirby P, Glass and McHugh JJA) held that the words 'all reasonable precautions' had to be read down to give effect to the commercial purpose of the contract. The insured was required to avoid recklessness, that is, to take such steps to protect the jewellery as were reasonable having regard to the dangers which he recognised. Kirby P was of the opinion that the word 'all' in the condition must be read down by reference to two conditions:

> The first is the companion adjective 'reasonable'. It is only 'all reasonable' precautions that must be taken. The second consideration is the purpose of the policy, in which the condition appears. Clearly, its purpose is to permit the insured, whilst maintaining possession of his personal property, such as the jewellery here in question, to pass the risk of loss to the insurer. If the insurer wished to insist that items generally, or items of a particular value, must be deposited with a bank before it is at risk, it should say so. Likewise, if it wished only to be at risk when the property was in a locked safe or other secure receptacle, it should make provision to that effect in its policy. Were it to do so, it would make its conditions clearer to the insured. But it might also forfeit the market because many insureds might consider such conditions unacceptable. The respondent might, for example, have wished from time to time to wear some of the valuable rings. It is this recognition, that the insured will retain and use possession of the property the subject of the insurance, that undermines the insurer's argument that a rigorous obligation was imposed by the condition. Such an obligation would be contrary to the normal expectations of persons insured under such a policy. It would impose on the insured the obligation of 'precautions' which go beyond those that are 'reasonable' in the circumstances of policies such as this.[33]

Accordingly, the commercial object or function of the clause and its relation to the contract as a whole must be taken into consideration when construing the intent of specific clauses within a given policy.

Courts have further ruled that, as an insurance policy is a commercial document, fair and reasonable construction of a clause requires that it accord with sound commercial principles and good business sense.[34]

33 *Ibid*, at 74-504. See also *Haines House Haulage Co v Goldstar Insurance Co Ltd* (1989) 5 ANZ Insurance Cases 60-937.

34 MacGillivray and Parkington, 1988, p 439; *National Protector Fire Insurance Co Ltd v Nivert* [1913] AC 507, at 513; *Minucoe v London, Liverpool & Globe Insurance Co Ltd* (1925) 36 CLR 513; *MGICA Ltd v United City Merchants (Aust) Ltd* (1986) 4 ANZ Insurance Cases 60-937.

Derrington and Ashton[35] state that practical business considerations and common sense may be operative canons of construction in giving to an ill-drafted clause a meaning which the parties as sensible business people must have intended. For example, in *Boys v State Insurance General Manager*[36] the insurer rejected a claim that it argued breached a condition in the policy requiring notification of other insurance. The policy in question was an indemnity policy whereas the other policy covered the replacement cost of the house concerned. The court, in holding that no duty to give notice arose as it was not a case of double insurance (for example, different risks were covered), stated that conditions should be interpreted in a way which is reasonable and gives business efficacy.

5.2.4 Doctrine of reasonable expectations

Like Australian courts, the United States judiciary has struggled to achieve a workable balance between providing adequate consumer protection to signatories of standard form insurance contracts while still retaining adequate respect for the sanctity of contract. Given the gross disparity in bargaining power in most insurance contracts[37] and the degree of complexity and nature and effect of policy terms, it is not surprising that this tension between legal formalism and legal functionalism should be particularly acute in the insurance context.

In the UK, such conflicts between sanctity of contract on the one hand and preservation of the objective of fairness and justice for individual insureds on the other has not been of perhaps the same level of concern due to the role of the Ombudsman's Office in that jurisdiction. As Steyn LJ stated in *First Energy (UK) Ltd v Hungarian International Bank Ltd*:[38]

> The theme that runs through our law of contract is that the reasonable expectations of honest men must be protected. It is not a rule or a principle of law. It is the objective which has been and still is the principal moulding force of our law of contract. It affords no license to a judge to depart from binding precedent. On the other hand, if the *prima facie* solution to a problem runs counter to the reasonable expectations of honest men, this criterion sometimes requires a rigorous re-examination of the problem to ascertain whether the law does indeed demonstrate unfairness.

35 Derrington and Ashton, 1990, p 102.

36 [1980] 1 NZLR 87.

37 'Consumer' insurance contracts here refers to contracts of motor vehicle insurance (property damage), home buildings insurance, home contents insurance, sickness and accident insurance, consumer credit insurance and travel insurance. See the Insurance Contracts Act 1984 (Australia), ss 34, 35 and the Insurance Contracts Regulations (SR No 162 of 1985, as amended).

38 [1993] 2 Lloyd's Rep 194, 196 (CA).

Although this observation arose in relation to a banking dispute, Clarke[39] observes that in the United Kingdom, the Insurance Ombudsman Bureau has approached these words as the 'guiding light'.[40] Accordingly, some of the considerable strain that might otherwise befall consumer-insureds have been side stepped. Despite the triteness of the observation, however, benevolent construction and intervention are not synonymous with legislative reform of disclosure requirements.

Some US courts and, increasingly, their Canadian equivalents, have sought to embrace an alternative means of resolving these types of issues in the standard form insurance context. Through the Doctrine of Reasonable Expectations, the rights of consumers who are party to a policy which contains provisions which, if read closely and literally, would result in the defeat of their claim, have been arguably realigned to take into account this initial premise of parties' intentions. It is, however, an approach that is distinct from traditional rules of construction. Unlike the latter, which are uncontroversial and based on the need to deliver a policy consistent with the terms indicated by the proposal,[41] the doctrine of reasonable expectations constitutes a principle that applies a measure on the basis of what the parties would have expected. This allows for much greater overriding of the written word. It arises in the context where the contract's technical language is severely at odds with the understanding or expectations of the non-drafting party.[42] It is least controversial when it is defensively invoked against language of the document that, if applied literally, would produce a result largely devoid of value to the insured, that is – a result which would defeat his or her 'reasonable expectation' of the purpose of the contract. This doctrine is said to reside uneasily amongst the *contra proferentem* rule of construction, the sufficiency of notice cases[43] associated more broadly with exemption clauses and the doctrine of unconscionability. In practice, it probably functions more like the rule against absurdity found in the commercial purpose rules which are discussed above.[44]

---

39 Clarke, 1997, p 369.

40 Report 1993, para 6.1. See also Report 1990, para 2.4 and para 2.6 cited in Clarke, 1997, p 369, note 204.

41 See, for example, *Steadfast Insurance Co Ltd v F & B Trading Co Ltd* (1971) 125 CLR 578, at 586; *Randell v Atlantica Insurance Co Ltd* [1985] 80 FLR 253; *Re Bradley and Essex and Suffolk Accident Indemnity Society* [1912] 1 KB 415, at 430; *Inn Cor International Ltd v American Home Assurance Co* (1947) 42 DLR (3d) 46.

42 Jerry (1998) 5 Connecticut Law Review 21, at 22, offers the following call to arms on the issues of interpretation of standard form insurance contracts when noting that his dialectic constitutes 'a battle for the heart and soul – not only of contract law, or insurance law – but of American jurisprudence generally'.

43 *Thornton v Shoe Lane Parking Ltd* [1971] 2 QB 163; *Interfoto Picture Library Ltd v Stiletto Visual Programmes Ltd* [1989] QB 433.

44 See cases discussed below.

Section 211 of the *Restatement (Second) of Contracts* in the United States sets forth the principles on which this doctrine rests by stating that an insured remains bound by a specific provision of a contract of adhesion when:

(1) Except as stated in sub-s (3), where a party to an agreement signs or otherwise manifests assent to a writing and has reason to believe that like writings are regularly used to embody terms of agreement of the same type, he adopts the writing as an integrated agreement with respect to the terms included in the writing.

(2) Such a writing is interpreted wherever reasonable as treating alike all those similarly situated, without regard to their knowledge or understanding of the standard terms of the writing.

(3) Where the other party has reason to believe that the party manifesting such assent would not do so if he knew that the writing contained a particular term, the term is not part of the agreement.[45]

The drafters offer the following comment on the interpretation of this provision:

> Although customers typically adhere to standardized agreements and are bound by them without even appearing to know the standard terms in detail, they are not bound to unknown terms which are beyond the range of reasonable expectations. A debtor who delivers a check to his creditor with the amount blank does not authorize the insertion of an infinite figure. Similarly, a party who adheres to the other party's standard terms does not assent to a term if the other party has reason to believe that the adhering party would not have accepted the agreement if he had known that the agreement contained the particular term. Such a belief or assumption may be shown by the prior negotiations or inferred from the circumstances. Reason to believe may be inferred from the fact that the term is bizarre or oppressive, from the fact that it eviscerates the non-standard terms explicitly agreed to, or from the fact that it eliminates the dominant purpose of the transaction. The inference is reinforced if the adhering party never had an opportunity to read the term, or if it is illegible or otherwise hidden from view.[46]

Unlike the *contra proferentem* rule this doctrine is not dependent upon the existence of an ambiguity in the contract. Rather, it is a legal concept that United States courts employ in 10 jurisdictions. It has been employed in instances where no ambiguity was involved to nullify certain provisions of

---

45 The *Restatement (Third) of Contracts* is at this time currently being drafted amidst considerable academic speculation that these provisions will be extended to incorporate more accurately Keeton's original formulation of the principle (see Keeton (1970) 83 Harvard Law Review 961 and 1281) and/or may possibly be reformulated to include a separate provision for insurance contracts only. Movement is also afoot to revise s 2-206 of the *Uniform Commercial Code* in this direction. See White (1997) 75 Washington University Law Quarterly 315.

46 *Restatement (Second) of Contracts*, s 211, cmt F (1981).

standard form policies that are unfair to those who have had no opportunity but to adhere to the agreement and would consequently be deprived of the benefit of their bargain.

Its formal recognition as a principle arose initially out of a two part Harvard Law Review article published in 1970 by Professor (now Judge) Keeton.[47] He argued that in principle: '[t]he objectively reasonable expectations of applicants and intended beneficiaries regarding the terms of insurance contracts will be honoured even though painstaking study of the policy provisions would have negated those expectations.'[48]

Judicial adoption of this premise was first formally articulated in 1961 in *Kievit v Loyal Protective Life Insurance Co.*[49] The New Hampshire Court concluded that the clause in issue would, if literally interpreted, render the policy 'of little value to a [man of 48] since disability or death resulting from accidental injury would in all probability be in some sense contributed by the infirmities of old age'. (This should be compared with the reasoning of the House of Lords in the 1998 case of *Cook v Financial Ins Co*,[50] which is discussed below.)

This was not an entirely new approach since Learned Hand J in *Gaunt v John Hancock Mutual Life Insurance Co* anticipated it with the comment that emphasised the need to read the proffered contract from the insured's point of view. He said:

> An underwriter might so understand the phrase, when read in its context [to start coverage at a later date], but the application was not to be submitted to underwriters; it was to go to persons utterly unacquainted with the niceties of life insurance, who would read it colloquially. It is the understanding of such persons that counts ... A man must indeed read what he signs, and he is charged, if he does not; but insurers who seek to impose upon words of common speech an esoteric significance intelligible only to their craft, must bear the burden of any resulting confusion.[51]

Judicial interpretation of the nature of this doctrine varies substantially. In its most conservative form, courts have invoked it as a rule of construction to resolve an ambiguous phrase or term in accordance with the insured's reasonable expectations, which is the *contra proferentem* rule.[52] In contrast the

47 Keeton (1970) 83 Harvard Law Review 961 and 1281.

48 *Ibid*, at 967.

49 34 NJ 475; 170 A 2d 22 (1961).

50 [1998] 1 WLR 1765.

51 *Gaunt v John Hancock Mutual Life Insurance Co* 160 F 2d 599 (2d Cir), cert denied, 331 US 849 (1947), at pp 1185–86.

52 See, for example, *Carly v Lumberman's Mutual Casualty Co* 521 A 2d 1053 (Conn App Ct 1987); *Eli Lilly & Co v Home Ins Co* 482 NE 2d 467 (Ind, 1985); *Allstate Ins Co v Elwell* 513 A 2d 269 (Me, 1986); *Rodriguez v General Accident Ins Co* 898 SW 2d 379 (Mo, en banc, 1991); *Kracl v Aetna Cas & Sur Co* 374 NW 2d 40 (Neb, 1985); *National Union Fire Ins Co v Reno's Executive Air Inc* 682 2d 1380 (Nev, 1984); *Max True Plastering Co v United States Fidelity & Guar Co* 912 P 2d 861 (Okla, 1996).

courts generally look to the overall purpose of the contract, or the reasonable expectations the insured brings to the transaction, in order to identify phrases that may be ambiguous[53] in the context of what an average insured would believe them to be.[54] Contrary to the *contra proferentem* rule it does not search out ambiguous words or phrases in order to determine whether the language can support an alternative meaning – under this process the language itself may be clear. What is sought is a clause or language that bestows a condition that would have caused the insured, *if* he or she had understood the language, not to enter the contract. That the standard is that of the average insured is vital in Keeton's view as a higher standard could potentially penalise a policy holder who took the time to read and understand the document(s).[55]

In its most aggressive application, the doctrine promotes reasonable expectations even over express policy language to the contrary.[56] In *C & J*

53 Australian and New Zealand courts have similarly mirrored this reasoning in a number of cases. In *Legal & General Insurance Australia Ltd v Eather* (1986) 4 ANZ Insurance Cases 60-749; 6 NSWLR 390, the court was required to interpret the meaning of the words 'all reasonable precautions to avoid or minimise injury, loss or damage' in relation to the theft of jewellery. The court held that this phrase had to be read down to give effect to the commercial purpose of the contract. The insured was required to avoid recklessness, that is, to take such steps to protect the jewellery as were reasonable having regard to the dangers which he recognised. Kirby P, in particular, was of the opinion that the word 'all' must be read down to achieve this effect, thereby bringing in the objective of the contract to clarify this seemingly ambiguous word. It is submitted that within the facts of this case, the level of 'ambiguity' identified for reading down purposes would possibly fall more happily under the ambit of the reasonable expectations approach. See also *Tru-Line Plumbing Ltd v CML Fire & General Insurance Co Ltd* (1982) unreported, High Court, Auckland, New Zealand, 26 February, M191/81; *Fraser v BN Furman (Productions) Ltd* [1967] 1 WLR 898; *Alex Kay Pty Ltd v General Motors Acceptance Corp and Hartford Fire Insurance Co* [1963] VR 458; *Boys v State Insurance General Manager* [1980] 1 NZLR 87; *Re Etherington and Lancashire and Yorkshire Accident Insurance Co* [1909] 1 KB 591 (literal meaning of words must not be allowed to prevail where it would produce an unrealistic and generally unanticipated result).

54 A similar result has been achieved by at least one court using the rubric of implied warranty. See *C & J Fertilizer Inc v Allied Mut Ins Co* 227 NW 2d 169 (Iowa, 1975), at 178–79. In this case, the Iowa court in dealing with an insurance policy looked to the broad purpose of the whole contract and concluded that as the insurer is said to have impliedly warranted that the provisions within the contract are consistent with the broad purpose of the document, an implied warranty of fitness existed and had been breached. Implied warranties are, however, rarely applied to insurance contracts for privity purposes (as they potentially can give rise to unexpected third party rights of suit against the insurer) and for doctrinal purposes. In the latter instance, it is not clear whether an implied warranty arises in contract law, tort law or both. As the positioning of the claim affects both remedies and statutes of limitations, the jurisprudential implications are of significant complexity.

55 Keeton, 1971, section 6.3(b), at 351. Keeton goes on to advocate the more stringent corollary that 'If the enforcement of a policy provision would defeat the reasonable expectations of the great majority of policy holders to whose claims it is relevant, it will not be enforced even against those who know of its restrictive terms', *ibid*, at section 6.3(a).

56 See, for example, *Reliance Ins Co v Moessner* 121 F 3d 895 (3rd Cir, 1997); *State Farm Mut Auto Ins Co v Falness* 29 F 3d 966 (9th Cir, 1994); *Regional Bank of Colorado v St Paul Fire and Marine Ins Co* 35 F 3d 494 (10th Cir, 1994); *Bering Strait School Dist v RLI Ins Co* 873 P 2d 1292 (Alaska 1994); *Darner Motor Sales Inc v Universal Underwriters' Ins Co* 682 P 2d 388 (Ariz, 1984); *Clark-Peterson Co v Independent Ins Assocs* 492 NW 2d 675 [contd]

Fertilizer Inc v Allied Mutual Insurance Co,[57] a small businessman sought to claim for a burglary loss under his general storekeeper's policy. Although burglary losses were covered, the definitional section required that 'visible marks ... or physical damage to, the exterior of the premises' be present. As the premises appeared to have been entered through a unmarked plexiglass door, which was subsequently shown to be able to be forced open without leaving scratch marks, cover was refused. In upholding the insured's claim, the Iowa Supreme Court looked to the doctrine of reasonable expectations in overriding the specific definitional language. The court tried to reconstruct the policy's expectation of the insured based on the bargain struck at the time he purchased the policy. It noted the evidence of a conversation at the time of the inspection of the premises prior to the issue of the policy when the insured was told that 'there had to be visible evidence of burglary'. This conversation, however, did not explicitly tell the insured that the evidence had to be visible marks or physical damage to the *exterior* of the building.

From this the court concluded that the 'negotiation was for ... the insurer's promise "To pay for loss by burglary" ... so long as it was not an "inside job". But there was nothing relating to the negotiations [which would have led the insured] to reasonably anticipate ... another exclusion denying coverage when, no matter how extensive the proof of a third party burglary, no marks were left on the exterior of the premises'. Further, the definition was not the common or legal definition of burglary. The court concluded that: '[T]he most that the plaintiff might have reasonably anticipated was a policy requirement of visual evidence (abundant here) indicating the burglary was an "outside" not an "inside" job.'

The same result may have been achieved by a less radical course. If the preliminary conversation had the force it was apparently given, it may have founded a claim for rectification of the policy or a claim for specific performance of preliminary for the contract to insure, which the subsequent policy failed to do.

Whether individual courts will register on this continuum is further complicated by the absence of doctrinal refinement or identification of salient factors. One commentator argues that the doctrine is often invoked 'as a kind of "mantra" to justify the desired outcome, but without the support of sufficient explicit legal analysis'.[58] As a result, it may be viewed as an equitable process that considers the surrounding circumstances, public policy and fair treatment, much like the equitable doctrine of unconscionability.

56 [contd] (Iowa, 1992); *Transamerica Ins Co v Royle* 565 P 2d 820 (Mont, 1983); *Atwood v Hartford Accident & Indem Co* 365 A 2d 744 (NH, 1976); *Sparks v St Paul Ins Co* 495 A 2d 406 (NJ, 1985); *West Virginia v Janicki* 422 SE 2d 822 (WVa, 1992).

57 227 NW 2d 169 (Iowa, 1975).

58 See Rahdert (1986) 18 Connecticut Law Review 323, at 370.

In summary, at this time, the majority of American courts have neither expressly adopted nor expressly rejected use of the doctrine.[59] Since its inception 30 years ago, less than a quarter of states in the US have clearly recognised it as a substantive rule of insurance law that permits courts to ignore unambiguous terms in standard form insurance contracts that would otherwise defeat the insured's expectations. In part this seeming judicial reluctance may be attributable to confusion over its function, particularly with respect to that of the *contra proferentem* rule.

It is also arguable that a number of courts are reluctant to embrace contract reformation for consumer protection purposes with perhaps the same zeal that was to be found in the consumer oriented judgments of the 1960s. In respect of the doctrine's most radical applications, it would not be the first time in the United States' legal experience that a principle intended to be a shield for weaker parties has been transformed into a sword for aggressive litigation purposes. The courts' awareness of the Pandora's Box potential of this doctrine may be implicit in what one commentator has described as the doctrine's 'failure to thrive'.[60]

Nevertheless there is emerging evidence that it is establishing itself in the United Kingdom and Canada. Canadian precedent over the last decades reveals a significant body of precedent affording judicial recognition to the doctrine's existence and its distinction from the *contra proferentem* rule.[61] In 1993, the Supreme Court of Canada's limited affirmation on this point in *Reid Crowther v Simcoe & Erie General Insurance Co*,[62] citing United States precedent, set out the now frequently invoked principle that:

> In each case the courts must examine the provisions of the particular policy at issue (and the surrounding circumstances) to determine if the events in

59 See, for example, *Collins v Farmers' Inc Co* 822 P 2d 1146, at 1162, noting: 'this court has not explicitly adopted the doctrine of reasonable expectations, at least by name, in any of its forms. Neither has this court explicitly rejected it ... At some point, this court will have to address this series of conflicting precedents in our cases which today's majority opinion simply ignores.' (Unis J, dissenting.)

60 Henderson (1998) 5 Connecticut Law Review 69, at 71.

61 See, for example, *Consolidated-Bathurst Export Ltd v Mutual Boiler and Machinery Insurance Co* [1980] 1 SCR 888; *Wigle v Allstate Insurance Co of Canada* (1984), 49 OR (2d) 101 (leave to appeal to SCC refused [1985] 1 SCR); *Elite Builders Ltd v Maritime Life Assurance* (1985) BCD Civ 2114-01; *United Realty Ltd v Guardian Insurance Co of Canada* [1986] BCD Civ 1933-02; *Scott v Wawanesa Mutual Insurance Co* [1989] 1 SCR 1445; *Fletcher v Manitoba Public Insurance Co* [1990] 3 SCR; *Chilton v Co-operators General Insurance Co* (1997) 143 DLR (4th) 647; *University of Saskatchewan v Firemans' Fund Insurance Co of Canada* [1998] 5 WWR 276 (Sask CA), at 289; *Kildonan Tree Service Ltd v Sovereign General Insurance Co* (1997) Man D Lexis 505; [1997] Man D 470.55.55.35-03; *Montigny v Montigy and the General Accident Assurance Company of Canada* (1999) ACWS 3d 468; *Brissette Estate v Westbury Life Insurance Co; Brissette Estate v Crown Life Insurance Co* [1992] 3 SCR 87; *Smith v Crown Life Insurance Co* (1999) ACWS 3d 423; *Tansey Estate v Mutual Life Assurance Co of Canada* (1999) BCD Civ 470.55.50.40-01; *Scalera v Oppenheim* (2000) SCC 24; Can Sup Ct Lexis 24.

62 [1993] 1 SCR 252.

question fall within the terms of the coverage of that particular policy. This is not to say that there are no principles governing this type of analysis. Far from it. In each case, the courts must interpret the provisions of the policy at issue in light of general principles of interpretation of insurance policies, including but not limited to:

(1) the *contra proferentem* rule;

(2) the principle that coverage provisions should be construed broadly and exclusion clauses narrowly; and

(3) the desirability, at least where the policy is ambiguous, of giving effect to the reasonable expectations of the parties.[63]

The third principle is a weak version of the *contra proferentem* rule, but it is significant that it expressed in terms of 'reasonable expectations' and it applies that as a measure. Consideration of the preponderance of cases generated on this basis indicates Canadian courts can best be described as following what is referred to above as the most 'conservative' application of this rule.

In the United Kingdom, although shying away from actual invocation of the doctrine by name, the House of Lords in *Cook v Financial Insurance Co*,[64] held that a self-employed builder's certificate of insurance for disability insurance 'must be construed in the sense in which it would have been reasonably understood by him as the consumer'. Additionally, paralleling Keeton's directive that such a principle be invoked when 'painstaking' readings of policy materials are necessary to achieve clear understandings of the final result, UK courts have refused to give meaning to clauses inconspicuously printed in non-contractual written material[65] or 'tucked away at the end of the policy'.[66] This position is similarly recognised in ss 5–8 of the Unfair Terms in Consumer Contracts Regulations 1999 in relation to standard form contract terms wherein legibility, intelligibility and 'unfairness' are controlled. This said, although these provisions clearly go a substantial distance in the protection of consumers, it is questionable whether they are adequate to pick up the type of scenario set forth in *Kievit*, wherein the clause itself was understandable and legible as well as 'fair' in that it carried the valid objective of protecting against 'inside jobs' through specified evidentiary requirements. Whether an English insured would therefore be entitled to the same degree of protection under such literally worded circumstances seems questionable. Professor Malcolm Clarke,[67] in reviewing the mounting ground

63 [1993] 1 SCR 252, at 269.

64 [1998] 1 WLR 1765, 1768, *per* Lord Lloyd, with Lord Steyn and Lord Hope in agreement.

65 *Stephen v International Sleeping-Car Co Ltd* (1903) 19 TLR 621; *Thornton v Shoe Lane Parking* [1971] 2 QB 163; *Interfoto Picture Library Ltd v Stiletto Visual Programs Ltd* [1989] 2 QB 433.

66 *Woolfall & Rimmer Ltd v Moyle* [1942] 1 KB 66, 73. See also Insurance Ombudsman, Annual Report 1990, paras 2.4, 2.6.

67 See Clarke, 1999, at 15-5B2.

swell of precedent in this direction and considering Steyn LJ's comments regarding the protection of reasonable expectations of honest men set forth in *First Energy (UK) Ltd v Hungarian International Bank Ltd*,[68] probably concurs in this respect to the extent that his most recent text contains the observation that it may indeed 'now be the time to draw these strands together in England to form a rule of reasonable expectations applied to insurance contracts'.[69]

5.2.5 The way forward

It remains to be seen to what extent this doctrine will establish itself. Other more predictable strategies have been deployed by legislatures around the world to ensure that reasonable expectations are met and to protect insureds against unexpected exclusions or obligations. The most common strategy is to prescribe the standard terms and conditions that all policies in a particular market must contain. This approach, used extensively in compulsory insurance such as workers' compensation and third party motor vehicle insurance, delivers peace of mind that certain minimum cover is provided. Derogation from standard cover is permitted, only where clear notice is given.[70] This is discussed in detail below.

Finally, it is instructive to consider the position under German law. Commentators[71] observe:

> Not only can a German judge achieve justice through the interpretation of the contract, but he also has another powerful statutory tool for the purpose. The Civil Code requires that obligations be performed according to standards of good faith. There seems to be an increasing tendency of German courts to use this provision as an indirect way to modify contractual stipulations they regard at unfair.[72]

The same potential exists in other jurisdictions. The duty of utmost good faith underpins the insurance relationship and while case law in this area is overwhelmingly concerned with the failure or alleged failure by the insured to disclose material information in a pre-contract setting, many cases such as the House of Lords decision in *Banque Financière de la Cité SA v Westgate (UK) Insurance Co Ltd*[73] confirm the application of this duty to all contractual

68 [1993] 2 Lloyd's Rep 194, at 196.

69 Clarke, 1999, at 15–30.

70 See, for example, the Insurance Contracts Act 1984 (Australia), s 35.

71 Kimball and Pfenningstorf (1964) 39 Indiana Law Journal 675; Lucke, in Finn (ed), 1987, Chapter 5.

72 Kimball and Pfenningstorf, *ibid*, at 724.

73 [1991] 2 AC 249. See however *Manifest Shipping Co Ltd v Uni-Polaris Shipping Co Ltd (The Star Sea)* [2001] Lloyd's Rep 1R where the continuing duty of utmost good faith was narrowly construed. Lord Hobhouse distinguished a lack of good faith which [contd]

matters. Similarly the passage of legislation like the Insurance Contracts Act 1984 (Australia),[74] enshrining utmost good faith provisions in all insurance contracts to which the Act applies, gives Australian courts the opportunity to take a more interventionist and reconstructive role in relation to insurance contracts, their terms and conditions and the insured's reasonable expectations.[75]

Particular mention should be made in this context to *Beverley v Tyndall Life Insurance Co Ltd*[76] where the Full Court of the Supreme Court of Western Australia decided that the insurer's duty of utmost good faith to an insured obliged it to follow rules of procedural fairness, and to disclose to the insured all the material upon which the insurer intended to rely in sufficient time to allow the insured to respond to any adverse material. The key issue was the definition of 'disability' in an insurance contract, and as this depended upon the insurer's being satisfied that the insured was disabled, it was in a very real sense acting as a judge in its own cause. This was, therefore, a particularly appropriate circumstance in which to apply the duty of utmost good faith.

In summary, reconciling contractual language with the 'spirit' of a given deal is effectively a *leit motif* of 20th century contract jurisprudence. Aligning parties' expectations with the language employed in agreements is necessarily a difficult balance, both layers being capable of semantic ambiguity.[77] The tension between respecting the sanctity of contract – legal formalism – and that of recognising the ultimate objective of fairness and justice for individual plaintiffs – legal functionalism – is a recurrent theme in all jurisdictions. What emerges broadly from the examination of cases and discussions above is a growing willingness on part of the courts in the United States, Canada and the United Kingdom to reconsider the relative weightings assigned, at least as regards standard form insurance contracts, to the interests of individual justice over the sanctity of contract. However, there is reluctance, evident from

73 [contd] was material to the making of the contract itself (or some variation of it) and a lack of good faith during the performance of the contract. The remedy for the former was avoidance. The latter, because it derived from the contract, attracted only those remedies provided by the laws of contract. See Insurance Law Monthly Volume 13, March 2001, p 6.

74 See ss 12–14.

75 See, for example, *Moss v Sun Alliance Australia Ltd* (1990) 6 ANZ Insurance Cases 60-967; *Gugliotti v Commercial Union Assurance Co of Australia* (1992) 7 ANZ Insurance Cases 61-104; *Australian Associated Motor Insurers Ltd v Ellis* (1990) 6 ANZ Insurance Cases 60-987; *Kelly v New Zealand Insurance Co Ltd* (1993) 7 ANZ Insurance Cases 61-197; *Ibrahim v Greater Pacific Life Insurance Co Ltd* (1996) 9 ANZ Insurance Cases 61-330; cf *Re Zurich Australian Insurance Ltd* (1999) 10 ANZ Insurance Cases 61-429.

76 (1999) 10 ANZ Insurance Cases 61-453.

77 Clarke, 1997, p 363, nicely encapsulates this common jurisdictional dichotomy by observing that: '[t]he concern of the philosopher or semanticist is with the truth of such language. The terms of contract (Seller will deliver goods to Buyer at Seller's warehouse) may be similar in form to the law of science (ice will melt at 0 degrees Celsius), but they are fundamentally different in significance. The language of a contract is not directed at describing experience but at controlling human behaviour ordinarily the behaviour of the contracting parties. The concern of a court is not with the truth of this language but with the expectations that it arouses in the parties.'

the jurisprudential struggle in various jurisdictions in the United States, with the doctrine of reasonable expectations. At one extreme it provides protection of reasonable expectations even in instances where express language to the contrary exists in the policy. At the other extreme it is simply used as a rule of construction to resolve ambiguities.

The major problem with the development of a more interventionist approach to the reconstruction of contractual obligations based upon utmost good faith provisions is uncertainty. It was this factor of uncertainty that led the Australian Law Reform Commission[78] to reject a general power of review of contractual terms. General insurers were concerned that a general power of review would lead to great uncertainty and would further complicate the process of setting appropriate rates.[79] A broadly based application of the good faith provisions in the construction and modification of contractual provisions would engender as much uncertainty as a general power of review.

The major limitation upon such an approach and the reasonable expectations doctrine and with constructional devices such as the *contra proferentem* rule is that they can only be deployed in the context of litigation. The insured has to take the initiative and incur the expense and risk in an endeavour to cure what he or she perceives to be ambiguities or obligations that are not in accord with information provided or understandings reached in the pre-contract setting. Against this it may be said that a willingness by courts to modify contractual obligations on the basis of the statutory good faith provisions or in the context of reasonable expectations could encourage insurers towards more careful drafting of policies and a greater level of caution when seeking to invoke their strict terms.[80]

5.3 STANDARD COVER

Difficulties with the construction and readability of insurance policies have led the Australian legislature to prescribe standard cover in six areas of domestic insurance. While a multitude of rules of construction exists, the application of any particular rule of construction is uncertain because it must depend on the words actually used, including other parts of the policy, and because it is also a matter of judicial assessment in the circumstances of the case under consideration.[81] The volume of case law concerned with

78 *Report on Insurance Contracts* (No 20, 1982), at para 51.

79 *Ibid*.

80 See, for example, Kimball and Pfenningsdorf (1964) 39 Indiana Law Journal 675.

81 See, for example, *Manufacturers' Mutual Insurance Ltd v Queensland Government Railways* (1968) 118 CLR 314.

construction of insurance policies is ample testimony to the fact that these contracts of adhesion[82] give rise to numerous complex misunderstandings.

While the Australian Law Reform Commission[83] was firmly in favour of insurers' attempts to simplify their policy wordings, it did not espouse the cause of compulsion in this direction. The Commission recognised that readability formulae should be approached with caution and accepted that the abandonment of technical wording could exacerbate, rather than diminish, difficulties in certain circumstances. Setting standards of comprehensibility, it asserted:

> [W]ould involve considerable rewriting in fields where that might seem unnecessary, given the nature of the typical insured and of the advice available to him. Even in areas of domestic insurance, it would offer no protection to those who did not read their policies or who were, despite simplification, unable to understand them. It would also impose on insurers the risk of being made subject to unexpected liability through drafting errors or through the abandonment of technical wordings.[84]

The Commission considered the possibility of the courts being given a general power to review the terms of insurance contracts. Reform along these lines was rejected however as being a potential source of great uncertainty, of further complicating the process of setting rates, and of being strictly unnecessary in light of the requirement that both parties must act in utmost good faith towards one another.[85]

Another avenue of reform in this area pointed to administrative control of the form and the substance of certain insurance contracts.[86] While this would provide some protection to policy holders against unusual exclusions or obligations, a pre-clearance scheme or one based on subsequent disapproval would be very expensive, and the latter would also have the demerits of uncertainty and would inhibit innovation.[87]

The Commission decided, therefore, that many misunderstandings about insurance could be cured or alleviated through the prescription of standard cover in certain designated areas. The unavailability of policy terms at the time when cover is effected, the problems of illegibility and incomprehensibility,

---

82 That is, contracts in which one of the parties has no choice but to adhere to the terms dictated by the other party. See Kimball and Pfenningstorf (1964) 39 Indiana Law Journal 675, at 676.

83 Australian Law Reform Commission, *Report on Insurance Contracts* (No 20, 1982), para 42.

84 *Ibid*, para 43.

85 *Ibid*, para 51.

86 The Insurance and Superannuation Commissioner has limited power to require certain forms to be withdrawn if they do not comply with the Life Insurance Act 1945 (Australia), s 77.

87 Australian Law Reform Commission, *Report on Insurance Contracts* (No 20, 1982), para 53.

and even of ignorance of the existence of unusual and unexpected exclusions or obligations, could be redressed, fully or in part, by the imposition of standard covers – with the rider that derogation from such standard terms would be permitted only where clear warning was given.[88]

The Commission explained its recommendation as follows:

> The argument for the introduction of standard policies or terms in areas of domestic insurance where expert advice is not usually available and where the insured himself is unlikely to be able to understand individual terms, let alone appreciate the significance of the contract as a whole. The imposition of standard contracts would simplify insurance for insureds and would protect them against unusual and unexpected exclusions and obligations. It might also increase the efficiency of insurers and reduce their costs in a variety of ways. Competition could proceed on the basis of price, reputation and service.[89]

It was recognised that the introduction of standard cover would have anti-competitive effects,[90] but the Commission maintained that the benefits that would accrue through its provision – such as to the risks covered and to the minimum amount of cover – would more than outweigh any such disadvantages.

The legislature accepted the Commission's recommendation that standard cover be prescribed in six areas of consumer insurance, and this is dealt with in the Insurance Contracts Act 1984 (Australia)[91] and the Insurance Contracts Regulations 1985 (Australia).[92] Standard cover is provided in respect of motor vehicle insurance (property damage), home buildings insurance, home contents insurance, sickness and accident insurance, consumer credit insurance and travel insurance.[93]

The combined effect of the Act and the Regulations is that where an insured makes a claim under a prescribed contract (that is, a contract to which the standard cover provisions apply) and that claim is in respect of loss arising from an event prescribed in the Regulations, the insurer must pay the insured the minimum amount specified in the Regulations. The insurer cannot rely on the terms of the contract to deny liability or reduce the amount of liability below a certain prescribed minimum *unless* the insurer proves that before the contract was entered into, the insured was clearly informed in writing

88 *Ibid*, para 69.

89 *Ibid*, para 55.

90 *Ibid*. While flexibility in responding to the marketplace by the development of new and improved products might be inhibited, the Commission was of the opinion that the public benefit was served through a standard cover regime.

91 Insurance Contracts Act 1984 (Australia), ss 34–37.

92 SR No 162 of 1985; as amended by SR No 444 of 1990.

93 SR No 162 of 1985; regs 5–28. Special attention is drawn to the particular notice requirements in relation to consumer credit insurance; see the Insurance Contracts Act 1984 (Australia), s 71A.

(whether by providing the insured with a document containing the provisions, or the relevant provisions, of the proposed contract or otherwise). Or, in the alternative, that the insured knew, or that a reasonable person in the circumstances could be expected to have known, that the insurer was liable only for the lesser amount or that the particular risk was not covered by the contract of insurance.[94]

Crucial to an understanding of these standard cover provisions are the pivotal expressions 'prescribed contract', 'prescribed event' and 'minimum amount'. The expression 'prescribed contract' is defined to mean 'a contract of insurance that is included in a class of contracts of insurance declared by the regulations to be class of contracts in relation to which [Division 1 of Part V of the Act dealing with "standard cover"] applies'.[95]

As mentioned above, the Regulations have declared six widely used types of insurance cover to be classes of contracts to which the standard cover rules apply. 'Prescribed event', in relation to any of these classes of insurance, 'means an event that is declared by the regulations to be a prescribed event in relation to that contract'.[96] For example, in the case of motor vehicle insurance the legitimate expectations of an insured are secured in that an insured is covered against the prescribed events of theft of, or accidental damage to, the vehicle or its accessories, against liability for property damage caused to third parties arising out of the use of the motor vehicle or a trailer or caravan attached to the motor vehicle.[97]

As a corollary, expectations based on the common course of insurance practice in the relevant field are not ignored. The insured's liability in the motor vehicle insurance area is excluded in respect of depreciation, wear and tear, rust and corrosion, where the insured is driving the motor vehicle and is under the influence of intoxicating liquor or of a drug, or where the destruction or damage or incurrence of liability occurs at a time when the vehicle is being used (with the express or implied consent of the insured) in racing, pacemaking, hill-climbing and so on.[98] So, in prescribing events that are covered and excluding others for each of the prescribed classes of insurance, account has been taken not only of an insured's likely expectations based on the relevant class or description of insurance, but also of

94 Insurance Contracts Act 1984 (Australia), s 35(1)(2). As amended by the Statute Law (Miscellaneous Provisions) Act (No 1) 1985, s 3; Statute Law (Miscellaneous Provisions) Act (No 2) 1985, ss 2(8), 3.

95 Insurance Contracts Act 1984 (Australia), s 34.

96 *Ibid*.

97 Insurance Contracts Regulations 1985 (Australia), reg 6. The cover against liability for property damage extends to a person driving or using the motor vehicle with the express or implied consent of the insured, and to persons who incur such a liability (otherwise than under the contract) as employer, principal or partner, respectively.

98 Insurance Contracts Regulations 1985 (Australia).

expectations based on the common course of insurance practice in the relevant area.[99]

From the insurer's point of view, it represents a fair limitation on the cover in accordance with common practice, and with the added flexible protection of further special limits which the insurer may impose in appropriate cases, subject only to the reasonable precaution protecting the insured that the insurer draw such special provisions to the insured's attention. This would seem to be a small but reasonable attempt to avoid the unfairness experienced in practice in which the insured is unaware of such special limitations. Whether it will overcome the problems that some insureds will not acquaint themselves of the standard policy and/or will not read the insurer's notice of special terms is very doubtful; but protection can extend fairly only to what might be expected of persons showing some reasonable care for their own interests.

The third vital component in the standard cover 'matrix' is 'minimum amount', and this is defined to mean 'the amount declared by the regulations to be the minimum amount in relation to a class of claims in which that claim is included'.[100] For example, in respect of home buildings insurance the minimum amount in respect of a claim arising out of an event such as a fire is the amount sufficient to indemnify the person who made the claim; moreover, the minimum amount is taken to include the reasonable cost of emergency accommodation, demolition and removal of debris, and identifying and locating the cause of destruction or damage concerned if it is necessary to do so to effect a repair.[101] Most minimum amount provisions specify particular limits; for instance, where a claim is made under a contract of motor vehicle insurance in respect of liability incurred to pay compensation for property damage arising out of the use of the motor vehicle, the minimum amount in respect of the claim is the amount, not exceeding $5,000,000, sufficient to indemnify the person who made the claim in respect of his or her liability.[102] This minimum amount also comes within the matters that may be varied by the insurer by notice under s 35(2).

The general scheme, therefore, is that for the widely used classes of insurance cover which lie beneath the umbrella of 'prescribed contracts', the insurer must provide a minimum cover in respect of any loss or damage arising out of the occurrence of a 'prescribed event'. However, this general scheme is inoperative in those cases where s 35(2) of the Insurance Contracts Act 1984 (Australia) is successfully invoked by an insurer – that is, where the

99 Australian Law Reform Commission, *Report on Insurance Contracts* (No 20, 1982), para 76.

100 Insurance Contracts Act 1984 (Australia), s 34.

101 Insurance Contracts Regulations 1985 (Australia), reg 12.

102 *Ibid*, reg 8(2); see also regs 12(3), 16(2), 20(3).

insurer can prove that he clearly informed the insured in writing, or the insured knew, or a reasonable person in the circumstances could be expected to have known, that the insurer was liable only for a lesser amount or that the particular risk was not covered by the contract of insurance, the insurer may escape the standard cover constraints.

Pursuant to s 69 of the Insurance Contracts Act 1984 (Australia) the insurer may comply with the requirement of notice 'in writing' about a particular maximum amount or lack of cover by giving the information orally. This is only permissible where it is not reasonably practicable for the information to be given in writing at the time the contract was entered into, and in any event must also be given in writing within 14 days after the day the contract was entered into.

On the question of whether a particular risk and consequent claim come within the purview of s 35, the regulations are to be construed as though they were provisions of a contract put forward by the insurer.[103] Consequently, the *contra proferentem* rule remains in application to the construction of standard cover, and in the event of irreducible ambiguity, will see such provisions being read against the insurer. This position reflects the Australian Law Reform Commission's opinion that notwithstanding standard cover provisions the contractual nature of the relationship between insurer and insured remains.

And yet, clearly a fundamental premise of the *contra proferentem* rule has been ignored. The standard cover provisions are in statutory form. They are not in fact terms drafted by the insurer. Application therefore of the *contra proferentem* rule against the insurer seems logically misplaced as neither party would be directly responsible for creating linguistic ambiguity[104] arising out of the statutory provisions. A court should be permitted to employ a more equitable (and possibly less expedient) canon of construction.

In applying the terms of s 35 regard is to be had to the regulations in force at the date on which the contract is entered into and any subsequent amendment will be disregarded for the purposes of that particular contract.[105]

The imposition of standard cover in areas of domestic insurance is designed to counter the problems stemming from: (i) the vast variety and heterogeneity of policy terms to be found in any one given area of insurance; (ii) the presence of unexpected and idiosyncratic terms, conditions, or exclusions in policies; and (iii) consumer ignorance of the nature and extent of cover obtainable in any given area in the insurance market. Any derogation in

103 Insurance Contracts Act 1984 (Australia), s 36.

104 See, for example, *Kodak (Aust) Pty Ltd v Retail Traders Mutual Indemnity Insurance Association* (1942) 42 SR (NSW) 231; *Green v Windman* (1964) VR 297; *Re Linsley and Co-operative Association* (1976) 62 DLR (3d) 408.

105 Insurance Contracts Act 1984 (Australia), s 35(4).

scope or quantum of cover will have to be brought to the attention of the insured to be effective, unless, of course, the insured knew, or a reasonable person in the circumstances could be expected to have known that the policy in question offered less than, or something different from, the standard cover. This latter escape route has become a fertile ground of legal endeavour as counsel attempt to attribute varying standards of knowledge and comprehension to this hypothetical being.[106]

As far as written notice of any derogation from standard cover is concerned, the real danger is that the given notice is so lengthy and comprehensive that an insured will not have the time, energy and/or inclination to read it. The Australian Law Reform Commission rejected such a criticism largely on the assumption that controls over length, legibility and comprehensibility of notices would ensure that this problem would not arise.[107] However, it is quite clear from s 35(2) (as amended by the Statute Law (Miscellaneous Provisions) Acts, No 1 and No 2 of 1985) that by handing a prospective insured a copy of the proposed contract there is notice of derogation from standard cover. Depending on the length and/or clarity of this document a prospective insured may or may not become aware of such derogation. Apart from the requirement of clarity, which may have some influence, no controls over length or comprehensibility appear in the Act or Regulations. The best course of action therefore would generally be for an insurer who wishes to provide less than standard cover to provide the prospective insured with a copy of the proposed policy at the pre-contract stage, and to accompany it with a notice drawing attention to and explaining the effect of departures from standard cover. Given the length and style of documentation that such an action would comprise, it is improbable the contents would be readily understood or appreciated by the prospective insured for the reasons outlined in Chapter 2.

The means of disclosing derogation from standard cover is vitally important. It is submitted that permitting disclosure 'by giving the insured a copy of the policy' largely negates the thrust of the standard cover reform. If standard cover is the appropriate way to address consumer ignorance as to the wide variety of policy terms and conditions then the disclosure mechanism needs to be reconsidered.

---

106 See the Annual General Report of the General Insurance Enquiries and Complaints Scheme; discussed in Chapter 6 below.

107 *Report on Insurance Contracts* (No 20, 1982), para 72.

MARKETPLACE PERSPECTIVES: AN AUSTRALIAN CASE STUDY

6.1 INTRODUCTION

This chapter examines the experience of insurers, insureds and representative groups in relation to the formation of consumer insurance contracts. In particular, issues arising out of disclosure of information, the obligation of insurers to inform insureds of their duty of disclosure, and the efficacy of the standard cover provisions under the Insurance Contracts Act 1984 (Australia) will be analysed. Through consideration of areas of conflict that arise frequently during the course of an insured/insurer relationship, operational issues relating to the formation of consumer insurance contracts can be addressed.

This chapter is broken into the following components:

- General Insurance Enquiries and Complaints Scheme.
- Australian Consumers' Association.
- Case Study: Home Contents Insurance.
- Insurance Council of Australia.

6.2 GENERAL INSURANCE ENQUIRIES AND COMPLAINTS SCHEME

6.2.1 General

The Insurance Industry Complaints Council was created in 1991 and was an initiative of the Insurance Council of Australia and the Life Insurance Federation of Australia. This Council comprises a Chair, appointed by the Federal Minister for Consumer Affairs on the unanimous recommendation of the Insurance Council of Australia and the Life Insurance Federation of Australia; an appointee of the Insurance Council of Australia; an appointee of the Life Insurance Federation of Australia; and two members with experience in consumer affairs appointed by the Federal Minister for Consumer Affairs.

The Council monitors the performance of a national complaints resolution scheme and has a duty to ensure that this scheme is independent. Separate schemes are established for the life insurance industry and the general insurance industry. Relevant to this work is the General Insurance Enquiries and Complaints Scheme whereby any person who feels that a general insurer has unfairly dealt with his or her claim may use the conciliation and adjudication services offered under this scheme. Conciliation services are provided by a number of Consumer Consultants while determination services are available through Claims Review Panels, Referees and Adjudicators. The Scheme is free to insureds.

Under the Scheme an insured may refer a complaint to panels within three months of an insurer's giving its final decision on a claim. The insurer is bound by Panel determinations of $105,000 or less, but determinations do not bind the insured, whose recourse to normal legal channels remains unaffected. Panels have jurisdiction to recommend settlements up to $250,000. The General Insurance Enquiries and Complaints Scheme and the secretariat to the Scheme, Insurance Enquiries and Complaints Ltd, has achieved a high level of confidence and recognition as evidenced by the Federal Government's 1997 decision to endorse Insurance Enquiries and Complaints Ltd as also being responsible for administering and monitoring the General Insurance Code of Practice.[1]

This monograph is, of course, focused upon pre-contract formation issues in relation to consumer insurance contracts. However, the General Insurance Enquiries and Complaints Scheme (while concerned with dissatisfied claimants) has built up an invaluable database deriving from 204,424 enquires/complaints in the period from 1 July 1992 to 30 June 1998. Many of these enquiries and complaints relate to policy coverage issues, non-disclosure and the presence and interpretation of conditions and exclusions. Moreover, the Panels deal with general insurance matters of a non-commercial nature. The terms of reference include motor vehicle policies, home buildings and contents, travel, sickness and accident, consumer credit and other insurance of a personal and domestic nature. Accordingly, the data and reports of the General Insurance Enquiries and Complaints Scheme provide good insight into many operational issues relating to the formation of prescribed insurance contracts.

6.2.2 Statistics

The number of enquiries and requests for advice directed to the General Insurance Enquiries and Complaints Scheme has grown steadily over the years. Since its inception in 1992, the Scheme has logged over 200,000 enquiries, a quarter of which were registered in its most recent calendar year.

1 The Insurance Act 1973 (Australia) was amended by the Financial Laws Amendment Act 1997 (Australia) to require all general insurers who write code business to comply with the code. 'Code business' is the standard cover class described in s 34 of the Insurance Contracts Act 1984 (Australia) plus contracts of insurance that insure personal and domestic property.

Table 1: IEC enquiries

Year	No of Enquiries
1992–1993	14,626
1992–1994	22,496
1992–1995	31,104
1992–1996	37,895
1992–1997	41,691
1992–1998	56,612
Total	204,424

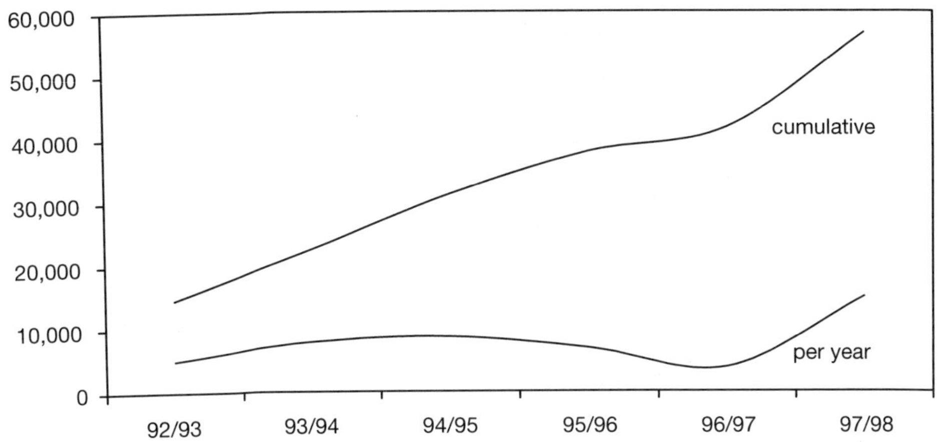

A subset of these enquiries and requests for advice will amount to or constitute complaints. The process whereby complaints are handled is reflected in Table 2.

The existence of the General Insurance Enquiries and Complaints Scheme has had a positive effect upon the internal claims review processes of individual companies; that is, the Insurance Industry Complaints Council reports that the industry is placing greater reliance on internal measures to

Table 2: Complaints flow chart[2]

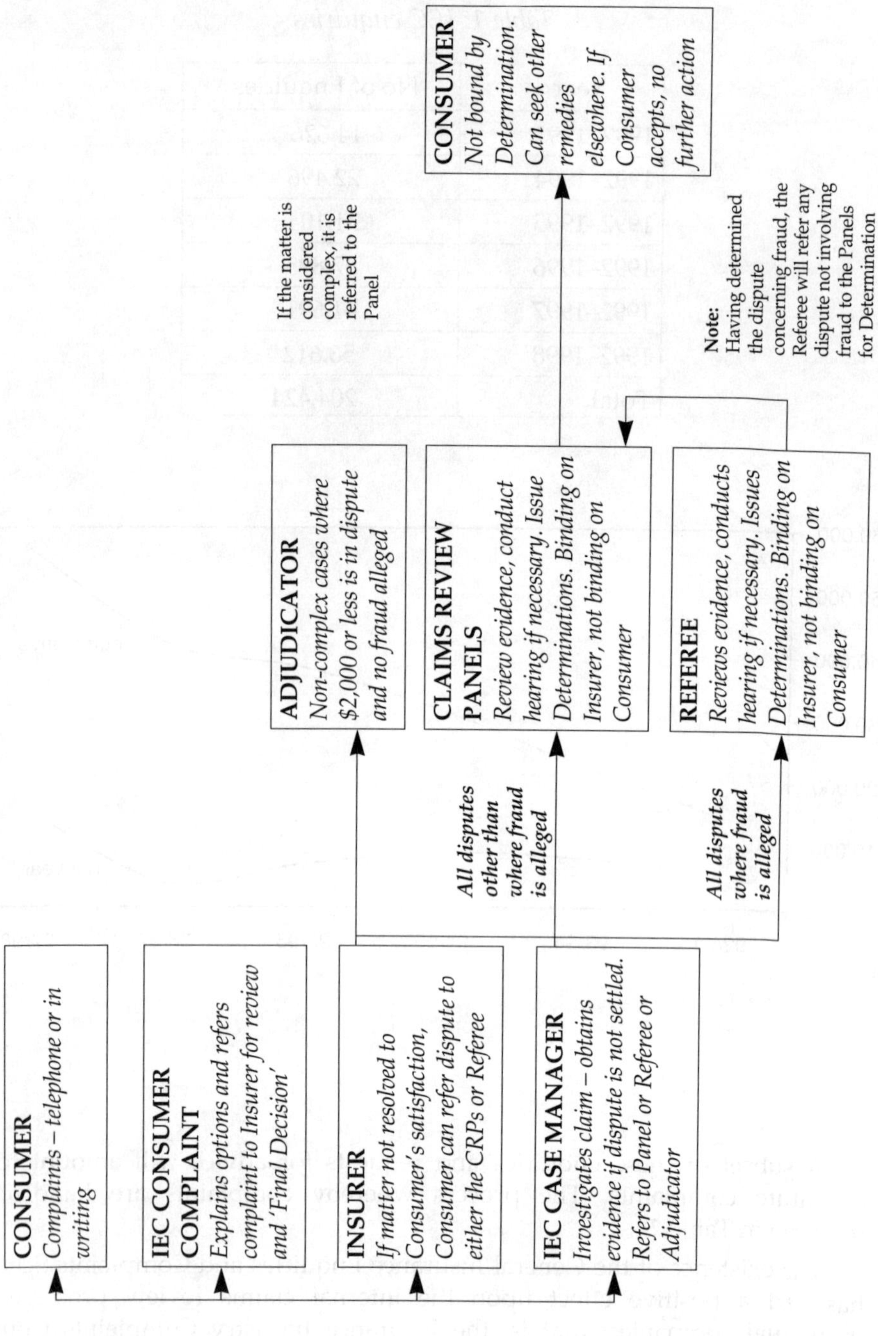

2 This chart is taken from the General Insurance Enquiries and Complaints Scheme Annual Report 1998, p 28.

avoid the need for insureds to seek redress with the Scheme.[3] However, there has been a steady growth in the number of referrals to Claims Review Panels, Adjudicators and Referees. Referrals are reflected in the table below.

Table 3: Referrals

Year	Referrals
1992–1993	377
1992–1994	435
1992–1995	616
1992–1996	931
1992–1997	1578
1992–1998	1838

It is particularly interesting in this context to analyse the reasons why insurers denied liability and hence the basis for the referral. This information is recorded in respect of the period from 1 July 1995 to 30 June 1998 in Table 4 below.

Table 4: Reasons for denial of liability

Reason	Year					
	1995/1996		1996/1997		1997/1998	
Fraud	163	18%	234	15%	238	13%
Not covered by policy	209	22%	256	16%	244	13%
Condition/Exclusion	226	29%	658	42%	817	44%
Non-disclosure	104	11%	124	8%	181	10%
No policy contract	52	6%	79	5%	90	5%
No proof of loss	9	1%	22	1%	30	2%
Quantum dispute	121	13%	196	12%	225	12%
Other	7	0.7%	9	0.6%	13	0.7%
Total	931	100%	1578	100%	1838	100%

3 See the comments of Lionel Bowen AC, Chairperson Insurance Industry Complaints Council, General Insurance Enquiries and Complaints Scheme Annual Report 1994, p 2. Moreover, the Code of Practice for the General Insurance industry required insurers to have in place by 1 July 1995 an Internal Dispute Resolution process. This process significantly reduced the number of complaints in need of determination by the Claims Review Panel, Adjudicator or Referee. See the General Insurance Enquiries and Complaints Scheme Annual Report 1996, p 16.

From the above, it is worth noting that non-disclosure and disputes as to policy coverage account for over 60% of the matters referred to Claims Review Panels for determination. This is discussed in greater detail below. A further statistic of interest is the fact that over 75% of the matters referred relate to motor vehicle, home buildings, home contents and travel insurance.

6.2.3 Insureds

Every Annual Report of the Insurance Industry Complaints Council on the operation of the General Insurance Enquiries and Complaints Scheme draws attention to the tendency of consumers not to read their policy carefully and to be more interested in the size of the premium than in the cover they are receiving. For example, the 1996 Annual Report[4] notes:

> Despite the widespread use of 'plain English' policies, which are intended to be comprehensible to lay persons, it remains true that policies are complex documents and there is an inbuilt resistance on the part of consumers to try and grapple with the details of the policy ... Consumers appear to become aware of the limitations of their policy belatedly, after an event has occurred rather than when they purchase their policy.

The Annual Reports recount numerous examples of problems occasioned through insureds' failure to read the insuring clauses, the exceptions to cover and the overall conditions of their policies. Travel insurance has given rise to particular problems with the most common ground for complaint arising in instances where a claim is refused because the insured is said to have failed to take reasonable precautions in respect of lost property or to have left it unattended in a public place.

Closely following this ground is that of cases where liability is denied because of a pre-existing illness or condition. The General Insurance Claims Review Panels are very critical of the limited information provided to purchasers of travel insurance.[5] As a starting point, the Panels are strongly of the view that the promotional material on policy documents should more accurately reflect the limitations of the policy. Moreover, travel agents should be trained to explain to insureds at least the salient features of the policy.[6] However, as the Panel notes: '... constant themes running through the

4 The General Insurance Enquiries and Complaints Scheme Annual Report 1996, pp 8–9.

5 The General Insurance Enquiries and Complaints Scheme Annual Report 1997, pp 6–7; the General Insurance Enquiries and Complaints Scheme Annual Report 1999, p 9; the General Insurance Enquiries and Complaints Scheme Annual Report 1993, p 10.

6 The General Insurance Enquiries and Complaints Scheme Annual Report 1993, p 10.

disputes are the failure of consumers to read the policy and their over optimistic expectations of the cover.'[7]

Similar problems emerge in relation to home buildings and home contents insurance cover. Malicious damage under home policies and the exclusion relating to tenants tends to escape the attention of landlords taking out cover, and variations as to what constitutes an insured event in water damage claims are common causes of complaint to the General Insurance Enquiries and Complaints Scheme.[8]

Consumer credit insurance is also a major concern, especially where the insurance is obtained contemporaneously with the purchase of a motor vehicle; that is, where a purchaser takes out insurance protection against the possibility of either unemployment or disablement during the period of the loan. The transaction is usually affected simultaneously with the sale of the motor vehicle, an application for finance and arranging comprehensive insurance on the vehicle. As the Panel notes: '... the consumer may thus drive out of the car yard having just entered into four important but separate legal contracts.'[9]

Unfortunately, many claims arising under consumer credit insurance contracts are denied as a result of non-disclosure of a previous medical condition, or recurrence of a previous medical condition within a nominated period of time after commencement of the policy (usually 90–180 days). The failure by insureds to read and/or comprehend the nature and extent of their consumer credit cover is compounded by the circumstances in which such transactions are commonly concluded.

6.2.4 Section 22 matters

The General Insurance Enquiries and Complaints Scheme Annual Reports record many deficiencies with the operation of s 22 of the Insurance Contracts Act 1984 (Australia). Section 22(1), as originally cast, imposes an obligation on the insurer to inform the insured clearly, in writing, before the contract is entered into, of the general nature and effect of the duty of disclosure. By virtue of the Insurance Laws Amendment Act 1998 (Australia) this requirement was augmented; namely, if s 21A applies to the contract, the insurer must also clearly inform the insured in writing of the general nature and effect of s 21A.

The General Insurance Claims Review Panel asserts that s 22 is proving ineffectual. The first reason given is that most insureds are unaware that renewal requires fresh disclosure of relevant matters that have occurred since the last renewal. The second reason is that even if consumers were aware that they had a duty of disclosure it is not clear that they would know what to

7 *Ibid*, at p 8.
8 See Annual Report 1996, p 9.
9 See Annual Report 1997, p 8.

disclose.[10] The Panel has emphasised the need for insurers to ask what they want to know rather than leaving it to the insured to guess at what should be disclosed.[11]

Accordingly, the Panel has been critical of disclosure statements that simply state:

> Before you enter into a contract of general insurance with [us] you have a duty, by law, to disclose to [the insurer] every matter that you know, or could be expected to know, is relevant to [the insurer] whether to accept the risk of the insurance and, if so, on what terms.
>
> You have the same duty to disclose those matters to [the insurer] before you renew, extend, vary or reinstate a contract of general insurance.

Such a statement serves to remind the insured of the duty of disclosure but does little more than this. Conversely the Panel noted with approval the approach adopted by one insurer who sought to assist its policy holders in the following way. On the face of the renewal notice for a motor vehicle policy, the consumer is told in very clear print: 'Your current insurance policy ends on [the due date] at 4 pm. To make sure your policy continues please pay for your renewal before that date. You have a legal duty to make sure that all the details on this certificate are correct. Please write any changes on the payment slip below. If you want to talk about your insurance with us please ring [number given].'

On the back of the notice the following is printed:

It is important that we have correct details. If anything is wrong you may not be covered properly or you may be paying the wrong amount. Please write any changes in the box on the payment slip or ring us before you pay.

Here is what we have on our current records. Is it right?	• Your vehicle is insured for personal use
Have any of these things happened in the past year? If yes, please tell us immediately	• Has your vehicle been modified? • Have you, or any regular driver of your vehicle, had physical or mental problems that affect driving? • Had an accident or driving offence?
The amount you are asked to pay for your insurance may change	• If you lodge a claim for damage or loss occurring before [the due date] we may increase the amount you have to pay to renew your policy and the amount of excess shown on this certificate • If you only pay for six months insurance, the amount for the next six months may be different
If you are late paying	• You are not covered after [the due date] until we receive your payment • If you have not paid by [the due date plus 60 days] you will have to complete a new insurance proposal form and have your vehicle inspected by us

10 General Insurance Claims Review Panel Annual Report 1993, p 20.

11 The General Insurance Enquiries and Complaints Scheme 1998, p 6.

This approach is much more in accord with cl 4.2 of the General Insurance Code of Practice that provides:

> Insurers shall use forms or have procedures for collecting information in relation to the provision of cover that:
>
> (a) identifies all usual information that the insurer ordinarily requires to be disclosed and which the insurer wishes to know prior to providing cover;
>
> (b) clearly informs consumers of their duty of disclosure and the consequences of non-disclosure;
>
> (c) expresses questions in plain language and, where instructions are necessary, provides information on how the questions are to be answered; and
>
> (d) provides adequate space or opportunity to answer questions or, if there is inadequate space or opportunity, provides advice as to how the additional information is to be provided.

The Panel has encountered situations where an insurer has not included in a proposal a question inquiring as to an insureds previous criminal history, relying instead on a question which asks whether there is 'any other information' the insured believes should be disclosed to the insurer. Insureds have then not disclosed criminal histories and the insurer has denied liability on this basis. In support of its denial, the insurer has presented the Panel with copies of its underwriting guidelines and examples of declinatures which establish that had it known of the insured's criminal background, it would not have underwritten the risk. In these cases, the Panel has found in favour of the claimant. It has done so because the insurer should have asked the appropriate questions. The insured was entitled to believe that if the insurer wanted to know about criminal history, it would have asked about it. The Code of Practice specifically covers this situation.

Finally, where the cover note or proposal is completed over the telephone, the requirements of s 69 apply, under which oral communication about the duty of disclosure has to be followed up by the dispatch of the information in writing within 14 days. The Panel notes that in cases where the information about the duty of disclosure is communicated orally, the parties are frequently in dispute as to whether the insurer has informed the insured of the general nature and effect of the duty of disclosure. This is particularly so in connection with cover notes completed over the telephone when a loss has been sustained in the cover note period. In dealing with such cases, the Panel makes the point that it would be assisted if insurers were able to present the checklist which their staff are required to use, showing quite clearly that the substance of s 22(1) has been included for recital and explanation of the proponent.[12]

---

12 General Insurance Claims Review Panel Annual Report 1994, p 16. Chair of the General Insurance Claims Review Panel, Mr P Hardman, reported at the Australian Insurance Law Association's Annual Conference 1999 that 'with 90% of new motor, home [contd]

6.2.5 Section 21 matters

The General Insurance Claims Review Panel commented in 1994 that:

> The purpose of a proposal is to obtain information an insurer requires in order to decide whether to accept the risk and the terms of the cover. In the Panel's view, questions in proposals should be framed in specific, rather than general terms and they should be accurately directed to the information required in relation to the insurer's underwriting guidelines. The Panels have commented before that it is not appropriate to put to an insured general questions which operate as a fishing net. Nor is it appropriate to rely on a general statement in the proposal as to the insured's duty of disclosure.[13]

Accordingly, the Panel has given a cautious welcome[14] to the new s 21A of the Insurance Contracts Act 1984 (Australia). This section, according to the Explanatory Memorandum, is designed to redress the imbalance and improve the capacity of an insured to comply with the duty of disclosure in respect of prescribed contracts by requiring insurers to ask specific questions in respect of a proposed contract of insurance, in default of which the insurer is deemed to have waived the duty of disclosure.

The Panel acknowledges that this section may make it easier for insureds to comply with the duty of disclosure on policy inception. The Panel points out that the new section is not intended to apply to renewal contracts which creates an odd situation as the duty of disclosure by the insured in renewable contracts arises each time the contract is renewed. In addition, the duty of disclosure at the time of the renewal is not assisted by the proposal form, and insureds are perhaps more likely to overlook the need to disclose a particular matter without any guidance in the form of specific questions.[15]

The Panel can foresee cases where the new section imposes a more difficult standard for consumers. Under the new scheme they will be required to answer correctly the questions asked of them on the proposal form.

At the next stage (renewal) where the duty of disclosure arises freshly, it appears that they will be required to disclose – rather than answer questions about – material that they were not required to tell the insurer about in the

12 [contd] and contents policies being made over the phone, some insurers had embarked on the potentially treacherous activity' of abbreviating the duty of disclosure, which they must read to potential policy holders. Mr Hardman said disputes arose over whether the disclosure was properly advised. There were also disputes over what was or was not said, and even insurers which sent a confirmation of details but did not require it to be checked and signed became embroiled in disputes. See 1999 AILA News, Conference edition, p 6.

13 General Insurance Claims Review Panel 1994, p 13.

14 General Insurance Enquiries and Complaints Scheme Annual Report 1998, p 6.

15 *Ibid*, p 6.

first instance. In the Panel's view, that is a recipe for confusion.[16] The Panel comments:

> Perhaps it is expected that the Code of Practice will assist the insured in that they will be given better documentation. On the other hand, there will be two standards of disclosure – one at the time of first entering into a contract of insurance and another at each periodical renewal under the current s 21 rules. This leads to the irony that, to avoid possibly breaching the duty of disclosure, insureds will be better off changing their insurer each year.[17]

The Panel has drawn attention to other problems associated with s 21 of the Insurance Contracts Act 1984 (Australia). These include:

(a) too many people, that is, insurer's agents and employees are involved in the process of completing proposals. If an insurer, for reason of customer relations, wants to encourage this practice it is vulnerable in a non-disclosure dispute to a claimant stating that he or she told the insurer's representative of the matters allegedly not disclosed, and that the person simply omitted to transmit the information to the company;

(b) in a telemarketing situation it is essential that insurers, as soon as practicable, provide written confirmation of what has allegedly transpired over the telephone. If insured persons have received such a document, and have failed to inform the insurer of any errors, they must accept the consequences;

(c) insurers must check their records to ensure all questions have been answered in the proposal. In several cases claimants have been able to avoid the consequences of non-disclosure, by establishing that an insurer has waived the requirement of disclosure, by not insisting on an answer to a question and accepting partially completed proposals;

(d) many insurers still refrain from asking people to disclose criminal convictions and then allege fraudulent non-disclosure when they do not do so. An insurer in this situation has two hurdles to overcome. First, it must prove in the circumstances that there was a duty to disclose such information pursuant to s 21 of the Insurance Contracts Act 1984 (Australia) and, secondly, that the failure to disclose was fraudulent. Insurers are advised to ask the question.[18]

The Annual Reports of the General Insurance Enquires and Complaints Scheme over the past six years make it clear that considerable work still has to be done by the insurance industry in the area of proposal drafting and in the processes that are employed in the completion of proposal forms. Questions should be specific enough to procure the required information. For example,

16 *Ibid*, p 7.

17 General Insurance Enquiries and Complaints Scheme Annual Report 1998, p 8.

18 General Insurance Enquiries and Complaints Scheme Annual Report 1996, pp 10–11.

the general nature of questions asked of proponents such as 'are you in good health?' or 'is your house in good condition and repair?' are unsatisfactory in the absence of definitions or guidance as to what the insurer means by 'good health', 'good condition' or other terms of such general nature. The Annual Reports also highlight the fact that many, if not most, insureds believe that their duty of disclosure ends when a proposal has been completed and accepted by the insurer.[19]

6.2.6 Format, language and content of policies

The experience of Panels, as mentioned above,[20] is that 'consumers are primarily interested in how much the insurance policy costs, not what it contains – or the exclusions'.[21] Consequently, the Reports of the General Insurance Enquiries and Complaints Scheme are filled with examples where claimants have been disappointed to discover that their insurance cover has not matched their expectations.

Some common examples include ignorance of an under 25 driver exclusion until after a $15,000 accident, exclusion of pre-existing illness in a personal accident policy and burglary coverage only applying if there was evidence of 'forcible entry at the point of entry'. Moreover, it is clear that many insureds are unaware that policy entitlements vary considerably between insurers – a common cause of complaint that arises when neighbours, friends or relatives compare their outcomes in similar circumstances, not factoring in different policy entitlements.

The standard cover regime erected by s 35 of the Insurance Contracts Act 1984 (Australia) was intended to address these problems. As discussed in Chapter 5, the basic rationale behind standard cover is that the insurer is required to provide cover against risks specified in the Regulations to the Act in respect of prescribed insurance contracts. The Act also provides that insurers may derogate from the standard cover, provided the insured has been clearly informed in writing of the provisions of the contract before it was entered into. The fact that this notice of derogation may be achieved by providing the insured with a document containing the provisions, or the relevant provisions,[22] of the proposed contract, has emasculated the standard cover regime.

19 *Ibid*, p 10; the General Insurance Enquiries and Complaints Scheme Annual Report 1997, p 9; the General Insurance Enquiries and Complaints Scheme Annual Report 1998, p 10.

20 See Chapter 6.2.3 above.

21 General Insurance Enquiries and Complaints Scheme Annual Report 1998, p 7.

22 Insurance Contracts Act 1984 (Australia), s 35(2).

The Claims Review Panel reports in their most recent Annual Report:

> Most insurance policies of the [motor vehicle, home buildings, home contents, consumer credit, personal accident and travel insurance] classes ... do not provide standard cover ... Many claims officers may not know what standard cover is, and the relationship between the clauses in their policies and standard cover policies.[23]

The Claims Review Panel is very critical of the operation of s 35(2) that permits standard cover to be by-passed through the simple expedient of giving the insured a copy of the policy. This clearly is inadequate notice were it not expressly authorised by the legislative provision. In the circumstances the Claims Review Panel poses the question 'whether the legislature, the industry and the consumer movement still believe the terms of these statutory policies remain appropriate for ... the new millennium?'[24]

The problem may, of course, be more one of the implementation of the standard cover regime. It is evident that the simple provision of a policy document does not 'clearly inform' an insured of differences in the levels of cover provided under that policy as measured against the standard cover statutory version. It is unrealistic to assume that many (if any) insureds are knowledgeable enough about policies to become aware of derogations from standard cover or to make any meaningful assessment. The Claims Review Panel[25] has urged Parliament and the superior courts to look at this issue, and has suggested that the following matters are relevant when deciding whether a requirement to inform clearly is satisfied:

1 The extent of variation from standard cover. The more significant or harsh the variation, the greater, in the Panel's opinion, is the requirement to clearly inform.

2 The language used in the policy and the simplicity or complexity of the policy terms.

3 The length of the policy.

4 The size and colour of the print and the general formatting of the policy.

5 Whether the relevant policy terms were changed or varied during the time an insured person has held the particular policy.

6 The layout of the policy and how well it may be indexed.

7 The particular circumstances of the policy holder may also be relevant. For example, is the insurer aware of any disability of a policy holder?[26]

---

23 General Insurance Enquiries and Complaints Scheme 1998, p 7.

24 *Ibid.*

25 *Ibid*, p 10.

26 *Ibid.*

This is a useful list of considerations. One other matter that may be added relates to the prior history of dealings between the insurer and insured, or particular knowledge that the insurer may have of the insured's use of the property, motor vehicle or other subject of the insurance or of any other conduct or circumstance that may adversely affect the cover. A heightened duty to inform the insured about any such derogation from standard cover may arise commensurate with the impact such derogation may have or the insured's idiosyncratic needs or on the cover.

The Claims Review Panels have commended insurers efforts to make their documentation more 'user friendly' by adopting plain language styles and by redesigning the format. There are, however, numerous ongoing and, in some instances, new problems. An example of the latter is where elaborate brochures are provided in an endeavour to clarify the scope of the cover. In practice some of this documentation can be misleading – for example, by highlighting particular areas of cover without sufficient reference or indication of a related exclusion.[27] Another example of a 'new' problem is where, despite an improvement in policy layout and wording, underwriting guidelines and claims procedures reflect the pre-reform approach and old documentation.

Poor drafting continues to be a major problem. A common drafting problem is where a broad statement of what is covered is made and only subsequently qualified by detailed exclusions many pages later in the policy.[28] Examples of poor or confusing language abound. Numerous disputes arise as to the use of 'conviction' which, on its narrow meaning, implies that a charge has been processed in court and a conviction has been imposed. Persons with traffic infringements which have resulted in an accumulation of demerit points and/or summary fines would, on this meaning, be entitled to indicate that they had no convictions. The Claims Review Panel[29] in reporting many disputes in this regard emphasise that insurers have an obligation to ask precisely what they want to know about an insured's driving record, and that questions should be directed at fines/charges/traffic infringements if confusion is to be avoided.

There also continues to be problems with personal accident claims with varying definitions of 'permanent total disablement'. This form of cover is normally arranged by a person engaged in his or her own business and is designed to provide a compensatory weekly benefit to cover loss of income or

27 General Insurance Enquiries and Complaints Scheme 1996, p 7.

28 *Ibid*, p 6.

29 *Ibid*, p 5.

to offset additional costs incurred in maintaining the business whilst incapacitated. The definitions of total disablement vary enormously:

> ... the disability must have continued for one year from the date of inquiry and at that time is certified by a duly qualified medical practitioner as being beyond hope of improvement and entirely preventing you forever from engaging in any business, profession, occupation or employment for which you are reasonably qualified by training, experience or education;
>
> or
>
> total disablement is disablement which entirely prevents you from engaging in your usual occupation, profession or business.

In the first definition, for example, the words 'beyond hope of improvement' imposes an absolute test that is virtually impossible to meet. Temporary relief from pain could constitute an improvement. In relation to the second definition, insurers have contended that the injured person must be unable to have any involvement in the conduct of his or her business, including the giving of orders to his or her replacement or other workers, if the insured is said to be 'entirely' prevented from engaging in the business. In effect, totally disabled in the context of such a definition means comatose or so isolated that the insured is unable to have any involvement or make any direction in matters of his or her occupation, profession or business. As the Claims Review Panels point out, definitions of this kind would undoubtedly not have been accepted by the prospective insured if the limitations of the cover had been understood when the cover was sought.[30]

Numerous other examples of poor drafting and 'tough' clauses appear in the Annual Reports. Two further instances are worth recording. Proponents for home buildings or home contents insurance are commonly required to advise in proposal documents whether their house is 'in good condition and repair'. A condition in the policies normally makes such good condition and repair an ongoing obligation of the insured. The Claims Review Panel[31] has considered numerous instances where insurers have argued misrepresentation at the time of the claim basing their arguments on confidential underwriting guidelines as to the meaning of 'good condition and repair' – in most instances this phrase was nowhere defined in the proposal or policy.

The final example relates to the common exclusion in motor vehicle policies excluding liability where the vehicle is driven by an intoxicated person. Some exclusions have been framed more generally[32] to exclude the

30 General Insurance Claims Review Panel Annual Report 1993, p 11; General Insurance Claims Review Panel 1994, pp 18–19.

31 General Insurance Claims Review Panel Annual Report 1993, p 12.

32 The Insurance Contracts Regulations 1985 (Australia), reg 7(ix) entitles an insurer to exclude liability in the standard cover motor vehicle policy where the insured knew or reasonably should have known at the time of giving his consent that the driver was under the influence.

insurer's liability even in circumstances where the insured did not give consent to the person to drive the vehicle or was unaware of the driver's condition.

Finally, the format and structure of many policies is productive of much confusion and can inhibit the most determined effort to understand the contents. This problem is exacerbated when the same document performs the dual roles of marketing brochure and policy document. A good example is afforded by the Claims Review Panel[33] in relation to travel insurance. Luggage was lost whilst being transported unaccompanied by rail. The policy brochure stated on p 2: 'We'll cover you against accidental loss or damage to your luggage.' A number of limits for particular types of items and sums involved were stated. Late in the document at pp 16 and 17, the same promise was repeated but this time with many more qualifications including a specific exclusion for unaccompanied luggage. As the Panel points out, p 2 is marketing material emphasising the positive aspects of the cover and the serious policy terms appear later. The Panel comments that: 'there being no indication that the promise made on p 2 was subject to further qualifications, it is difficult to expect a consumer to understand that it is not meant literally – especially as the pagination of the document is continuous and there is no clear separation.'[34]

6.3 AUSTRALIAN CONSUMERS' ASSOCIATION

6.3.1 General

The Australian Consumers' Association is an independent, non-governmental organisation that provides information on a wide range of consumer issues. It is the publisher of *Choice* magazine, well known for its product and service testing. The Association conducted a major survey of home buildings and home contents insurance cover in 1998. As both of these covers fall within the umbrella of standard cover, aspects of the Association's findings relevant to this work are recorded here.

The Australian Consumers' Association reiterates a theme common to that found in the General Insurance Enquiries and Complaints Annual Reports discussed above; namely, that it is very important for insureds to read and

33 General Insurance Enquiries and Complaints Scheme 1996, p 6.
34 *Ibid*.

understand their policies to ensure that their personal situations are covered. Although the most common claims for home and contents insurance in Australia are theft, fire, weather (including storm and rain damage), burst pipes, fusion of electric motors and accidental breakage of glass, such as windows and doors, not all policies cover these events.[35] Moreover, the Association points to the exclusion of flood cover from the overwhelming majority of policies. Only seven policies of the 40 surveyed covered flood, and with most to those it is an option that the insured had to pay an additional premium for. As discussed below,[36] the absence of flood cover is a very significant departure from 'prescribed events' under standard cover provisions.[37]

The Association's survey concludes that 43% of persons insured do not have sufficient cover to completely rebuild or replace their house or contents. Additionally, there is wide variation as to how depreciation operates in the context of contents policies – the best depreciate no, or very few, items, the worst either have a very long list, or depreciate everything over 15 years old. Insureds are advised to check carefully whose property is covered under contents insurance. For example, some policies cover belongings of a guest in a range from $300 to $5,000, while other insurers exclude liability for anyone other than the insured and his or her family. Even in this connection, there is a wide variety. The broadest definition includes grandparents and grandchildren, while the narrowest does not include a *de facto* spouse.[38]

In conclusion, there is significant variation in the policies considered by the Australian Consumers' Association. A careful reading of the policy document is necessary to gain a proper understanding of the cover provided and of the limitations to and/or exclusions from cover. Similar policies are often available at quite significant price differentials. For example, the Association cites examples in each state and territory where some large savings are available as in Western Australia where $798 on house buildings insurance and $120 on house contents insurance could be saved by switching between existing very similar policies. As explored earlier, consumers are often not sufficiently equipped to take advantage of such opportunities as they lack the information and expertise to evaluate the relative merits of competing insurance products.

35 See *Choice*, November 1998, p 21.

36 See Section 6.4.2.

37 See Insurance Contracts Regulations (SR 162 of 1985), regs 10, 14.

38 *Choice*, November 1998, p 22.

Table 5: Policy features[39]

Company (in alphabetical order within policy types)	Where they're available	DISCOUNTS			HOUSE POLICY				CONTENTS POLICY			
		Combined*	Older person	No-claim bonus	Other**	Landslip cover***	Earth-quake excess ($)	Additional emergency accomm	Unspecified valuables limit ($)****	Tools of trade limit ($)	Visitors' contents limit ($)	Legal liability limit ($, million)
DEFINED EVENTS POLICIES												
AAMI	ACT, NSW, Qld, SA, Tas, Vic	X	50+	X	Security	X	500	X	1,000	1,000		10
AMP Home Insurance Options	All states	X	50+	X (B)	Security		200	(J)	2,000	750	500	10
ANSVAR Household	All states	X	55+		Security	X	300	X	1,000	500	500	10
AUSTRALIAN PENSIONERS	ACT, NSW, Qld, SA, Tas, Vic, WA		55+				0	X	1,000	500	500	10
AUSTRALIAN UNITY – First Option	ACT, NSW, Qld, SA, Tas, Vic, WA	X	55+	X	Security		200	X	1,000	1,000	500	10
COMMERCIAL UNION – First Choice	All states		Aged pensioners		Security	X	250	X	1,000	500	5,000	20
CUNA Home and Contents	ACT, NSW, Qld, SA, Vic		55+ & retired				300	X	1,000	1,000	500	10
DIRECDIAL Household Policy	ACT, NSW, Qld, SA, Tas, Vic, WA	X			Security		500	X	1,000	1,000	300	10
FAI Classic	All states	X	50+	X	Security, Web buy	X	500	X	1,000	750	500	10
FAI Vital	All states	X	50+	X	Security, Web buy	X	500	X	1,000	750		10

GIO Home and Contents	ACT, NSW	X	55+ (C)				300	X	2,000			10
HBA Cover A	Vic		50+		Security IIBA fund members	X	250 (H)	X	1,000	500		5
HBF Home and Contents	WA	X			Security	X	500	(J)	500			5
IBN Silver Star	All states	X	55+	X	Security	X	200	X	1,000	5,000	5,000	20
MERCANTILE MUTUAL MercPak	All states	X (B)	55+ (D)	X (B)	Security (B)	X	200	X (K)	1,000	1,000 (M)	500 (M)	20
MUTUAL COMMUNITY Cover A	NT, SA		50+		Security	X	250 (H)	X	1,000	500		5
NATIONAL Home and Contents	All states	X					200	X	1,000	5,000	500	10
NRMA Home and Contents	ACT, NSW, Qld, Vic	X	55+	X	Security	X	500	X	1,000	Full		10
RAA-GIO Home and Contents	SA, Broken Hill (NSW)	X	55+	X	Security	X	100	(J)	5%			10
RACQ-GIO Household	Qld	X	55+ (E)	X			300 (H)	X	(L)	1,000		10
RACT Home and Contents	Tas		55+		Security	X	200	X	1,000	Full		10
RAVC Fair Deal	ACT, Southern NSW, Vic			X	Security, other ins	X	0	X	1,000	500		10
REWARD Home and Contents	All states			(G)	Security		50		1,000	1,000		10
SGIC Home and contents	SA, WA (as SGIO)	X (B)	55+ (B)		Security, other ins (B)		1,000	X	1,000	500	500	10

Table 5: Continued

Company (in alphabetical order within policy types)	Where they're available	DISCOUNTS			HOUSE POLICY				CONTENTS POLICY			
		Combined*	Older person	No-claim bonus	Other**	Landslip cover***	Earth-quake excess ($)	Additional emergency accomm	Unspecified valuables limit ($)****	Tools of trade limit ($)	Visitors' contents limit ($)	Legal liability limit ($, million)
DEFINED EVENTS POLICIES												
SUNCORP Essential	ACT, NSW, Qld, SA, Vic	X	55+		Other ins		0	X	1,000	500		5
TIO Home and Contnets	NT, SA		Aged pensioners		Security		200	X	1,000	1,000	1,000	10
TRANSPORT INDUSTRIES – Homeplan	All states	X			Security		200	X	1,000	1,000	500	10
WESTERN QBE Home	ACT, NSW, Qld, SA, Tas, Vic, WA	X	(F)	X	Security		200	X	1,000	500		10
WESTPAC Quality Care	All states	X	55+	X	Security		500	X	1,000	200	2,000	10
ZURICH Personal Assistance	All states	X			Other ins		1,000	X	1,000	5,000	5,000	5
ACCIDENTIAL DAMAGE POLICIES												
AMP Home Insurance Options	All states	X	50+	X (B)	Security		200	(J)	2,000	750	500	10
AUSTRALIAN ALLIANCE – Household Extra	ACT, NSW, Qld, SA, Tas, Vic, WA		55+		Security		0	X	1,000	500	500	10
AUSTRALIAN UNITY Triple A	Vic	X	55+	X	Security, other ins	X	0	X	1,000	1,000	500	20
FAI Progressive	All states	X	50+	X	Security, Web buy	X	500	X	1,500	1,000	750	10

HBA Cover B	Vic		501		Security HBA fund members	X	250 (H)	X	1,000	500	500	5
IBN Gold Star	All states	X	55+	X	Security	X	200	X	1,500	5,000	5,000	20
MERCANTILE MUTUAL MercPak	All states	X (B)	55+ (D)	X (B)	Security (D)	X	200	X (K)	1,000	1,000 (M)	500 (M)	20
MUTUAL COMMUNITY Cover B	NT, SA		50+		Security	X	250 (H)	X	1,000	500	500	5
SGIC Home and Contnets (A)	SA		551		Security, other ins	X	1,000	X	1,000	500	500	10
SUNCORP Maximum	ACT, NSW, Qld, SA, Vic	X	55+		Other ins		0	X	1,000	1,000		10

In relation to the above table, the following key describes elements of that table:

* 'Combined' means a discount is available if you take out both house and contents insurance with this company.

** 'Security' means a discount for having bars, key locks, alarms, etc. Different companies have different requirements.
'Web buy' is a discount for purchasing your insurance via the internet.
'Other insurance' is a discount for buying car, boat or other insurance with the same company.

*** In all cases, landslip cover is only provided if another event, such as an earthquake or storm, has occurred immediately before it.

**** You must specify any individual valuable with a value equal to, or above, this amount. The collective limit for unspecified valuables may be higher.

(A) The building must be insured for more than $100,000, the contents for more than $30,000.
(B) This discount doesn't apply in all states.
(C) NSW/ACT Senior's Card holders also qualify for the discount and there is less depreciation applied.
(D) Higher discounts apply if you're 60+ and not living in Sydney (or NSW), or if you're 55+ and retired.
(E) Higher discounts apply for Queensland Senior's Card holders.
(F) Members of the National Seniors Association.
(G) Reward gives a no-claim bonus after five years; this is not a premium discount, but a form of investment.
(H) This is in addition to the ordinary excess.
(J) Accommodation is only offered as part of the sum insured, not in addition to it.
(K) In Tasmania, accommodation is only offered as part of the sum insured, not in addition to it.
(L) RACQ-GIO has category limits for unspecified valuables of $1,500 – for example, paintings or pictures up to a value of $1,500 in total.
(M) $5,000 in SA and the NT.

6.4 HOME CONTENTS INSURANCE: A CASE STUDY

6.4.1 Introduction

This section examines the home contents insurance cover provided by the six insurers who together have in excess of 75% of the Australian home contents insurance market.[40] The cover provided by these insurers is assessed against the standard home contents insurance cover prescribed in the Insurance Contracts Regulations 1985.[41]

Home contents insurance is defined in reg 13 as:

> ... contracts that provided insurance cover (whether or not the cover is limited or restricted in any way) in respect of loss of or damage to the contents of a residential building where the insured or one of the insureds is a natural person, but does not include a contract that provides insurance cover only or primarily in respect of specified personal effects.

The seven policies discussed below all qualify as home contents insurance policies in terms of this broad definition.

6.4.2 Prescribed events

Regulation 14 states as follows:

> The following, except in so far as they are excluded by reg 15, are declared to be prescribed events in relation to a contract referred to in reg 13:
>
> (a) destruction of, or damage occurring to, the contents of the residential building which is specified in the contract, at a time when they are in the residential building or on the site of the residential building, being destruction or damage that is caused by or results from:
>
> (i) fire or explosion;

39 This table is taken from *Choice*, November 1998, p 23.

40 For statistical data, refer to the KPMG 1999 Insurance Industry Survey, the KPMG 1998 Insurance Industry Survey and the 1997 KPMG Insurance Industry Survey. The policies identified for discussion are:

- CGU Insurance Group: First Choice Home Insurance (06H REV 02 11/98).
- Commercial Union Assurance Company of Australia Ltd: Home Insurance Policy (Item 1966 8/98).
- HIH Insurance Group/CIC Insurance: Home Cover Insurance Policy (3065 3.99 V4.0).
- NRMA Insurance Ltd: Home Contents Insurance Policy (Edition 10 NSW & ACT; Edition 3 Qld P 100707 8/99).
- QBE Insurance Ltd: Home Contents Insurance Policy (WQBE 841 10/99).
- Suncorp General Insurance Ltd: Home Insurance Policy (Per 014 12/96).

41 See Division 3; regs 13–16.

(ii) lightning or thunderbolt;

(iii) earthquake;

(iv) theft, burglary or housebreaking or an attempt to commit theft, burglary or housebreaking;

(v) a deliberate or intentional act;

(vi) bursting, leaking, discharging or overflowing of fixed apparatus, fixed tanks or fixed pipes used to hold or carry liquid of any kind;

(vii) riot or civil commotion;

(viii) an action of a person acting maliciously;

(ix) impact by or arising out of the use of a vehicle (including an aircraft or water-borne craft);

(x) impact by:

(a) space debris or debris from an aircraft, a rocket or a satellite;

(b) an animal (other than an animal kept on the site or a domestic animal);

(c) a falling tree or part of a tree; or

(d) a television or radio aerial that has broken or collapsed; or

(xi) storm, tempest, flood, the action of the sea, high water, tsunami, erosion or land slide or subsidence:

(a) accidental damage that is breakage of glass forming part of an item of furniture (including fixed or unfixed glass table tops), at a time when it is in the residential building or on the site of the residential building;

(b) loss by theft, burglary or housebreaking of contents while in the residential building on the site;

(c) where:

(i) the insured is a tenant or lessee of the residential building; or

(ii) the residential building is a unit (however described) created by the subdivision of strata (however described) in a building and the insured is the owner of the unit;

the insured or a member of the insured's family ordinarily residing with the insured incurring a liability as occupier of the home building to pay compensation or damages to some other person.

In general, the policies identified for consideration cover these prescribed events. More specifically, there are very fundamental derogations from standard cover and some significant qualifications to cover. Of particular importance is the standard cover provision in reg 14(a)(xi) whereby destruction of, or damage occurring to, the contents of a residential building caused by or that results from a storm, tempest, flood, the action of the sea, high water, tsunami, erosion or landslide or subsidence is declared to be a defined event. None of the policies provide *flood* cover. The Suncorp Home Insurance Policy provides that flood cover may be added as an optional extra, subject to the insurer inspecting the insured address.

The absence of flood cover was brought home to Australian insureds in the aftermath of the Coffs Harbour flood, and the major floods in the Townsville (Qld), Katherine (NT) and Wollongong (NSW) regions. A very careful reading of the policy conditions and exclusions is required to discern what events, if any, are covered under the umbrella of reg 14(a)(xi) prescribed events. Consider, for example, the clause in the HIH/CIC Home Cover insurance policy:

28 Storm, rainwater or run-off

We will pay for loss or damage caused by storm, rainwater or run-off:

'**storm**' means violent wind (including cyclones and tornadoes), thunderstorms and hail that may be accompanied by snow;

'**rainwater**' means rain falling naturally from the sky onto the building(s) and/or ground;

'**run-off**' means rainwater that has collected on or has flowed across normally dry ground or has overflowed from:

- swimming pools, saunas or spas, or
- normally dry stormwater gutters and/or normally dry drains, which have been built or approved by a government or public authority;

'**flood**' means the inundation of normally dry land by water that has escaped or been released from the normal confines of any natural watercourse, lake or lagoon whether or not altered or modified, or of any resevoir [sic], canal or dam.

We will not pay for loss or damage:

(a) caused by:
  - flood, or
  - flood water combined with run-off and/or rainwater;

(b) caused by action of the sea, high water, tidal wave or tsunami;

(c) caused by:
  - soil movement including erosion, landslide, mudslide or subsidence, or
  - shrinkage or expansion of earth or land;

(d) to gates, fences and retaining walls;

(e) to swimming pool covers, their liners or their solar domes;

(f) to the external paintwork or other exterior coatings of the building(s) caused by rainwater;

> (g) caused by water seeping, percolating or otherwise penetrating into the building(s) as a result of:
>
> - structural defects,
> - faulty design of the buildings, or
> - your failure to adequately maintain the buildings;
>
> (h) caused by wind, rainwater, hail or snow entering the building(s) through an open window or door or any opening not made by the storm;
>
> (i) caused by water entering your building(s) through an opening made for the purpose of alterations, extensions, renovations or repairs.
>
> We will also pay up to a maximum amount of $500, for any one incident, for the removal of trees (or portion of a tree) damaged by storm, rainwater or run-off which caused loss or damage covered under this policy.
>
> If the tree causing the loss or damage to your property is not located at your address, we will only pay for the cost of removal of that portion of the tree which remains on your property after the incident.
>
> We will not pay for the removal of a tree stump from the ground or any part of a tree that has not fallen.
>
> An excess will apply to this insured event.

Although this is one of the clearer statements of what is covered in the policies under consideration, it is readily apparent that far less than the cover that is contemplated in reg 14(a)(xi) is provided, and it is necessary to turn to pp 30–32 of the policy to acquire this important information.

Another example of an important departure from the standard cover prescribed events of reg 14 occurs in relation to damage or destruction to contents of a residential building caused by, or resulting from, a person acting maliciously. The Suncorp Home Insurance Policy provides in cl 8 that:

> You are covered for any action of a person acting maliciously, as long as you report it to the police as soon as possible.
>
> You are not covered for any action of any person who lives in the insured building or home, or who has entered the insured address with the consent of any person who lives in the insured building or home.

The QBE policy condition in this regard, cl 1.6, refers to vandalism and similarly excludes liability for vandalism by the insured, the insured's family or tenants – as well as persons visiting with permission. The exclusion of liability for malicious acts, including vandalism, by tenants or boarders is not necessarily in the contemplation of insureds and again it is only on a careful reading of policy documents that one discerns the insurer's intent. As to the obligation imposed by the Suncorp policy that the insured report promptly the 'actions of person acting maliciously' as a condition for cover, the circumstances in which compliance may be required gives rise to humorous mental imagery.

Numerous other minor variations and qualifications occur. All policies provide cover for earthquakes but the excess applicable varies from zero to $500. All policies provide for loss or damage caused by fire but a variety of qualifications to this cover exist. One policy excludes damage 'which arises gradually out of repeated exposure to fire or smoke' while another policy states that 'scorching is not covered, unless caused by an accidental fire to other property'.

While not of great practical significance in the Australian context, all policies exclude cover for loss or damage caused by tidal wave or tsunami. Of more significance, five of the policies exclude liability for loss or damage caused by or arising from the action of the sea or high water and one policy remains totally silent as to whether this is covered or not. Finally, there is a widely divergent approach as to how erosion, landslide and subsidence are treated across the six major home contents covers – ranging from outright exclusion of liability for such prescribed events through to qualified or partial cover being extended in certain circumstances.

6.4.3 Exclusions

Regulation 15 states as follows:

The following are excluded:

(a) depreciation;

(b) wear and tear, rust or corrosion;

(c) the action of insects of vermin;

(d) destruction or damage, or the incurring of a liability as mentioned in para 14(d), as a result of:

(i) the expropriation of the contents;

(ii) war or warlike activities;

(iii) the use, existence or escape of nuclear weapons material, or ionizing radiation from, or contamination by radioactivity from, any nuclear fuel or nuclear waste from the combustion of nuclear fuel;

(iv) the use of the residential building for the purposes of a business, trade or profession; or

(v) tree lopping or felling by the insured or a person acting with the express or implied consent of the insured;

(e) destruction or damage intentionally caused, or a liability as mentioned in para 14(d) intentionally incurred, by:

(i) the insured; or

(ii) a member of the insured's family ordinarily residing with the insured, or a person acting with the express or implied consent of any of them;

(f) where the residential building is unoccupied and has been unoccupied for a continuous period of more than 60 days – destruction or damage occurring otherwise than as mentioned in sub-para 14(a)(ii) or (iii) or (vii) to (ix) (inclusive), or the incurring of liability as mentioned in para 14(d);

(g) destruction of, or damage occurring to:

  (i) an electrical machine or apparatus as a result of the electric current in it; or

  (ii) any property as a result of it undergoing a process necessarily involving the application of heat;

(h) accidental breakage of:

  (i) a television picture tube or screen;

  (ii) the picture tube or screen of an electronic visual display unit;

  (iii) a ceramic or glass cooking top of a stove;

  (iv) glass in a picture frame, a radio set or a clock;

(i) (no entry)

(j) theft by a person ordinarily residing with the insured at the time of the theft;

(k) in the case of destruction or damage that is caused by or results from bursting, leaking, discharging or overflowing of fixed apparatus, fixed tanks or fixed pipes used to hold or carry liquid of any kind or impact by a television or radio aerial that has broken or collapsed – damage to the apparatus, tanks or pipes or the television or radio aerial, respectively;

(l) (no entry)

(m) the incurring of a liability as mentioned in para 14(d):

  (i) to the insured or a member of the insured's family ordinarily residing with the insured; or

  (ii) as a result of –

    (a) the insured; or

    (b) a member of the insured's family ordinarily residing with the insured,

  or a person acting with the express or implied consent of any of them, using a vehicle (including an aircraft or water-borne craft) on the site.

What is particularly noticeable in all the policies under consideration is that the exclusions are more comprehensive and extensive than those contained in the standard cover provisions. Reference has already been made to the fundamental exclusion of flood cover. Another very important area where exclusions have been included relates to burglary, housebreaking and theft. The exclusion in reg 15(j) excludes the insurer's liability where a theft is by a person ordinarily residing with the insured at the time of the theft.

Consider the exclusion contained in the HID/CIC Home Cover Insurance Policy:

> We will pay for loss or damage caused by theft, burglary or housebreaking.
> We will not pay:
>
> (a) if the actual or attempted theft, burglary or housebreaking:
> - is committed by:
>   - you, your domestic servants, or your tenants;
>   - the invitees of you, your domestic servants, or your tenants; or
>   - any person who is acting with your express or implied consent;
> - takes place in the internal or external common areas of residential flats, home units, town houses or any other type of multiple occupancy residences; or
> - relates to contents in the open air;
>
> (b) for the theft of money or other negotiable instruments unless there is visible evidence of forcible entry to the buildings.
>
> An excess will apply to this insured event.

These more extensive exclusions pose particular problems for landlords, tenants and persons sharing houses or other accommodation. In addition, the common exclusion of cover for cash, tools of trade or negotiable instruments is not well known to the insureds.

Other exclusions common to several of the policies under consideration are exclusion of cover for loss or damage as a result of non-compliance with year 2000 computer and software requirements and the cost of reinstalling or replacing electronically stored files. Moreover, all policies exclude cover for the fusion of electric motors (including refrigeration units, electronic components, printed circuit boards) unless specifically arranged for the payment of an additional premium.

6.4.4 Minimum amounts

Regulation 16 states as follows:

(1) Subject to these Regulations, for the purposes of s 34 of the Act, the minimum amount in respect of a claim made under a contract referred to in reg 13, being a claim arising out of an event referred to in para 14(a), (b) or (c), is declared to be the amount sufficient to indemnify the person who made the claim, reduced, in the case of destruction or damage occurring as a result of an earthquake, by $200.

(2) For the purpose of s 34 of the Act, the minimum amount in respect of a claim made under a contract referred to in reg 13, being a claim that arises out of an event referred to in para 14(d), is declared to be the amount, not exceeding $2,000,000, sufficient to indemnify the person who made the claim in respect of his or her liability.

(3) Where there is more than one such claim arising out of the same event, being an event referred to in para 14(d), then, for the purposes of s 34 of the Act, the minimum amount in respect of a claim made after the first to those claims has been made is declared to be the amount sufficient to indemnify the person who made the claim or the amount ascertained by subtracting from $2,000,000 the amount or the sum of the amounts, as the case may be, that the insurer has paid, or is liable to pay, in respect of the claim or claims arising out of that event that have already been made, whichever is the lesser.

In accordance with this Regulation, the minimum amount payable by an insurer in respect of a claim arising out of an event like a fire is the amount required to indemnify the insured for the loss of his or her contents. A particular limit of $2 million is specified. The general scheme, therefore, is that the insurer must provide a minimum cover in respect of any loss or damage arising out of a 'prescribed event'. The only deductible recognised in the Regulations is that of $200 in the case of destruction or damage occurring as a result of an earthquake.

The policies under consideration depart significantly from the standard established under the Regulations. Particularly dramatic is the inclusion in the NRMA Home Contents Insurance Policy (at pp 34–35) of the following average clause:

> Underinsuring your general contents
>
> You should take care to insure your general contents for their full replacement value because it may affect how much we pay you if you make a claim.
>
> Your general contents are underinsured if their sum insured is below 80% of their full replacement value. It means that you must bear the loss for the portion you did not insure.
>
> We use this formula only when the amount of your claim is more than 5% of your general contents sum insured.
>
> $$\frac{\text{Sum insured of your general contents}}{\text{80\% of full replacement value of your contents}} \times \text{the cost of replacing your general contents} = \text{the amount we pay}$$
>
> **For example:**
>
> | | |
> |---|---|
> | If you have insured your general contents for: | $50,000 |
> | **But** their full replacement value is: | $90,000 |
> | *then* | |
> | 80% of the full replacement value is | $72,000 |
> | **and some of your contents are stolen,** | |
> | and the cost of replacing them is | $27,000 |
> | *then we use the formula* | |
>
> $$\frac{\$50,000}{\$72,000} \times \$27,000 = \$18,750$$
>
> | | |
> |---|---|
> | Then the most we would pay is | $18,750 |
> | and you bear the loss for the portion you did not insure | $18,750 |

or

Your contents are totally destroyed by a fire, and the cost of replacing them is $90,000

then we use the formula

$$\frac{\$50{,}000}{\$72{,}000} \times \$90{,}000 = \$62{,}500$$

Then the most we would pay is the general contents sum insured $50,000

and you bear the loss for the portion you did not insure $40,000

Average clauses serve valuable incentive and actuarial functions for insurers. Their inclusion arguably benefits individual policy holders by providing significant incentive towards full insurance. Such clauses are also identified as being of assistance in achieving rating stability and a measure of equity between different insureds; that is, full insurance spreads claims more equally over the whole body of policy holders.

Against this, however, are several potentially serious disadvantages for insureds. First, for many insureds, its operating principle combined with complexities inherent in calculating its effect render it effectively incomprehensible. Secondly, inflation and rapidly escalating property values and building costs may result in a significant divergence between the amount of cover initially sought – and generally rolled over with annual renewals – and the property value reflected at the time of the loss. Finally, the assumption that insureds are indeed dissuaded from underinsuring by the inclusion of average clauses presupposes not only that insureds understand their effect but also that insureds are in a financial position to increase their cover. As one commentator notes: 'both these assumptions may be flawed and yet they are the cornerstones of the pro-average advocacy.'[42]

Such a clause has a drastic effect upon the cover extended to the insured. The New Zealand legislature has prohibited the inclusion of average clauses in contents policies,[43] and their operation in Australia has been qualified.[44] It is most unfortunate that such a clause should appear without careful attention being drawn to its existence and the consequences of its operation.

42 Tarr (1985) 11 New Zealand Universities Law Review 362, at 370. See also Contracts and Commercial Law Reform Committee, *Aspects of Insurance Law* (2) (1983), para 8; Australian Law Reform Commission, *Report on Insurance Contracts* (No 20, 1982), at para 268.

43 Insurance Law Reform Act 1985 (NZ), s 15(1).

44 Section 44(1) of the Insurance Contracts Act 1984 (Australia) provides that an insurer may not rely upon an average clause unless, before the contract was entered into, the insurer clearly informed the insured in writing of the nature and effect of the provision. This enables the insurer to insert an average clause in houseowners'/householders insurance, subject to prior notification, and subject to the additional limitation in s 44(2) that an average clause should only apply where, and to the extent that, the sum insured is less than 80% of the true value at the time when the contract was entered into. Moreover, pursuant to s 44(3), the amount of any reduction under an average clause is to be calculated by reference to a formula based on the difference between *80% of the value of the property* at the time the contract was entered into and the sum insured and *not* between the *full amount of the value* and the sum insured. Which approach – [contd]

Another common and notable departure from the 'minimum amount' rules established in reg 16 is the limitation as to the value of contents contained in the policies under consideration. For example, special items such as jewellery, antiques, paintings, oriental rugs and collections are subject to specified limits of cover. Cover in excess of these specified limits is only available where the insured has had the items individually listed due to them being of an unusual nature or a higher value than would normally be covered. In the event of a claim the insured must be able to provide evidence of value and ownership of such specified contents items. There is nothing unreasonable about the inclusion of these specified contents clauses – the intent is to protect the insurer against inflated and fraudulent claims. However, there is an issue about the notice given to insureds as to the existence of such limitations upon cover and this problem surfaces on a regular basis.[45]

Finally, in relation to 'minimum amount' rules in reg 16, the regulation only contemplates an excess or deductible of $200 in respect of destruction or damage occurring as a result of an earthquake. The policies under consideration contain numerous additional excess provisions.

In conclusion to this chapter, therefore, experience at the 'coal face', as it were, seems to indicate that despite statutory intervention on behalf of consumers considerable scope remains for confusion over policy contents. In part this is attributable to some consumers' failure to spend adequate time carefully considering their policies and the supplemental information insurers may distribute in this respect. As the study above shows, however, even the more intrepid policy holders might be forgiven in certain respects for being less than informed in relation to the actual contents of their contracts. The cumulative effects of multi-paged documents laced with legal and technical terminology is likely, for reasons discussed in Chapter 2, to prove an understandable stumbling block for the average consumer and is borne out by contemporary experience in the Australian market.

Against this, the standard cover regime appears to have had one positive effect; namely, that there is some uniformity between the policies under consideration as to coverage. However, the exceptions and variations (in some cases very significant) without adequate foreshadowing of these departures from the standard derogate from the benefits said to underpin standard cover.

---

44 [contd] the Australian or the New Zealand – is preferable is debatable. Given that an underlying major dissatisfaction with average clauses is that many, if not the overwhelming majority, of the public do not appreciate or understand the significance of such provisions, mandatory disclosure of the existence and attributes of these clauses does defuse the basis of complaint – but only if disclosure is effected in a meaningful way. On the other hand, the straightforward statutory prohibition against the use of average clauses in policies affecting dwelling houses and contents does have the merit of simplicity and puts the matter beyond doubt.

45 See, for example, *Legal & General Insurance (Aust) Ltd v Eather* (1986) 4 ANZ Insurance Cases 60-749; *Young v Commercial Union General Insurance Co Ltd* (1988) 5 ANZ Insurance Cases 60-875.

CONCLUSIONS

7.1 DISCLOSURE OF INFORMATION

Discussion in Chapters 2, 3, 4 and 5 highlights the significant asymmetry of information and knowledge between insurers and insureds in relation to consumer insurance contracts. In some respects the insured is in a superior position in that he or she is aware of the particular circumstances encompassing the subject matter of the insurance contract and any specific risks to which it is exposed or where particular liability may be incurred. Conversely, the insurer is in an advantageous position as regards the scope and content of the insurance cover being sought. The insured is aware of the primary features of the transaction (such as the type of cover, the quantum of the cover and the premium payable) but is unlikely to have a clear (or any) understanding of subordinate terms such as average clauses, subrogation provisions and the myriad of exclusions, excesses and limitations upon liability potentially contained in the associated multi-paged document(s).

Against this background legislative intervention must be assessed. The common law duty of disclosure and its evolution, as analysed in Chapters 3 and 4, is closely tied to the emergence of the modern contract of insurance. In this respect, the role Lloyd's and its subsequent marine insurance competitors played cannot be underestimated. The merchants' practices used at Lloyd's in the 18th century and adopted by the common law had a profound impact upon insurance law. Its printed marine policy of 1779, which differed in only a few particulars from that adopted as the statutory form in various Marine Insurance Acts,[1] effectively set the benchmark for information disclosure requirements between insured and insurer for the ensuing development of the entire insurance industry. Lloyd's and the courts at the time[2] emphasised the dependency of insurers upon the full and accurate disclosure by insureds of information relative to the risk. The common law duty of disclosure that was enshrined in the Marine Insurance Act 1906 (UK) and faithfully adopted in the Marine Insurance Acts of Australia, Singapore, Malaysia, Thailand, New Zealand and elsewhere reflected this emphasis by measuring materiality by reference to circumstances which would influence the judgment of a prudent insurer in fixing the premium or determining whether it will take the risk.[3]

1 See, for example, the Marine Insurance Act 1906 (UK); Marine Insurance Act 1908 (NZ); Marine Insurance Act 1909 (Australia).

2 See, for example, *Carter v Boehm* (1766) 3 Burr 1905 at 1909; 97 ER 1162.

3 Marine Insurance Act 1909 (Australia), s 24(2).

Two centuries later, the Insurance Contracts Act 1984 (Australia) wrought significant change to this approach by focusing instead upon what the insured knew to be material to the decision of the insurer as to whether to accept the risk, or what a reasonable person in the circumstances could be expected to know to be a matter so relevant.[4] Effectively, therefore, a reasonable insured test of materiality replaced the common law prudent or reasonable insurer test. This shift has been further bolstered by the recent enactment of s 21A of the Insurance Contracts Act 1984 (Australia).[5] In essence, as discussed in Chapters 3 and 4, the insured's obligation to disclose information in relation to prescribed or consumer contracts of insurance is restricted to answering specific questions that are relevant to the decision of the insurer whether to accept the risk and, if so, on what terms.[6]

The pendulum in Australia has therefore swung a long way in relation to prescribed contracts of insurance; that is, in relation to these six classes of consumer insurance contracts. Similarly, this shift is evident in the United States, where in the preponderance of cases, fraud must be demonstrated before an insurer can rescind a consumer insurance contact on the ground of concealment. As a general rule if the insurer makes no inquiry and the insured makes no misrepresentations as to the facts in question, concealment not amounting to actual fraud in relation to those facts is not a ground for rescission of the insurance contract, as the insured may assume that the insurer has satisfied itself as to the risk. The shift in Australia and the approach taken by the courts in the United States reflects the reality that contemporary insurers, unlike those of the 1700s and 1800s, have recourse to information disclosure mechanisms discreet from the insured him or herself. There is no doubt that insurers have access to detailed statistical data relevant to contracts of home buildings insurance, home contents insurance, motor vehicle insurance, sickness and accident insurance, travel insurance and consumer credit insurance. Moreover, sophisticated investigative facilities and personnel are available to examine claims and to detect fraud. Actuarial analysis has refined the process of estimating risk/loss and setting premiums with appropriate regard to a range of variables. Prudential margins are incorporated into loss forecasts to cater for unforeseen contingencies. Having regard to these factors, asymmetry of knowledge relative to the particular transaction being negotiated is less significant. The only knowledge that the insurer does not have is particular knowledge that the insured may have or be aware of in relation to the particular property or potential liability that he or she wishes to insure. This deficiency can be cured by the insurer asking particular questions.

---

4 Insurance Contracts Act 1984 (Australia), s 21(1).

5 Inserted by the Insurance Laws Amendment Act 1998 (Australia), s 3.

6 Insurance Contracts Act 1984 (Australia), s 21A(2), (3), (4).

In this context, there is, in my opinion, no necessity for a legislative framework to continue to support a general duty of disclosure. The provisions of the Insurance Contracts Act 1984 (Australia) provide remedies to regulate the parties' rights in the event that a non-disclosure or misrepresentation of a material matter has a causative effect on the transaction. General insurers offering prescribed insurance covers are by virtue of their size and market position more than capable of procuring information through proposals and other sources to protect their legitimate interests and to calculate the risk accurately. The conjoint approach adopted by ss 21 and 21A of the Insurance Contracts Act 1984 (Australia) does not achieve anything more than this; but these provisions are unduly complex and they do impose a cost upon insurers and, ultimately, their insureds. This is discussed below in 'Notice of the duty of disclosure'. Moreover, there are sound pragmatic reasons to extinguish general disclosure responsibilities in relation to prescribed insurance contracts. As discussed in Chapter 6, these contracts are increasingly effected or renewed through telemarketing and canvassing.[7] The General Insurance Enquiries and Complaints Scheme has registered a growing number of complaints and disputes as to the nature and extent of oral disclosures in this context.[8] This, it is suggested, supports a narrower approach as to what information should be provided; namely, only that which is specifically solicited by direct questioning. Even within these narrower confines, there are going to be disputes as to what was or what was not said and disclosed.

Accordingly, it is recommended that in relation to consumer contracts of insurance the insured's obligation to provide information is restricted to answering specific questions from the insurer relevant to the decision of the insurer as to whether to accept the risk, and if so, on what terms. The consequences of a failure to respond accurately and/or completely would be determined by reference to remedies in Division 3 of the Insurance Contracts Act 1984 (Australia).[9] No general duty of disclosure nor necessity to provide notice of such duty would be required in relation to consumer contracts of insurance. In addition to cost savings generated through this approach, certainty would be delivered to insureds and insurers as to what information should be provided.

In light of these observations perhaps the National Consumer Council in the United Kingdom, in advocating reforms that correspond with those contained in the Insurance Contracts Act 1984 (Australia), might better serve the interests of consumers by instead recommending the abolition of a general duty of disclosure in consumer insurance contracts.

---

7 For example, Mr P Hardman, Chairman of the General Insurance Claims Review Panel reports that 90% of new motor, home and contents policies are being made over the telephone. See 1999 AILA News, Conference Edition, p 6.

8 See, for example, The General Insurance Enquiries and Complaints Scheme Annual Report 1996, p 11.

9 Sections 28–33.

7.2 NOTICE OF THE DUTY OF DISCLOSURE

It follows from the recommendation in para 7.1, that no notice of the duty of disclosure should be required in relation to prescribed or consumer insurance contracts.

This will alleviate a significant burden upon insurers, especially in light of the recent decision in *Suncorp General Insurance Ltd v Cheihk*,[10] where it was emphasised that the duty of disclosure must be 'clearly' made known to the insured in writing. This requirement of clarity and the compliance costs associated with the obligation generally are not inconsiderable. This cost is further increased by the additional requirement imposed by s 22(1) of the Insurance Contracts Act 1984 (Australia), as amended,[11] to clearly inform the insured in writing of the general nature and effect of s 21A. This is no easy task as this section can only be described as one of the more convoluted drafting results in recent years.

7.3 STANDARD COVER

The principal rationale behind the Australian Law Reform Commission's recommendations and the legislature's decision to establish standard cover in six prescribed areas was to alleviate misunderstandings over the terms and conditions of individual policies.[12] The Commission notes:

> The argument for the introduction of standard policies or terms is strongest in areas of domestic insurance where expert advice is not usually available and where the insured himself is unlikely to be able to understand individual terms, let alone appreciate the significance of the contract as a whole. The imposition of standard contracts would simplify insurance for insureds and would protect them against unusual and unexpected exclusions and obligations.[13]

The prescription of standard policies also created a benchmark as to what constituted a fair, basic policy in these six areas of insurance.

Under the standard cover regime recommended by the Commission that was adopted in the legislation an insurer, although able to derogate from the standard prescribed, can only do so if it specifically draws to the insured's attention the relevant limit on, or exclusion from, the standard cover.[14] As

10 (1999) 10 ANZ Insurance Cases 61-442 (NSW CA).

11 By the Insurance Laws Amendment Act 1998 (Australia), Sched 1, item 84.

12 *Report on Insurance Contracts* (No 20, 1982), para 48.

13 *Ibid*, at para 55.

14 *Ibid*, at para 57.

discussed in Chapter 5, the insurer can provide the requisite notice of derogation pursuant to s 35(2) of the Insurance Contracts Act 1984 (Australia) by providing the insured with a copy of the proposed contract. Given that even the preponderance of agents are unaware of the standard cover provisions, it is little wonder that this 'disclosure mechanism' is hardly an efficient means to alert the average insured as to departures from the relevant prescribed standard.

There is little doubt, though, that standard cover in these key areas possesses the potential to benefit both insurer and insured. As discussed in Chapter 2, although standard contracts *per se* can be both fair and efficient to both parties, in situations where asymmetry of information is pervasive, such as happens in the case of consumer insurance contracts, market failure can produce inefficiencies on both sides.

From the perspective of insureds, prescribed contracts can help remedy the comparative advantage that accrues to insurers through their relative size and resource base relative to individual consumers. In specific terms, such provisions can assist consumers:

(1) who are likely otherwise to be uninformed about the risks allocated by terms set out in insurer drafted standard form contracts, to choose terms that correctly reflect their preferences;

(2) who are likely otherwise to be unaware of the array of prices and terms that the firms in the market can offer to achieve more easily the objectives sought. Consumers who lack this information may accept poor bargains because they do not know that better ones exist, and insurers consequently will have little incentive to offer better deals because these will not increase sales;

(3) to better understand the legal relationship they have established between themselves and their insurer. As many (if not most) consumers are to varying extents unlikely to read and comprehend the language of the multi-page policy documents, insurers have an incentive to exploit this ignorance by using hidden terms that will disadvantage consumers if circumstances permit these terms to be invoked. Standard cover provides a solution to this latter problem while simultaneously helping to provide a document that potentially represents a more balanced representation of terms or agreement between parties – *if* consumers had had the ability to negotiate such at the outset.

The use of prescribed terms therefore provides a beneficial reform to the problem that the consumer, as the significantly weaker party, is not in a position to negotiate all the contract provisions supplied in any given standard form contract. In effect, the prescribed terms take up the role described in Chapter 2; the standard provisions become the informed marginal consumer that acts as a watchdog for the overall benefit of all consumers.

From the perspective of insurers, the use of standard terms are similarly beneficial in that:

(1) such provisions help cure the market failure that arises out of consumers' inability to distinguish between good and bad products. Accordingly, 'good' insurers will receive the benefits of consumers' more accurate understanding of the product market and, in specific, of the actual benefits being bestowed by their products. Such awareness further enhances the incentive to create new and improved products thereby creating more effective competition.

(2) consumers will have a better understanding of their legal obligations and the corresponding duties therein attached. For example, increased understanding of the role of disclosure and its inherent responsibilities allows insurers to tailor their inquiries more accurately and curtail ambiguities that might otherwise arise. Moreover, use of standard provisions can help improve the 'goodwill' between insurer/insured that can be undermined by the use of individual insurer produced lengthy and complicated contracts. This, in turn, enables the insurer to concentrate more on genuine market differentiation such as better service provision or creation of positive consumer brand name recognition.

The crucial issue, therefore, is how to make these standard cover provisions work. One option would be to follow the approach adopted in respect of compulsory insurance such as workers compensation insurance and motor vehicle third party insurance; that is, on the basis of public interest no derogation from prescribed standard cover would be permitted and the minimum terms and conditions specified in the Act and Regulations would have to be provided by all insurers. Competition between insurers in this scenario could proceed on the basis of price, reputation, service and benefits provided over and above the standard. Alternatively, if an approach preserving greater flexibility is preferred and insurers are to be allowed to offer less than standard cover, then disclosure of such derogation must be made more meaningful. 'Clearly informed' must mean more than simply providing a policy document that reflects less than the standard cover.

On balance, it is recommended that the latter approach be adopted. The anti-competitive effect of insisting upon the standard terms and conditions in every case would not satisfy the public benefit test, as argued by the then Trade Practices Commission,[15] and insistence upon such uniformity may have a negative impact upon certain categories of insureds. For example, if flood cover must be included in all home buildings and home contents insurance polices, inevitably premiums would rise and there would be a cross-subsidy of insureds living in flood prone areas by those whose properties are not so affected. The option to purchase flood cover in the

15 Australian Law Reform Commission, *Report on Insurance Contracts* (No 20, 1982), para 56.

knowledge, because of clear information to this effect by the insurer, that the house and contents cover does not include such cover, would put the onus and cost upon those insureds who live in flood prone areas and not upon all insureds.

It is therefore recommended that the insurer be obliged to inform the insured clearly in writing of any derogation from standard cover. Such derogation should be contained in a separate notice drawn to the insured's attention and acknowledged by the insured. Otherwise the scheme adopted in the Act is satisfactory and represents a fair balance of the competing interests of the parties.

7.4 CONSTRUCTION AND THE INSURED'S EXPECTATIONS

It remains to be seen whether the Australian courts will use the opportunity afforded by the utmost good faith provisions in ss 13 and 14 of the Insurance Contracts Act 1984 (Australia) to take a more interventionist and reconstructive role in relation to insurance contracts and their terms and conditions. The requirements that obligations be performed according to standards of utmost good faith and that parties act towards one another in respect of all contractual matters in good faith does enable the court to use these provisions to modify the enforcement of obligations where it regards such enforcement as betraying the requisite standard of conduct under the Act.

The evidence in Australia thus far is sparse. In *Moss v Sun Alliance Australia Ltd*[16] the court, relying upon the implied term to act in good faith, allowed damages in addition to interest to compensate an insured for late payment of an indemnity in relation to business premises destroyed by fire. In *Australian Associated Motor Insurers Ltd v Ellis*[17] the court found that an insurer was in breach of the implied duty found in s 13 because it had failed to notify an insured of the consequences of breaching a provision in a motor vehicle policy relating to modification of the vehicle without the insurer's consent. In *Beverley v Tyndall Life Insurance Co Ltd*[18] the court decided that the insurer's duty of utmost good faith obliged it to follow rules of procedural fairness in determining the issue of an insured's disability. Conversely, in *Re Zurich Australian Insurance Ltd*,[19] Chesterman J declined an invitation to find, at common law, a separately existing, independent general duty to act in good faith broad enough to circumscribe payment of the monetary limit of

16 (1990) 6 ANZ Insurance Cases 60-967.

17 *Ibid*.

18 (1999) 10 ANZ Insurance Cases 61-453.

19 (1999) 10 ANZ Insurance Cases 61-429. The policy considered in this case was effected in 1972 so that ss 13 and 14 of the Insurance Contracts Act 1984 (Australia) had no application.

indemnity under the policy and thereby extinguishing liability for any other costs, charges and expenses after such payment. In reviewing American authorities, he stated:

> In short, the American doctrine of good faith and fair dealing is so exotic a growth that if it is to be transplanted into the common law it should be done by a more accomplished gardener than I.[20]

In the United Kingdom, decisions such as *Manifest Shipping Co Ltd v Uni-Polaris Shipping Co Ltd (The Star Sea)*[21] and *HIH Casualty and General Insurance Ltd v Chase Manhattan Bank*[22] do not evince any enthusiasm by the courts to embrace a more extensive continuing duty of utmost good faith. A similar reluctance is evident from the jurisprudential struggle in various jurisdictions in the United States with the doctrine of reasonable expectations. At one extreme the doctrine provides protection of reasonable expectations even in instances where express language to the contrary exists in the policy – at the other extreme it is simply used as a rule of construction to resolve ambiguities.

The major problem with the development in Australia of a more interventionist approach to the reconstruction of contractual obligations based upon utmost good faith provisions is uncertainty. It was this factor of uncertainty that led the Australian Law Reform Commission[23] to reject a general power of review of contractual terms. General insurers were concerned that a general power of review would lead to great uncertainty and would further complicate the process of setting appropriate rates.[24] A broadly based application of the good faith provisions in the construction and modification of contractual provisions would engender as much certainty as a general power of review.

Moreover, the major limitation upon such an approach and with constructional devices such as the *contra proferentem* rule is that they can only be deployed in the context of litigation. The insured has to take the initiative and incur the expense and risk in an endeavour to cure what he or she perceives to be ambiguities or obligations not in accord with information provided or understandings reached in the pre-contract setting. Against this it may be said that a willingness by courts to modify contractual obligations on the basis of the statutory good faith provisions could encourage more careful drafting of policies and a greater level of caution when seeking to invoke their strict terms.[25]

20 At 74-838.

21 [2001] Lloyd's Rep 389 (HL).

22 [2001] Lloyd's Rep IR 702 (CA).

23 *Report on Insurance Contracts* (No 20, 1982), at para 51.

24 *Ibid*.

25 See, for example, Kimball and Pfenningsdorf (1964) 39 Indiana Law Journal 675, Chapter 5.

The disadvantages attendant upon a broadly based application of the good faith provisions to reconstruct contractual obligations outweigh any advantages. Such a process is too productive of uncertainty and is not, therefore, recommended.

7.5 EDUCATION AND COMPARISONS

The provision of information in the formation of consumer insurance contracts is vital to inform the decision making of the insured and the insurer. The greater the extent to which the contracting parties are knowledgeable as to the terms and conditions of the proposed contract, the more effectively the market can operate in fulfilling consumer demand. As discussed in reference to the general theory of contract, it is assumed that as individuals are best placed to judge their own interests society's common interest will automatically be enhanced through the amalgamation of individual benefits. It follows, therefore, that the better placed an individual is in terms of his or her own understanding of the transaction at hand, the better the resulting deal will be and the better off overall society is.

A corollary to this would also be that the closer 'the meeting of the minds' is at the outset as to what an individual insurance policy provides and prohibits, the less likely both parties are to have to bear extensive transaction costs associated with subsequent disputes over interpretation and enforcement. In times when cost efficient 'access to justice' is rapidly reaching the point of critical concern, such approaches that are designed to minimise possible 'fall out' problems are to be encouraged.

The position of the insured may be enhanced in a variety of ways. First, access to expert professional advice should facilitate an informed choice. Practically speaking, though, the services of brokers are not common in the consumer insurance contract area – the preponderance of these transactions are negotiated by telephone directly with the insured, with the insured not having the benefit of such independent, expert advice. Agents of the insurer in an endeavour to sell their principal's product cannot be relied upon to proffer any, let alone objective, advice about competing products in the marketplace.

Secondly, comparisons between competing products undertaken by third parties may inform an insured in choice or policy and insurer. The extensive survey published in *Choice*[26] canvassing home buildings and home contents insurance is an example. Similarly, reference to the Annual Report of organisations like the National Consumer Council in the United Kingdom and the General Insurance Enquiries and Complaints Scheme serves to inform and

26 November 1998, pp 18–35.

educate the insured about competing alternatives and problematic issues. It is common, also, in numerous overseas jurisdictions for comparative information to be published about competing insurers and their products.[27] This information is available electronically and accordingly is more easily accessible by prospective insureds.

Thirdly, the Insurance Council of Australia attempts to educate consumers on particular matters relating to insurance law and practice. Brochures dealing with home buildings and home contents insurance, for example, explain the types of cover available and the difference between replacement and indemnity cover. In addition, the Insurance Council issues fact sheets for distribution to educational and consumer groups. These materials do not resort to cost comparisons between competing insurers.

Fourthly, the position of insurers can be greatly enhanced through better trained and educated agents. Insurers receive information and evaluate the risk through their agents. The quality of information provided and, in consequence, the accuracy of the risk assessment reached is contingent upon the skill of the agent. For example, the dual pressures of a very competitive insurance market and the responsibilities cast upon insurers by the Insurance (Agents and Brokers) Act 1984 (Australia), have caused Australian insurers to devote considerable resources to the training of their agents.[28]

Finally, and with particular reference to consumer insurance contracts, the federal/national and state governments have an important educative role to play. For example, the significance of these standard covers in Australia to the majority of the population merits the dissemination of informative brochures through post offices and libraries emphasising the need for standard cover and awareness that certain covers may not meet the standard – flood cover being a particularly cogent example.

7.6 CONCLUSION

In conclusion, although it is recognised that misunderstanding and unrealised expectations between insured and insurers represents at one level a normal reflection of the human psyche – an individual's view of any given facts inherently being one of subjectivity – it is hoped that the asymmetry of information that currently exists in the insurance market can be better

27 See, for example, the California Department of Insurance at http://www.insure.com/complaints/cahome98.html.

28 The General Insurance Code of Practice 'by requiring the agency force in the insurance industry to be better trained, has improved the level of competency in the market place'. See Gill, M, Code Compliance Committee, Insurance Enquiries and Complaints Ltd 1997 Annual Review, p 3.

addressed by the above recommendations. The last two decades have brought a much more consumer oriented approach to the statutory governance of insurance transactions. This development, while a positive step in the legislative context in which it has been made, should not be construed as a condemnation of the practices of the insurance industry. Rather, it is a reflection of the advancements in economic development and technology that have taken place since the inception of the Anglo-Australian-American insurance industry. Technology has rendered significantly obsolete many of the concerns associated with assessing the risks attached to the preponderance on insurance products. At the same time, the emergence and prevalence of the standard form contract as the principal mechanism for doing business in the consumer insurance market has changed markedly the dynamics of insurance contracting. Added to this are such other dynamics as the massive capitalisation levels of the preponderance of contemporary insurers and the essential role insurance plays in the regulation and safeguarding of society. Establishing an appropriate balance of legal rights between insured and insurers in this context therefore can never be a static undertaking. It is one that will constantly require assessment and adjustment by both legislatures and courts.

As noted at the outset, insurance taken in its most basic form has much in common with gambling. That said, it is distinct from gambling in one very important respect: the ability to obtain insurance has proven to be one of the principal stimulants for the development of commerce. The ability to quarantine and limit potential losses associated with significant expenditure – whether it be for a home, a car or an intergalactic exploration – provides the necessary safety net to encourage the assumption of risk, and with it, development. As the Elizabethans so succinctly put it:

> [through the issuing of a policy of assurance] it has come to pass, upon the loss or perishing of any ship there follows not the undoing of any Man, but that the loss falls rather easily upon many, as opposed to heavily upon few … whereby all … are lured to venture more willingly and freely. [Elizabethan Statute of 1601, 43 Eliz C 12.]

INSURANCE CONTRACTS ACT 1984

Act No 80 of 1984 as amended

Consolidated as in force on 12 July 1999
(includes amendments up to Act No 44 of 1999)

Prepared by the Office of Legislative Drafting,
Attorney General's Department, Canberra

PART II – THE DUTY OF THE UTMOST GOOD FAITH

12 This Part not to be read down

The effect of this Part is not limited or restricted in any way by any other law, including the subsequent provisions of this Act, but this Part does not have the effect of imposing on an insured, in relation to the disclosure of a matter to the insurer, a duty other than the duty of disclosure.

13 The duty of the utmost good faith

A contract of insurance is a contract based on the utmost good faith and there is implied in such a contract a provision requiring each party to it to act towards the other party, in respect of any matter arising under or in relation to it, with the utmost good faith.

14 Parties not to rely on provisions except in the utmost good faith

(1) If reliance by a party to a contract of insurance on a provision of the contract would be to fail to act with the utmost good faith, the party may not rely on the provision.

(2) Sub-section (1) does not limit the operation of section 13.

(3) In deciding whether reliance by an insurer on a provision of the contract of insurance would be to fail to act with the utmost good faith, the court shall have regard to any notification of the provision that was given to the insured, whether a notification of a kind mentioned in section 37 or otherwise.

15 Certain other laws not to apply

(1) A contract of insurance is not capable of being made the subject of relief under:

(a) any other Act; or

(b) a State Act; or

(c) an Act or Ordinance of a Territory.

(2) Relief to which sub-section (1) applies means relief in the form of:

(a) the judicial review of a contract on the ground that it is harsh, oppressive, unconscionable, unjust, unfair or inequitable; or

(b) relief for insureds from the consequences in law of making a misrepresentation;

but does not include relief in the form of compensatory damages.

PART IV – DISCLOSURES AND MISREPRESENTATIONS

Division 1 – The duty of disclosure

21 The insured's duty of disclosure

(1) Subject to this Act, an insured has a duty to disclose to the insurer, before the relevant contract of insurance is entered into, every matter that is known to the insured, being a matter that:

(a) the insured knows to be a matter relevant to the decision of the insurer whether to accept the risk and, if so, on what terms; or

(b) a reasonable person in the circumstances could be expected to know to be a matter so relevant.

(2) The duty of disclosure does not require the disclosure of a matter:

(a) that diminishes the risk;

(b) that is of common knowledge;

(c) that the insurer knows or in the ordinary course of the insurer's business as an insurer ought to know; or

(d) as to which compliance with the duty of disclosure is waived by the insurer.

(3) Where a person:

(a) failed to answer; or

(b) gave an obviously incomplete or irrelevant answer to;

a question included in a proposal form about a matter, the insurer shall be deemed to have waived compliance with the duty of disclosure in relation to the matter.

21A Eligible contracts of insurance – disclosure of specified matters

(1) This section applies to an eligible contract of insurance unless it is entered into by way of renewal.

Position of the insurer

(2) The insurer is taken to have waived compliance with the duty of disclosure in relation to the contract unless the insurer complies with either sub-section (3) or (4).

(3) Before the contract is entered into, the insurer requests the insured to answer one or more specific questions that are relevant to the decision of the insurer whether to accept the risk and, if so, on what terms.

(4) Before the contract is entered into, both:

(a) the insurer requests the insured to answer one or more specific questions that are relevant to the decision of the insurer whether to accept the risk and, if so, on what terms; and

(b) the insurer expressly requests the insured to disclose each exceptional circumstance that:

(i) is known to the insured; and

(ii) the insured knows, or a reasonable person in the circumstances could be expected to know, is a matter relevant to the decision of the insurer whether to accept the risk and, if so, on what terms; and

(iii) is not a matter that the insurer could reasonably be expected to make the subject of a question under paragraph (a); and

(iv) is not a matter covered by sub-section 21(2).

(5) If:

(a) the insurer complies with sub-section (3) or (4); and

(b) the insurer asks the insured to disclose to the insurer any other matters that would be covered by the duty of disclosure in relation to the contract;

the insurer is taken to have waived compliance with the duty of disclosure in relation to those matters.

Position of the insured

(6) If:

(a) the insurer complies with sub-section (3); and

(b) in answer to each question referred to in sub-section (3), the insured discloses each matter that:

(i) is known to the insured; and

(ii) a reasonable person in the circumstances could be expected to have disclosed in answer to that question;

the insured is taken to have complied with the duty of disclosure in relation to the contract.

(7) If:

(a) the insurer complies with sub-section (4); and

(b) in answer to each question referred to in paragraph (4)(a), the insured discloses each matter that:

(i) is known to the insured; and

(ii) a reasonable person in the circumstances could be expected to have disclosed in answer to that question; and

(c) the insured complies with the request referred to in paragraph (4)(b);

the insured is taken to have complied with the duty of disclosure in relation to the contract.

Onus of proof – exceptional circumstance

(8) In any proceedings relating to this section, the onus of proving that a matter is an exceptional circumstance covered by sub-paragraph (4)(b)(iii) lies on the insurer.

Definition

(9) In this section:

eligible contract of insurance means a contract of insurance that is specified in the regulations.

22 Insurer to inform of duty of disclosure

(1) The insurer shall, before a contract of insurance is entered into, clearly inform the insured in writing of the general nature and effect of the duty of disclosure and, if section 21A applies to the contract, also clearly inform the insured in writing of the general nature and effect of section 21A.

(2) If the regulations prescribe a form of writing to be used for informing an insured of the matters referred to in sub-section (1), the writing to be used may be in accordance with the form so prescribed.

(3) An insurer who has not complied with sub-section (1) may not exercise a right in respect of a failure to comply with the duty of disclosure unless that failure was fraudulent.

Division 2 – Misrepresentations

23 Ambiguous questions

Where:

(a) a statement is made in answer to a question asked in relation to a proposed contract of insurance or the provision of insurance cover in respect of a person who is seeking to become a member of a superannuation or retirement scheme; and

(b) a reasonable person in the circumstances would have understood the question to have the meaning that the person answering the question apparently understood it to have;

that meaning shall, in relation to the person who made the statement, be deemed to be the meaning of the question.

24 Warranties of existing facts to be representations

A statement made in or in connection with a contract of insurance, being a statement made by or attributable to the insured, with respect to the existence of a state of affairs does not have effect as a warranty but has effect as though it were a statement made to the insurer by the insured during the negotiations for the contract but before it was entered into.

25 Misrepresentation by life insured

Where, during the negotiations for a contract of life insurance but before it was entered into, a misrepresentation was made to the insurer by a person who, under the contract, became the life insured or one of the life insureds, this Act has effect as though the misrepresentation had been so made by the insured.

26 Certain statements not misrepresentations

(1) Where a statement that was made by a person in connection with a proposed contract of insurance was in fact untrue but was made on the basis of a belief that the person held, being a belief that a reasonable person in the circumstances would have held, the statement shall not be taken to be a misrepresentation.

(2) A statement that was made by a person in connection with a proposed contract of insurance shall not be taken to be a misrepresentation unless the person who made the statement knew, or a reasonable person in the circumstances could be expected to have known, that the statement would have been relevant to the decision of the insurer whether to accept the risk and, if so, on what terms.

(3) This section extends to the provision of insurance cover in respect of:

(a) a person who is seeking to become a member of a superannuation or retirement scheme; or

(b) a person who is a holder, or is applying to become a holder, of an RSA.

27 Failure to answer questions

A person shall not be taken to have made a misrepresentation by reason only that the person failed to answer a question included in a proposal form or gave an obviously incomplete or irrelevant answer to such a question.

Division 3 – Remedies for non-disclosure and misrepresentation

28 General insurance

(1) This section applies where the person who became the insured under a contract of general insurance upon the contract being entered into:

(a) failed to comply with the duty of disclosure; or

(b) made a misrepresentation to the insurer before the contract was entered into;

but does not apply where the insurer would have entered into the contract, for the same premium and on the same terms and conditions, even if the insured had not failed to comply with the duty of disclosure or had not made the misrepresentation before the contract was entered into.

(2) If the failure was fraudulent or the misrepresentation was made fraudulently, the insurer may avoid the contract.

(3) If the insurer is not entitled to avoid the contract or, being entitled to avoid the contract (whether under sub-section (2) or otherwise) has not done so, the liability of the insurer in respect of a claim is reduced to the amount that would place the insurer in a position in which the insurer would have been if the failure had not occurred or the misrepresentation had not been made.

29 Life insurance

(1) This section applies where the person who became the insured under a contract of life insurance upon the contract being entered into:

(a) failed to comply with the duty of disclosure; or

(b) made a misrepresentation to the insurer before the contract was entered into;

but does not apply where:

(c) the insurer would have entered into the contract even if the insured had not failed to comply with the duty of disclosure or had not made the misrepresentation before the contract was entered into; or

(d) the failure or misrepresentation was in respect of the date of birth of one or more of the life insureds.

(2) If the failure was fraudulent or the misrepresentation was made fraudulently, the insurer may avoid the contract.

(3) If the insurer would not have been prepared to enter into a contract of life insurance with the insured on any terms if the duty of disclosure had been complied with or the misrepresentation had not been made, the insurer may, within three years after the contract was entered into, avoid the contract.

(4) If the insurer has not avoided the contract, whether under sub-section (2) or (3) or otherwise, the insurer may, by notice in writing given to the insured before the expiration of three years after the contract was entered into, vary the contract by substituting for the sum insured (including any bonuses) a sum that is not less than the sum ascertained in accordance with the formula ***SP/Q***, where:

S is the number of dollars that is equal to the sum insured (including any bonuses);

P is the number of dollars that is equal to the premium that has, or to the sum of the premiums that have, become payable under the contract; and

Q is the number of dollars that is equal to the premium, or to the sum of the premiums, that the insurer would have been likely to have charged if the duty of disclosure had been complied with or the misrepresentation had not been made.

(5) In the application of sub-section (4) in relation to a contract that provides for periodic payments, ***the sum insured*** means each such payment (including any bonuses).

(6) A variation of a contract under sub-section (4) has effect from the time when the contract was entered into.

30 Misstatements of age

(1) In this section, ***the standard formula***, in relation to a contract of life insurance means the formula ***SP/Q***, where:

S is the number of dollars that is equal to the sum insured (including any bonuses);

P is the number of dollars that is equal to the premium that has, or to the sum of the premiums that have, become payable under the contract; and

Q is the number of dollars that is equal to the premium, or to the sum of the premiums, that would have become payable under the contract if it or they had been ascertained on the basis of the correct date of birth or dates of birth.

(2) If the date of birth of one or more of the life insureds under a contract of life insurance was not correctly stated to the insurer at the time when the contract was entered into:

(a) where the sum insured (including any bonuses) exceeds the amount in dollars ascertained in accordance with the standard formula – the insurer may at any time vary the contract by substituting for the sum insured (including any bonuses) an amount that is not less than the amount in dollars so ascertained; and

(b) where the sum insured (including any bonuses) is less than the amount so ascertained, the insurer shall either:

(i) reduce, as from the date on which the contract was entered into, the premium payable to the amount that would have been payable if the contract had been based on the correct date of birth or correct dates of birth and repay the amount of overpayments of premium (less any amount that has been paid as the cash value of bonuses in excess of the cash value that would have been paid if the contract had been based on the correct date of birth or correct dates of birth) together with interest on that amount at the prescribed rate computed from the date on which the contract was entered into; or

(ii) vary the contract by substituting for the sum insured (including any bonuses) the amount in dollars so ascertained.

(3) In the application of sub-section (2) in relation to a contract that provides for periodic payments, ***the sum insured*** means each such payment (including any bonuses).

(4) A variation of a contract under sub-section (2) has effect from the time when the contract was entered into.

31 Court may disregard avoidance in certain circumstances

(1) In any proceedings by the insured in respect of a contract of insurance that has been avoided on the ground of fraudulent failure to comply with the duty of disclosure or fraudulent misrepresentation, the court may, if it would be harsh and unfair not to do so, but subject to this section, disregard the avoidance and, if it does so, shall allow the insured to recover the whole, or such part as the court thinks just and equitable in the circumstances, of the amount that would have been payable if the contract had not been avoided.

(2) The power conferred by sub-section (1) may be exercised only where the court is of the opinion that, in respect of the loss that is the subject of the proceedings before the court, the insurer has not been prejudiced by the failure or misrepresentation or, if the insurer has been so prejudiced, the prejudice is minimal or insignificant.

(3) In exercising the power conferred by sub-section (1), the court:

(a) shall have regard to the need to deter fraudulent conduct in relation to insurance; and

(b) shall weigh the extent of the culpability of the insured in the fraudulent conduct against the magnitude of the loss that would be suffered by the insured if the avoidance were not disregarded;

but may also have regard to any other relevant matter.

(4) The power conferred by sub-section (1) applies only in relation to the loss that is the subject of the proceedings before the court, and any disregard

by the court of the avoidance does not otherwise operate to reinstate the contract.

32 Non-disclosure or misrepresentation by member of scheme

This Division extends to the case where there was a failure to comply with the duty of disclosure, or a misrepresentation was made, to the insurer under a blanket superannuation contract in respect of a proposed member of the relevant superannuation or retirement scheme as though:

(a) the insurance cover provided by that contract in respect of that member were provided by an individual superannuation contract between the insurer as insurer and the trustee for the purposes of the scheme as the insured; and

(b) that contract had been entered into at the time when the proposed member became a member of the scheme.

32A Non-disclosure or misrepresentation by holder of RSA

This Division extends to the case where there was a failure to comply with the duty of disclosure, or a misrepresentation was made, to the insurer in relation to a holder, or a person applying to become a holder, of an RSA as though:

(a) the insurance cover provided in relation to that RSA in respect of that person were provided by a contract between the insurer as insurer and the RSA provider as the insured; and

(b) that contract has been entered into at the time when the holder became the holder, or the person applying to become the holder, became the holder.

33 No other remedies

The provisions of this Division are exclusive of any right that the insurer has otherwise than under this Act in respect of a failure by the insured to disclose a matter to the insurer before the contract was entered into and in respect of a misrepresentation or incorrect statement.

PART V – THE CONTRACT

Division 1 – Standard cover

34 Interpretation

In this Division:

minimum amount, in relation to a claim, means the amount declared by the regulations to be the minimum amount in relation to a class of claims in which that claim is included;

prescribed contract means a contract of insurance that is included in a class of contracts of insurance declared by the regulations to be a class of contracts in relation to which this Division applies;

prescribed event, in relation to a prescribed contract, means an event that is declared by the regulations to be a prescribed event in relation to that contract.

35 Notification of certain provisions

(1) Where:

(a) a claim is made under a prescribed contract; and

(b) the event the happening of which gave rise to the claim is a prescribed event in relation to the contract;

the insurer may not refuse to pay an amount equal to the minimum amount in relation to the claim by reason only that the effect of the contract, but for this sub-section, would be that the event the happening of which gave rise to the claim was an event in respect of which:

(c) the amount of the insurance cover provided by the contract was less than the minimum amount; or

(d) insurance cover was not provided by the contract.

(2) Sub-section (1) does not have effect where the insurer proves that, before the contract was entered into, the insurer clearly informed the insured in writing (whether by providing the insured with a document containing the provisions, or the relevant provisions, of the proposed contract or otherwise) or the insured knew, or a reasonable person in the circumstances could be expected to have known:

(a) where the effect of the contract, but for sub-section (1), would be that the liability of the insurer in respect of a claim arising upon the happening of the event would be less than the minimum amount – what the extent of the insurer's liability under the contract in respect of such a claim would be; or

(b) where the effect of the contract, but for sub-section (1), would be that the insurer would be under no liability in respect of such a claim – that the contract would not provide insurance cover in respect of the happening of that event.

(3) Regulations made for the purposes of this section take effect at the expiration of 60 days after the day on which they are notified in the *Gazette*.

(4) Where regulations made for the purposes of this section are amended after the day on which a particular contract of insurance is entered into, the amendments shall be disregarded in relation to the application of sub-section (1) to that contract.

36 Interpretation of regulations

If a question arises whether an event is a prescribed event, the relevant provisions of the regulations shall be construed as though they were provisions of a contract put forward by the insurer.

37 Notification of unusual terms

An insurer may not rely on a provision included in a contract of insurance (not being a prescribed contract) of a kind that is not usually included in contracts of insurance that provide similar insurance cover unless, before the contract was entered into the insurer clearly informed the insured in writing of the effect of the provision (whether by providing the insured with a document containing the provisions, or the relevant provisions of the proposed contract or otherwise).

INSURANCE CONTRACTS REGULATIONS

SR 1985 No 162 as amended

Made under the Insurance Contracts Act 1984

Consolidated as in force on 7 October 1998
(includes amendments up to SR 1998 No 195)

Prepared by the Office of Legislative Drafting,
Attorney General's Department, Canberra

PART I – PRELIMINARY

1 Citation (*see* Note 1)

These Regulations may be cited as the Insurance Contracts Regulations.

2 Interpretation

(1) In these Regulations, unless the contrary intention appears:

accidental damage, in relation to a thing, means damage that occurs to the thing fortuitously in relation to the insured;

accidental injury means an injury that occurs fortuitously to the insured person but does not include an injury that is caused by or results from a sickness or disease;

the Act means the Insurance Contracts Act 1984;

contents, in relation to a residential building, means:

(a) furniture, furnishings and carpets (whether fixed or unfixed);

(b) household goods;

(c) clothing and other personal effects;

(d) any of the following:

(i) a picture;

(ii) a work of art;

(iii) a fur;

(iv) a piece of jewellery;

(v) a gold or silver article;

(vi) a document of any kind;

(vii) a collection of any kind;

the value of all of which at the time when the relevant contract of insurance is entered into does not exceed $500; and

(e) swimming pools that are not fixtures, that are owned by the insured or by a member of the insured's family ordinarily residing with the insured, but does not include an article or thing to which the expression ***residential building*** extends;

expropriation, in relation to property, means the lawful seizure, confiscation, nationalization or requisition of the property;

home building means:

(a) a building used principally and primarily as a place of residence; and

(b) out-buildings, fixtures and structural improvements used for domestic purposes, being purposes related to the use of the principal residence;

on the site and, without limiting the generality of the expression, includes:

(c) fixed wall coverings, fixed ceiling coverings and fixed floor coverings (other than carpets);

(d) services (whether underground or not) that are the property of the insured or that the insured is liable to repair or replace or pay the cost of repairing and replacing; and

(e) fences and gates wholly or partly on the site;

but does not include:

(f) a hotel;

(g) a motel;

(h) a boarding house;

(j) a building that is in the course of construction;

(k) a temporary building or structure or a demountable or moveable structure;

(m) a caravan (whether fixed to the site or not); or

(n) a building that is let or rented by the insured, as lessor, as a business and is not the principal residence of the insured;

insured person, in relation to a contract of insurance, means a person specified in the contract as a person in respect of whose death, sickness, disease, injury or unemployment insurance cover is provided under the contract;

member of the insured person's travelling party means a member of the family of the insured person, or a person specified in the contract of insurance, travelling or intending to travel with the insured person on the specified journey;

motor vehicle means a vehicle that is designed:

(a) to travel by road;

(b) to use volatile spirit, steam, gas, oil, electricity or any other power (not being human power or animal power) as its principal means of propulsion; and

(c) to carry passengers;

and includes a motor cycle but does not include an omnibus or a tram or a motor vehicle the carrying capacity of which exceeds two tonnes;

personal belongings means baggage and other personal effects (including tickets, credit cards, traveller's cheques, travel documents and passports) that accompany the insured person on the specified journey (whether acquired before or during the journey) or have been collected from the insured person by a carrier in order to be taken on the specified journey, but does not include:

(a) currency notes, bank notes or coins; or

(b) goods so taken that are intended for trade;

residential building means:

(a) a building used principally and primarily as a place of residence; and

(b) out-buildings used for domestic purposes, being purposes related to the use of the principal residence;

on the site but does not include:

(c) a hotel;

(d) a motel;

(e) a boarding house;

(f) a building that is in the course of construction;

(g) a temporary building or structure or a demountable or moveable structure;

(h) a caravan (whether fixed to the site or not); or

(j) a building that is let or rented by the insured, as lessor, as a business and is not the principal residence of the insured;

site, in relation to a building, means the site specified in the relevant contract of insurance as the site on which the building is situated;

specified journey means a journey in relation to which insurance cover is provided by the relevant contract of insurance;

warlike activities means invasion, act of foreign enemy, hostilities (whether war is declared or not), civil war, rebellion, revolution, insurrection, military or usurped power, looting, sacking or pillage following any of these.

(2) Where a residential building is a part of a building that has been sub-divided under a law of a State or Territory that relates to the sub-division

of buildings into strata (however described), a reference in these Regulations to the contents of the residential building includes a reference to such of the fixtures and structural improvements in the part of the building as are not insured under a contract of insurance that provides insurance cover in respect of the destruction of, or damage occurring to, the building, being a contract under which the body corporate established by or under that law is the insured.

(3) A reference in these Regulations to a period during which a person is disabled is a reference to a period specified in a certificate given by a duly qualified medical practitioner that certifies that the person is disabled during that period.

2A Definition of *consumer credit insurance*

For the purposes of paragraph (b) of the definition of ***consumer credit insurance*** in sub-section 11(1) of the Act, the class of contracts referred to in regulation 21 is identified as consumer credit insurance.

Note For the purposes of paragraph (a) of the definition of ***consumer credit insurance*** (a class of contracts declared to be a class of contracts to which Division 1 of Part V of the Act applies), see regulation 21.

3 Prescribed form of writing to inform insured of duty of disclosure

For the purposes of section 22 of the Act, the form of writing prescribed to be used for informing an insured of the general nature and effect of the duty of disclosure is:

(a) in relation to a contract of general insurance – the form set out in Part I of Schedule 1; and

(b) in relation to a contract of life insurance – the form set out in Part II of Schedule 1.

4 Prescribed rate of interest – sub-paragraph 30(2)(b)(i) of the Act

For the purposes of sub-paragraph 30(2)(b)(i) of the Act, the rate of 11% per annum is prescribed.

PART II – STANDARD COVER

Division 1 – Motor vehicle insurance

5 Prescribed contracts

The following class of contracts of insurance is declared to be a class of contracts in relation to which Division 1 of Part V of the Act applies, namely, contracts that provide insurance cover (whether or not the cover is limited or restricted in any way) in respect of one or more of the following:

(a) loss of, or damage to, a motor vehicle;

(b) liability for loss of, or damage to, property caused by or resulting from impact of a motor vehicle with some other thing;

where the insured or one of the insureds is a natural person.

6 Prescribed events

The following, except insofar as they are excluded by regulation 7, are declared to be prescribed events in relation to a contract referred to in regulation 5:

(a) the occurrence within Australia of the destruction or, theft of, or accidental damage to, the motor vehicle specified in the contract;

(b) the occurrence within Australia of accidental damage to, or the theft of:

(i) a tool or appliance that is standard equipment for the motor vehicle specified in the contract; or

(ii) an accessory that forms part of that motor vehicle;

at a time when the tool, appliance or accessory is attached to or within the motor vehicle;

(c) the insured or a person:

(i) who, with the express or implied consent of the insured, was driving, using or in charge of the motor vehicle at the relevant time; or

(ii) who, at the relevant time, was an authorised passenger in the motor vehicle or, if the motor vehicle is a motor cycle, who, at the relevant time, was an authorised passenger on the motor vehicle;

incurring a liability (otherwise than under a contract) to pay compensation or damages in respect of loss of, or damage occurring to, property (not being the motor vehicle or a tool, appliance or accessory as mentioned in paragraph (b)) in Australia, being loss or damage that occurs as a result of the use of:

(iii) the motor vehicle; or

(iv) a trailer or caravan attached to the motor vehicle;

(d) a person who, at the relevant time, was an employer, principal or partner of the insured, incurring a liability (otherwise than under a contract) as employer, principal or partner, respectively, to pay compensation or damages in respect of loss of, or damage occurring to, property (not being the motor vehicle or a tool, appliance or accessory as mentioned in paragraph (b)) in Australia, being loss or damage that occurs as a result of the use of:

(i) the motor vehicle; or

(ii) a trailer or caravan attached to the motor vehicle.

7 Exclusions

The following are excluded:

(a) depreciation;

(b) wear and tear, rust or corrosion;

(c) structural failure or mechanical or electrical breakdown or failure;

(d) the tyres of the motor vehicle being damaged by application of brakes or by road punctures, cuts or bursting;

(e) destruction or damage, or the incurring of a liability as mentioned in paragraph 6(c) or (d), at a time when:

(i) the motor vehicle is being used in, or tested in preparation for, racing, pacemaking, a reliability trial or a speed or hill-climbing test by the insured or by some other person with the express or implied consent of the insured;

(ii) the motor vehicle, trailer or caravan is being used:

(A) in an experiment, test, trial or demonstration; or

(B) in the case of a motor vehicle, to tow some other vehicle;

in connection with the motor trade by the insured or by some other person with the express or implied consent of the insured;

(iii) the motor vehicle, trailer or caravan:

(A) is let on hire by the insured as lessor; or

(B) is being used in the course of the business of carrying passengers or goods for hire or reward by the insured or by some other person with the express or implied consent of the insured;

(iv) the motor vehicle, trailer or caravan is in the possession of a person as part of the person's stock in trade;

(v) the motor vehicle, trailer or caravan is being used for an unlawful purpose by the insured or is being so used by some other person with the express or implied consent of the insured;

(vi) the insured is driving the motor vehicle and is not authorised under the law in force in the State or Territory in which the motor vehicle is being driven, being a law with respect to the licensing of drivers of motor vehicles, to drive the motor vehicle;

(vii) a person other than the insured:

(A) is driving the motor vehicle with the express or implied consent of the insured; and

(B) is not authorised under the law in force in the State or Territory in which the motor vehicle is being driven, being a law with respect to the licensing of drivers of motor vehicles, to drive the motor vehicle;

and the insured knew or should reasonably have known, at the time when the consent was given or impliedly given, that that person was not so authorised;

(viii) the insured is driving the motor vehicle and is under the influence of intoxicating liquor or of a drug; or

(ix) a person other than the insured:

(A) is driving the motor vehicle with the express or implied consent of the insured; and

(B) is under the influence of intoxicating liquor or of a drug;

and the insured knew or should reasonably have known, at the time when the consent was given or impliedly given, that that person was or was to be at the relevant time under that influence;

(f) destruction or damage, or the incurring of a liability as mentioned in paragraph 6(c) or (d), as a result of:

(i) the expropriation of the motor vehicle, trailer or caravan;

(ii) war or warlike activities;

(iii) the use, existence or escape of nuclear weapons material, or ionizing radiation from, or contamination by radioactivity from, any nuclear fuel or nuclear waste from the combustion of nuclear fuel; or

(iv) the unroadworthy or unsafe condition of the motor vehicle, caravan or trailer concerned, being a condition that was known to the insured, or should reasonably have been known to the insured, at the time of the occurrence of the loss or damage or the incurring of the liability;

(g) destruction or damage intentionally caused by, or a liability as mentioned in paragraph 6(c) or (d) intentionally incurred by, the insured or a person acting with the express or implied consent of the insured;

(h) destruction or damage occurring as a result of the insured failing to take steps that are, in the circumstances, reasonable for the security of the motor vehicle after accidental damage has occurred to it;

(j) the incurring of a liability as mentioned in paragraph 6(c) or (d) (whether to the insured or to some other person) in respect of damage to property that belongs to, or is in the custody of, the person so liable;

(k) the incurring of a liability as mentioned in paragraph 6(c) or (d) by a person other than the insured at a time when that person is driving the motor vehicle and:

(i) is not authorised under the law in force in the State or Territory in which the motor vehicle is being driven, being a law with respect to the licensing of drivers of motor vehicles, to drive the motor vehicle; or

(ii) is under the influence of intoxicating liquor or of a drug;

(m) the incurring of a liability to pay compensation or damages in respect of loss or damage, where:

(i) the loss or damage occurred as a result of the use of a trailer or caravan attached to the motor vehicle; and

(ii) there were, at the time the loss or damage occurred, two or more trailers or caravans, or one or more trailers and one or more caravans, attached to the motor vehicle.

8 Minimum amounts

(1) Subject to these Regulations, for the purposes of section 34 of the Act, the minimum amount in respect of a claim made under a contract referred to in regulation 5, being a claim arising out of an event referred to in paragraph 6(a) or (b), is declared to be the amount sufficient to indemnify the person who made the claim.

(2) Subject to these Regulations, for the purposes of section 34 of the Act, the minimum amount in respect of a claim made under a contract referred to in regulation 5, being a claim that arises out of an event referred to in paragraph 6(c) or (d), is declared to be the amount, not exceeding $5,000,000, sufficient to indemnify the person who made the claim in respect of his or her liability.

(3) Where there is more than one such claim arising out of the same event, being an event referred to in paragraph 6(c) or (d), then, for the purposes of section 34 of the Act, the minimum amount in respect of a claim made after the first of those claims has been made is declared to be the amount sufficient to indemnify the person who made the claim or the amount ascertained by subtracting from $5,000,000 the amount or the sum of the amounts, as the case may be, that the insurer has paid, or is liable to pay, in respect of the claim or claims arising out of that event that have already been made, whichever is the lesser.

Division 2 – Home buildings insurance

9 Prescribed contracts

The following class of contracts of insurance is declared to be a class of contracts in relation to which Division 1 of Part V of the Act applies, namely, contracts that provide insurance cover (whether or not the cover is limited or restricted in any way) in respect of destruction of or damage to a home building, where the insured or one of the insureds is a natural person.

10 Prescribed events

The following, except in so far as they are excluded by regulation 11, are declared to be prescribed events in relation to a contract referred to in regulation 9:

(a) the destruction of, or damage occurring to, the home building on the site, being destruction or damage that is caused by or results from:

(i) fire or explosion;

(ii) lightning or thunderbolt;

(iii) earthquake;

(iv) theft, burglary or housebreaking or an attempt to commit theft, burglary or housebreaking;

(v) a deliberate or intentional act;

(vi) bursting, leaking, discharging or overflowing of fixed apparatus, fixed tanks or fixed pipes used to hold or carry liquid of any kind;

(vii) riot or civil commotion;

(viii) an action of a person acting maliciously;

(ix) impact by or arising out of the use of a vehicle (including an aircraft or a water-borne craft);

(x) impact by:

(A) space debris or debris from an aircraft, rocket or satellite;

(B) an animal (other than an animal kept on the site or a domestic animal);

(C) a falling tree or part of a tree; or

(D) a television or radio aerial that has broken or collapsed; or

(xi) storm, tempest, flood, the action of the sea, high water, tsunami, erosion or land slide or subsidence;

(b) accidental damage that is breakage of any fixed glass, fixed shower base, fixed basin, fixed sink, fixed bath, fixed lavatory pan or fixed cistern;

(c) loss by theft, burglary or housebreaking;

(d) the insured or a member of the insured's family ordinarily residing with the insured incurring a liability as owner or occupier of the home building to pay compensation or damages to some other person.

11 Exclusions

The following are excluded:

(a) depreciation;

(b) wear and tear, rust or corrosion;

(c) the action of insects or vermin;

(d) destruction or damage, or the incurring of a liability as mentioned in paragraph 10(d), as a result of:

(i) the expropriation of the home building;

(ii) war or warlike activities;

(iii) the use, existence or escape of nuclear weapons material, or ionizing radiation from, or contamination by radioactivity from, any nuclear fuel or nuclear waste from the combustion of nuclear fuel;

(iv) the use of the home building for the purposes of a business, trade or profession; or

(v) tree lopping or felling by the insured or a person acting with the express or implied consent of the insured; or

(e) destruction or damage intentionally caused, or a liability as mentioned in paragraph 10(d) intentionally incurred, by:

(i) the insured; or

(ii) a member of the insured's family ordinarily residing with the insured;

or a person acting with the express or implied consent of any of them;

(f) where the home building is unoccupied and has been unoccupied for a continuous period of more than 60 days – destruction or damage occurring otherwise than as mentioned in sub-paragraph 10(a)(ii) or (iii) or (vii) to (xi) (inclusive), or the incurring of liability as mentioned in paragraph 10(d);

(g) destruction of, or damage occurring to:

(i) a free-standing or retaining wall (whether or not part of the home building), or to a gate or fence, as a result of a storm or tempest;

(ii) an electrical machine or apparatus as a result of the electric current therein; or

(iii) any property as a result of it undergoing a process necessarily involving the application of heat;

(h) theft by a person ordinarily residing with the insured at the time of the theft;

(j) in the case of destruction or damage that is caused by or results from bursting, leaking, discharging or overflowing of fixed apparatus, fixed tanks or fixed pipes used to hold or carry liquid of any kind or impact by a television or radio aerial that has broken or collapsed – damage to the apparatus, tanks or pipes or the television or radio aerial, respectively;

(k) the incurring of a liability as mentioned in paragraph 10(d):

(i) to the insured or a member of the insured's family ordinarily residing with the insured; or

(ii) as a result of:

(A) the insured; or

(B) a member of the insured's family ordinarily residing with the insured;

or a person acting with the express or implied consent of any of them, using a vehicle (including an aircraft or water-borne craft) on the site.

12 Minimum amounts

(1) Subject to these Regulations, for the purposes of section 34 of the Act, the minimum amount in respect of a claim made under a contract referred to in regulation 9, being a claim arising out of an event referred to in paragraph 10(a), (b) or (c), is declared to be the amount sufficient to indemnify the person who made the claim reduced, in respect of destruction or damage occurring as a result of and within 48 hours after an earthquake, by $200.

(2) The amount declared by sub-regulation (1) to be the minimum amount in respect of a claim shall be taken to include the reasonable cost of:

(a) identifying and locating the cause of destruction or damage concerned if it is necessary to do so to effect a repair;

(b) demolition and removal of debris; and

(c) emergency accommodation.

(3) Subject to these Regulations, for the purposes of section 34 of the Act, the minimum amount in respect of a claim made under a contract referred to in regulation 9, being a claim that arises out of an event referred to in paragraph 10(d), is declared to be the amount, not exceeding $2,000,000, sufficient to indemnify the person who made the claim in respect of his or her liability.

(4) Where there is more than one such claim arising out of the same event, being an event referred to in paragraph 10(d), then, for the purposes of section 34 of the Act, the minimum amount in respect of a claim made after the first of those claims has been made is declared to be the amount sufficient to indemnify the person who made the claim or the amount ascertained by subtracting from $2,000,000 the amount or the sum of the amounts, as the case may be, that the insurer has paid, or is liable to pay, in respect of the claim or claims arising out of that event that have already been made, whichever is the lesser.

Division 3 – Home contents insurance

13 Prescribed contracts

The following class of contracts of insurance is declared to be a class of contracts in relation to which Division 1 of Part V of the Act applies, namely, contracts that provide insurance cover (whether or not the cover is limited or restricted in any way) in respect of loss of or damage to the contents of a residential building where the insured or one of the insureds is a natural person, but does not include a contract that provides insurance cover only or primarily in respect of specified personal effects.

14 Prescribed events

The following, except in so far as they are excluded by regulation 15, are declared to be prescribed events in relation to a contract referred to in regulation 13:

(a) destruction of, or damage occurring to, the contents of the residential building which is specified in the contract, at a time when they are in the residential building or on the site of the residential building, being destruction or damage that is caused by or results from:

(i) fire or explosion;

(ii) lightning or thunderbolt;

(iii) earthquake;

(iv) theft, burglary or housebreaking or an attempt to commit theft, burglary or housebreaking;

(v) a deliberate or intentional act;

(vi) bursting, leaking, discharging or overflowing of fixed apparatus, fixed tanks or fixed pipes used to hold or carry liquid of any kind;

(vii) riot or civil commotion;

(viii) an action of a person acting maliciously;

(ix) impact by or arising out of the use of a vehicle (including an aircraft or water-borne craft);

(x) impact by:

(A) space debris or debris from an aircraft, a rocket or a satellite;

(B) an animal (other than an animal kept on the site or a domestic animal);

(C) a falling tree or part of a tree; or

(D) a television or radio aerial that has broken or collapsed; or

(xi) storm, tempest, flood, the action of the sea, high water, tsunami, erosion or land slide or subsidence;

(b) accidental damage that is breakage of glass forming part of an item of furniture (including fixed or unfixed glass table tops), at a time when it is in the residential building or on the site of the residential building;

(c) loss by theft, burglary or housebreaking of contents while in the residential building on the site;

(d) where:

(i) the insured is a tenant or lessee of the residential building; or

(ii) the residential building is a unit (however described) created by the sub-division of strata (however described) in a building and the insured is the owner of the unit;

the insured or a member of the insured's family ordinarily residing with the insured incurring a liability as occupier of the home building to pay compensation or damages to some other person.

15 Exclusions

The following are excluded:

(a) depreciation;

(b) wear and tear, rust or corrosion;

(c) the action of insects or vermin;

(d) destruction or damage, or the incurring of a liability as mentioned in paragraph 14(d), as a result of:

   (i) the expropriation of the contents;

   (ii) war or warlike activities;

   (iii) the use, existence or escape of nuclear weapons material, or ionizing radiation from, or contamination by radioactivity from, any nuclear fuel or nuclear waste from the combustion of nuclear fuel;

   (iv) the use of the residential building for the purposes of a business, trade or profession; or

   (v) tree lopping or felling by the insured or a person acting with the express or implied consent of the insured;

(e) destruction or damage intentionally caused, or a liability as mentioned in paragraph 14(d) intentionally incurred, by:

   (i) the insured; or

   (ii) a member of the insured's family ordinarily residing with the insured;

   or a person acting with the express or implied consent of any of them;

(f) where the residential building is unoccupied and has been unoccupied for a continuous period of more than 60 days – destruction or damage occurring otherwise than as mentioned in sub-paragraph 14(a)(ii) or (iii) or (vii) to (ix) (inclusive), or the incurring of liability as mentioned in paragraph 14(d);

(g) destruction of, or damage occurring to:

   (i) an electrical machine or apparatus as a result of the electric current in it; or

   (ii) any property as a result of it undergoing a process necessarily involving the application of heat;

(h) accidental breakage of:

   (i) a television picture tube or screen;

   (ii) the picture tube or screen of an electronic visual display unit;

(iii) a ceramic or glass cooking top of a stove;

(iv) glass in a picture frame, a radio set or a clock;

(j) theft by a person ordinarily residing with the insured at the time of the theft;

(k) in the case of destruction or damage that is caused by or results from bursting, leaking, discharging or overflowing of fixed apparatus, fixed tanks or fixed pipes used to hold or carry liquid of any kind or impact by a television or radio aerial that has broken or collapsed – damage to the apparatus, tanks or pipes or the television or radio aerial, respectively;

(m) the incurring of a liability as mentioned in paragraph 14(d):

(i) to the insured or a member of the insured's family ordinarily residing with the insured; or

(ii) as a result of:

(A) the insured; or

(B) a member of the insured's family ordinarily residing with the insured;

or a person acting with the express or implied consent of any of them, using a vehicle (including an aircraft or water-borne craft) on the site.

16 Minimum amounts

(1) Subject to these Regulations, for the purposes of section 34 of the Act, the minimum amount in respect of a claim made under a contract referred to in regulation 13, being a claim arising out of an event referred to in paragraph 14(a), (b) or (c), is declared to be the amount sufficient to indemnify the person who made the claim, reduced, in the case of destruction or damage occurring as a result of an earthquake, by $200.

(2) For the purposes of section 34 of the Act, the minimum amount in respect of a claim made under a contract referred to in regulation 13, being a claim that arises out of an event referred to in paragraph 14(d), is declared to be the amount, not exceeding $2,000,000, sufficient to indemnify the person who made the claim in respect of his or her liability.

(3) Where there is more than one such claim arising out of the same event, being an event referred to in paragraph 14(d), then, for the purposes of section 34 of the Act, the minimum amount in respect of a claim made after the first of those claims has been made is declared to be the amount sufficient to indemnify the person who made the claim or the amount ascertained by subtracting from $2,000,000 the amount or the sum of the amounts, as the case may be, that the insurer has paid, or is liable to pay, in respect of the claim or claims arising out of that event that have already been made, whichever is the lesser.

Division 4 – Sickness and accident insurance

17 Prescribed contracts

The following class of contracts of insurance is declared to be a class of contracts in relation to which Division 1 of Part V of the Act applies, namely, contracts that provide insurance cover (whether the cover is limited or restricted in any way) in respect of the insured person contracting a sickness or disease or a specified sickness or disease or sustaining an injury or a specified injury, where the insured or one of the insureds is a natural person, other than:

(a) a life policy within the meaning of the Life Insurance Act 1995;

(b) a continuous disability insurance contract incorporated within a life policy within the meaning of the Life Insurance Act 1995;

(c) sickness and accident policies which are guaranteed 'renewable' at the option of the insured or where the insurer guarantees not to cancel the policy in response to a change in the risk where such a policy has been effected for a predetermined period of years in excess of one year; or

(d) a contract that is included in a class of contracts that is declared by some other regulation to be a class of contracts in relation to which that Division applies.

18 Prescribed events

The following, except in so far as they are excluded by regulation 19, are declared to be prescribed events in relation to a contract referred to in regulation 17:

(a) where the contract provides insurance cover (whether the cover is limited or restricted in any way) in respect of the insured person contracting a specified sickness or disease:

  (i) the death of the insured person; or

  (ii) the total disablement of the insured person from carrying out all the normal duties of his or her usual occupation;

  being death or disablement that results from the insured person contracting that sickness or disease;

(b) where the contract (not being a contract referred to in paragraph (a)) provides insurance cover (whether the cover is limited or restricted in any way) in respect of the insured person contracting a sickness or disease – the total disablement of the insured person from carrying out all the normal duties of his or her usual occupation, being disablement that results from the person contracting a sickness or disease;

(c) the death of the insured person, or the total disablement of the insured person from carrying out all the normal duties of his or her usual occupation, as a result of the insured person sustaining an accidental injury, being death or disablement that occurs within 12 months after the insured person sustains the injury;

(d) the partial disablement of the insured person from carrying out the normal duties of his or her usual occupation as a result of the insured person sustaining an accidental injury, being disablement that occurs within 12 months after the insured person sustains the injury.

19 Exclusions

The following are excluded:

(a) death or disablement that results from:

  (i) a deliberately self-inflicted injury;

  (ii) war or warlike activities;

  (iii) the use, existence or escape of nuclear weapons material, or ionizing radiation from, or contamination by radioactivity from, any nuclear fuel or nuclear waste from the combustion of nuclear fuel;

  (iv) the insured person:

    (A) being under the influence of intoxicating liquor or of a drug, other than a drug taken or administered by or in accordance with the advice of a duly qualified medical practitioner;

    (B) being addicted to intoxicating liquor or to a drug;

    (C) taking part in a riot or civil commotion;

    (D) acting maliciously; or

    (E) engaging in professional sporting activities;

(b) death or disablement occurring at a time when the insured person is flying, or engaging in aerial activities, otherwise than as a passenger in an aircraft that is authorised to fly under a law that relates to the safety of aircraft.

20 Minimum amounts

(1) Where the insured has expressly agreed that no amount is to be payable under the contract of insurance in particular circumstances, then, for the purposes of this regulation, the contract shall be read as though it specified an amount to be payable in those circumstances.

(2) Where a contract of insurance provides that an amount is payable by reference to a period other than a day, then, for the purposes of this regulation, the contract shall be read as though it specified as the daily amount an amount ascertained by dividing the amount payable for that period by the number of days in that period.

(3) Subject to these Regulations, for the purposes of section 34 of the Act, the minimum amount in respect of a claim made under a contract referred to in regulation 17, being a claim that arises as mentioned in Column 1 of the

following Table, is declared to be the amount ascertained in accordance with Column 2 of the Table in relation to that claim, reduced by an amount equal to the amount so payable in respect of the first 14 days of the period during which the insured person is disabled.

Column 1	Column 2
Description of claim	Minimum amount
1 A claim that arises out of the death of the insured person	The amount specified in the contract as the amount payable under the contract in respect of the death of the insured person or, where no amount is so specified, $25,000
2 A claim that arises out of the total disablement of the insured person	Where: (a) a daily amount is specified in the contract in respect of the total disablement of the insured person – that amount multiplied by the number of days during which the insured person is so disabled; or (b) where no amount is so specified – an amount equal to the amount of income lost by the insured person by reason of the disablement
3 A claim that arises out of the partial disablement of the insured person	Where: (a) a daily amount is specified in the contract in respect of the partial disablement of the insured person – that amount multiplied by the number of days during which the insured person is so disabled; or (b) where no amount is so specified – an amount equal to the amount of income lost by the insured person by reason of the disablement

Division 5 – Consumer credit insurance

21 Prescribed contracts

The following class of contracts of insurance is declared to be a class of contracts to which Division 1 of Part V of the Act applies, namely, contracts that provide insurance cover (whether the cover is limited or restricted in any way) in respect of:

(a) the death of the insured; or

(b) the insured:

 (i) contracting a sickness or disease;

 (ii) sustaining an injury; or

 (iii) becoming unemployed;

where:

(c) the insured or one of the insureds is a natural person; and

(d) the amount of the liability of the insurer under the contract is to be ascertained by reference to a liability of the insured under a specified agreement to which the insured is a party.

22 Prescribed events

The following, except in so far as they are excluded by regulation 23, are declared to be prescribed events in relation to a contract referred to in regulation 21:

(a) the total disablement of the insured person from carrying out all the normal duties of his or her usual occupation as a result of the insured person contracting a sickness or disease, being disablement that occurs within 12 months after the insured person contracted the sickness or disease;

(b) the death of the insured person, or the total disablement of the insured person from carrying out all the normal duties of his or her usual occupation, as a result of the insured person sustaining an accidental injury, being death or disablement that occurs within 12 months after the insured person sustains the injury;

(c) the insured person becoming unemployed.

23 Exclusions

The following are excluded:

(a) death, disablement or unemployment resulting from:

 (i) a deliberately self-inflicted injury;

 (ii) war or warlike activities;

(iii) expropriation of any property;

(iv) the use, existence or escape of nuclear weapons material, or ionizing radiation from, or contamination by radioactivity from, any nuclear fuel or nuclear waste from the combustion of nuclear fuel; or

(v) the insured person:

(A) being under the influence of intoxicating liquor or of a drug, other than a drug taken or administered by or in accordance with the advice of a duly qualified medical practitioner;

(B) being addicted to intoxicating liquor or to a drug;

(C) taking part in a riot or civil commotion;

(D) acting maliciously; or

(E) engaging in professional sporting activities;

(b) death or disablement occurring at a time when the insured person is flying, or engaging in aerial activities, otherwise than as a passenger in an aircraft that is authorised to fly under a law that relates to the safety of aircraft;

(c) the insured person becoming voluntarily unemployed;

(d) where the insured person is employed for a specified period or by reference to specified work – the insured person becoming unemployed at the expiration of the period or on the completion of the work.

24 Minimum amounts

(1) A reference in this regulation to the amount falling due under an agreement in respect of a day is a reference to the amount ascertained by dividing the amount of the payment that next falls due after that day under the agreement (excluding any arrears) by the number of days in the period commencing on the day on which the immediately previous payment under the agreement fell due and ending on the day on which that next payment falls due.

(2) Subject to these Regulations, for the purposes of section 34 of the Act, the minimum amount in respect of a claim made under a contract referred to in regulation 21, being a claim that arises as mentioned in Column 1 of the following Table, is declared to be the amount ascertained in accordance with Column 2 of the Table in relation to that claim, reduced by an amount equal to the amount so payable in respect of the first 14 days of the period during which the insured person is disabled.

Column 1 Description of claim	Column 2 Minimum amount
1 A claim that arises out of the death of the insured person	The amount due at the date of death (excluding any arrears) under the agreement specified in the contract
2 A claim that arises out of the total disablement of the insured person	The sum of the amounts falling due under the agreement specified in the contract in respect of each day during the period during which the insured person is so disabled
3 A claim that arises out of the insured person becoming unemployed	The sum of the amounts falling due under the agreement specified in the contract in respect of each day during the period during which the insured person is unemployed

Division 6 – Travel insurance

25 Prescribed contracts

The following class of contracts of insurance is declared to be a class of contracts in relation to which Division 1 of Part V of the Act applies, namely, contracts that provide insurance cover (whether or not the cover is limited or restricted in any way) in respect of one or more of the following:

(a) financial loss in respect of:

  (i) fares for any form of transport to be used; or

  (ii) accommodation to be used;

  in the course of the specified journey in the event that the insured person does not commence or complete the specified journey;

(b) loss of or damage to personal belongings that occurs while the insured person is on the specified journey;

(c) a sickness or disease contracted or an injury sustained by the insured person while on the specified journey;

where the insured or one of the insureds is a natural person.

26 Prescribed events

The following, except in so far as they are excluded by regulation 27, are declared to be prescribed events in relation to a contract referred to in regulation 25:

(a) financial loss on account of:
   (i) fares for any form of transport to be used; or
   (ii) accommodation to be used;

   in the course of the specified journey in the event that the insured person or a member of the insured person's travelling party, through unforeseen circumstances beyond the control of the insured person or member, respectively, cannot reasonably be expected to commence or complete the journey;

(b) loss of or damage occurring to personal belongings of the insured person during the course of the specified journey;

(c) the death of the insured person or a member of the insured's travelling party while on the specified journey;

(d) the insured person or a member of the insured's travelling party contracting a sickness or disease or sustaining an injury while on the specified journey.

27 Exclusions

The following are excluded:

(a) financial loss, loss of or damage to personal belongings or death, sickness or injury, occurring as a result of:
   (i) war or warlike activities;
   (ii) expropriation of any thing;
   (iii) the use, existence or escape of nuclear weapons material, or ionizing radiation from, or contamination by radioactivity from, any nuclear fuel or nuclear waste from the combustion of nuclear fuel; or
   (iv) the insured person or a member of the insured person's travelling party:
      (A) being under the influence of intoxicating liquor or of a drug, other than a drug taken or administered by or in accordance with the advice of a duly qualified medical practitioner;
      (B) being addicted to intoxicating liquor or to a drug;
      (C) taking part in a riot or civil commotion;
      (D) acting maliciously; or
      (E) engaging in professional sporting activities;

(b) financial loss, loss of or damage to personal belongings or death, sickness or injury, intentionally caused by:
   (i) the insured person; or
   (ii) a member of the insured person's travelling party;

   or by a person acting with the express or implied consent of any of them;

(c) financial loss as a result of:
   (i) the insured person failing to commence or complete the journey:
      (A) for financial, business or contractual reasons, being reasons related to the insured person or to a member of the insured person's travelling party; or
      (B) because of a sickness, disease or disability to which a person was subject at any time during the period of six months before the contract was entered into and continues to be subject to after that time;
   (ii) the insured person or a member of the insured person's travelling party being disinclined to travel; or
   (iii) contravention of, or failure to comply with, a law (including the law of a foreign country) by the insured person or a member of the insured person's travelling party;

(d) loss of or damage occurring to personal belongings as a result of:
   (i) depreciation;
   (ii) wear and tear, mildew, rust or corrosion;
   (iii) the action of insects or vermin;
   (iv) mechanical or electrical breakdown or failure of the personal belongings;
   (v) the personal belongings being cleaned, dyed, altered or repaired; or
   (vi) in the case of personal belongings that are fragile or brittle – the negligence of the insured;

(e) death occurring or injury sustained as a result of a sickness or disability to which the person concerned was subject at any time during the period of six months before the contract was entered into and continues to be subject to after that time;

(f) death occurring or injury sustained at a time when the person concerned is flying, or engaging in aerial activities, otherwise than as a passenger in an aircraft that is authorised to fly under a law that relates to the safety of aircraft;

(g) the insured person or a member of the insured's travelling party sustaining a deliberately self-inflicted injury.

28 Minimum amounts

(1) Subject to these Regulations, for the purposes of section 34 of the Act, the minimum amount in respect of a claim made under a contract referred to in regulation 25, being a claim that arises out of an event referred to in paragraph 26(a) or (b), is declared to be the amount sufficient to indemnify the person who made the claim in respect of his or her loss or damage.

(2) Subject to these Regulations, for the purposes of section 34 of the Act, the minimum amount in respect of a claim made under a contract referred to in regulation 25, being a claim that arises out of an event referred to in paragraph 26(c), is declared to be the amount sufficient to indemnify the person who made the claim in respect of the reasonable cost of:

(a) the funeral or cremation; or

(b) transporting the remains of the deceased person to the deceased's former place of residence.

(3) Subject to these Regulations, for the purposes of section 34 of the Act, the minimum amount in respect of a claim made under a contract referred to in regulation 25, being a claim that arises out of an event referred to in paragraph 26(d), is declared to be the amount sufficient to indemnify the person who made the claim in respect of the reasonable cost of:

(a) medical, surgical, hospital, ambulance and nursing home charges; and

(b) other medical treatment;

incurred during the specified journey as a result of the sickness, disease or injury.

Division 7 – Limits on minimum amounts

29 Limits on minimum amounts

Where the insured knew, or a reasonable person in the circumstances would have known, that a particular amount is the maximum amount that would be payable by the insurer under the contract of insurance whatever the circumstances, then, in relation to a claim under that contract, the minimum amount for the purposes of section 34 of the Act shall be the first-mentioned amount or the amount declared by the relevant provision of these Regulations to be the minimum amount in respect of the claim, whichever is the less.

SCHEDULE 1 – PRESCRIBED FORMS OF WRITING TO BE USED FOR INFORMING INSUREDS OF GENERAL NATURE AND EFFECT OF DUTY OF DISCLOSURE

(Regulation 3)

PART I – CONTRACTS OF GENERAL INSURANCE

Your duty of disclosure

Before you enter into a contract of general insurance with an insurer, you have a duty, under the Insurance Contracts Act 1984, to disclose to the insurer every matter that you know, or could reasonably be expected to know, is relevant to the insurer's decision whether to accept the risk of the insurance and, if so, on what terms.

You have the same duty to disclose those matters to the insurer before you renew, extend, vary or reinstate a contract of general insurance.

Your duty however does not require disclosure of matter:

- that diminishes the risk to be undertaken by the insurer;
- that is of common knowledge;
- that your insurer knows or, in the ordinary course of his business, ought to know;
- as to which compliance with your duty is waived by the insurer.

Non-disclosure

If you fail to comply with your duty of disclosure, the insurer may be entitled to reduce his liability under the contract in respect of a claim or may cancel the contract.

If your non-disclosure is fraudulent, the insurer may also have the option of avoiding the contract from its beginning.

PART II – CONTRACTS OF LIFE INSURANCE

Your duty of disclosure

Before you enter into a contract of life insurance with an insurer, you have a duty, under the Insurance Contracts Act 1984, to disclose to the insurer every matter that you know, or could reasonably be expected to know, is relevant to the insurer's decision whether to accept the risk of the insurance and, if so, on what terms.

You have the same duty to disclose those matters to the insurer before you renew, extend, vary or reinstate a contract of life insurance.

Your duty however does not require disclosure of a matter:

- that diminishes the risk to be undertaken by the insurer;
- that is of common knowledge;
- that your insurer knows or, in the ordinary course of his business, ought to know;
- as to which compliance with your duty is waived by the insurer.

Non-disclosure

If you fail to comply with your duty of disclosure and the insurer would not have entered into the contract on any terms if the failure had not occurred, the insurer may avoid the contract within three years of entering into it. If your non-disclosure is fraudulent, the insurer may avoid the contract at any time.

An insurer who is entitled to avoid a contract of life insurance may, within three years of entering into it, elect not to avoid it but to reduce the sum that you have been insured for in accordance with a formula that takes into account the premium that would have been payable if you had disclosed all relevant matters to the insurer.

BIBLIOGRAPHY

BOOKS

Anson, WR and Guest, A, *Anson's Law of Contract*, 25th edn, 1979, Oxford: OUP

Arrow, K (ed), *Essays in the Theory of Risk-Bearing*, 1970, Amsterdam: North Holland Pub Co

Bernstein, P, *Against the Gods: The Remarkable Story of Risk*, 1997, New York: John Wiley & Sons

Birds, J, *Modern Insurance Law*, 2nd edn, 1988; London: Sweet & Maxwell

Bishop, W, 'Negligent misrepresentation: an economic reformulation' in Burrows, P and Veljanovski, C (eds), *The Economic Approach to Law*, 1981, London: Butterworths

Black's Law Dictionary, 5th edn, 1979, St Paul, Minnesota: West Publishing Co

Brown, A, *Hazard Unlimited: The Story of Lloyds*, 3rd edn, 1973, London: Lloyd's of London Press

Burrows, P and Veljanovski, C (eds), *The Economic Approach to Law*, 1981, London: Butterworths

Cheshire, GC and Fifoot, CHS, *The Law of Contracts*, 6th NZ edn, 1984, Sydney: Butterworths

Clayton, G, *British Insurance*, 1971, London: Sweet & Maxwell

Clarke, M, *The Law of Insurance Contracts*, 1994, London: Lloyd's of London Press

Clarke, M, *The Law of Insurance Contracts*, 3rd edn, 1997, London: Lloyd's of London Press

Clarke, M, *The Law of Insurance Contracts*, Looseleaf, 1999, London: LLP Professional Publishing

Cooter, R and Ulen, T, *Law and Economics*, 1988, USA: HarperCollins

Cranston, R and Schick, A (eds), *Law and Economics*, 1982, Canberra: Dept of Law, Research School of Social Sciences, Australian National University

Derrington, D and Ashton, RS, *The Law of Liability Insurance*, 1990, Sydney: Butterworths

Finn, PD (ed), *Essays in Contract*, 1987, Sydney; Lawbook Co

Fridman, G, *The Law of Agency*, 5th edn, 1983, London: Butterworths

Grant, HR, *Insurance Reform: Consumer Action in the Progressive Era*, 1979, Iowa: Iowa State University Press

Hocker, PJ, Dufty, A and Heffey, PG, *Cases and Materials on Contract*, 1985, Sydney: Lawbook Co

Holdsworth, WS, *A History of English Law*, 1st edn, Vol 8, London: Methuen

Holmes, OW, *The Path of the Law*, 1921, Cambridge: Mass Press

Ivamy, ERH, *Marine Insurance*, 4th edn, 1985, London: Butterworths

Ivamy, ERH, *General Principles of Insurance Law*, 6th edn, 1993, London: Butterworths

Keeton, R, *Basic Text on Insurance Law*, 1971, St Paul, Minnesota: West Publishing Co

Keeton, RE and Widiss, AI, *Insurance Law: A Guide to Fundamental Principles, Legal Doctrines, and Commercial Practices*, 3rd edn, 1999, St Paul, Minnesota: West Publishing Co

Kelly, D StL and Ball, ML, *Principles of Insurance Law in Australia and New Zealand*, 1991, Sydney: Butterworths

Kelly, D StL and Ball, ML, *Principles of Insurance Law*, 2001, Sydney: Butterworths

Kimball, S, *Insurance and Public Policy*, 1960, Madison, Wisconsin: University of Wisconsin Press

Kronman, A and Posner, R (eds), *The Economics of Contract Law*, 1979, Boston: Little, Brown

MacGillivray, EJ and Parkington, M, *MacGillivray and Parkington on Insurance Law*, 8th edn, 1988, London: Sweet & Maxwell

MacGillivray, EJ and Parkington, M, *MacGillivray on Insurance Law*, 9th edn, 1997, London: Sweet & Maxwell (Legh-Jones, N (general ed); Longmore, A; Birds, J; Owen, D; Miller, M (eds))

Marks, F and Balla, A, *Guidebook to Insurance Law in Australia*, 2nd edn, 1987, Sydney: CCH Australia Ltd

McKinney's Consolidated Laws of New York – Insurance Law, 1966, New York: West Publishing Co

Park, JA, *A System of the Law of Marine Insurances*, 5th edn, London: Straun for Butterworths

Patterson, E, *Essentials of Insurance Law*, 1957, Brooklyn: Foundation Press

Posner, R, *Economic Analysis of Law*, 2nd edn, 1977, Boston: Little, Brown

Polinsky, A, *An Introduction to Law and Economics*, 2nd edn, 1989, Boston: Little, Brown

Roger Grant, H, *Insurance Reform: Consumer Action in the Progressive Era*, 1979, Ames, Iowa: Iowa State University Press

Samuelson, P (*et al*), *Economics*, 1992, Sydney: McGraw-Hill Book Co

Sutton, K, *Insurance Law in Australia and New Zealand*, 1980, Sydney: Lawbook Co

Sutton, K, *Insurance Law in Australia*, 2nd edn, 1991, Sydney: Lawbook Co

Tan, Lee Meng, *Insurance Law in Singapore*, 2nd edn, 1997, Singapore: Butterworths Asia

Tarr, AA and Kennedy, JR, *Insurance Law in New Zealand*, 2nd edn, 1992, Sydney: Lawbook Co

Tarr, AA, Tarr, JR (and Seddon, T (ed)), *Laws of Australia, Insurance and Income Security*, Title 22 Australia: CCH Pty Ltd

Trebilcock, M and Dewees, DN, 'Judicial control of standard form contracts' in Burrows, P and Veljanovski, C (eds), *The Economic Approach to Law*, 1981, London: Butterworths

Tullock, G, *The Logic of the Law*, 1971, New York: Basic Books (reprinted 1987: George Mason UP)

Turner and Sutton, *The Law Relating to Actionable Non-Disclosure*, 2nd edn, 1990, London: Butterworths

Williams, G, *Textbook of Criminal Law*, 2nd edn, 1983, London: Stevens & Sons

Woodruff, EH, *Casebook on Insurance*, 2nd edn, 1924, New York: Baker, Voorhs & Co

JOURNALS AND ARTICLES

Achampong, F, '*Uberrimae fidei* in English and American insurance law: a comparative analysis' (1987) 36 International and Comparative Law Quarterly 329

Akerlof, G, 'The market for lemons: qualitative uncertainty and the market mechanism' (1970) 84 Quarterly Law Journal of Economics 488

Ball, M, 'Misrepresentation and non-disclosure under the Insurance Contracts Act: *Advance (NSW) Insurance Agencies Pty Ltd v Matthews*' (1988) 1 Insurance Law Journal 77

Ball, M, 'Reducing claims under the Insurance Contracts Act 1984' (1992) 5 Insurance Law Journal 1

Beales, H, Craswell, R and Salop, S, 'The efficient regulation of consumer information' (1981) 24 Journal of Law and Economics 491

Bennett, H, 'The duty to disclose in insurance law' (1993) 109 LQR 513

Bennett, H, 'Utmost good faith in the House of Lords' (1995) 11 LQR 181

Birds, J, 'Duties of disclosure and breaches of warranty' (1989) 2 Insurance Law Journal 209

Birds, J, 'Insurers not liable in damages for failure to disclose' (1988) Journal of Business Law 421

Birds, J, 'Utmost good faith and insurers' (1990) Journal of Business Law 512

Birds, J and Hird, N, 'Misrepresentation and non-disclosure in insurance law – identical twins or separate issues?' (1996) 59 MLR 285

Borrowdale, A, 'Insurance Law Reform Acts in practice' (1987) NZLJ 30

Boxer, C, '*Pine top* just emerges above Atlantic' (1994) Solicitors Journal 936

Brooke, H, 'Materiality in insurance contracts' (1985) Lloyd's Maritime and Commercial Law Quarterly 437

The Hon Justice Brownie, 'The duty of utmost good faith, after the formation of the contract' (1993) 5 Insurance Law Journal 226

Brownsword, A, 'Two concepts of good faith' (1994) 7 Journal of Contract Law 16

Burge, P, 'Insurer's right to avoid a contract of insurance and insured's duty to make full disclosure reconsidered' (1993) 7 Journal of International Business Law N-149

Burrows, J, 'The Contractual Remedies Act 1979 – six years on' (1986) 6 Otago LR 220

Calabresi and Melamed, 'Property rules, liability rules and inalienability: one view of the cathedral' (1972) 85 Harvard Law Review 1089

Callaghan, A, 'The new insurance legislation', Seminar Paper for the Law Society of South Australia, 17 April 1985

Cayne, D and Trebilcock, MJ, 'Market considerations and consumer protection policy' (1973) 23 University of Toronto Law Journal 396

Clarke, M, 'The disclosure of criminal information to insurers' (1984) Lloyd's Comparative and Maritime Law Quarterly 100

Clarke, M, 'Insurance contracts and non-disclosure: *Pan Atlantic v Pine Top*' (1993) Lloyd's Maritime and Commercial Law Quarterly 297

Clarke, M, 'The marine insurance system in common law countries: status and problems' (1998) Paper: Marine Insurance Symposium Oslo 4–6 June

Cooter, R and Freeman, B, 'The fiduciary relationship: its economic character and legal consequences' (1991) 66 New York University Law Review 1045

Courtenay, DP, 'The innocent mortgagee: insurance without cost' (1989) 63 Australian Law Journal 587

Coase, R, 'The problem of social costs' (1960) 3 Journal of Law and Economics 1

Darby, M and Karni, E, 'Free competition and the optimal amount of fraud' (1973) 16 Journal of Law and Economics 67

Davis, RJ, 'The origin of the duty of disclosure under insurance law' (1991) 4 Insurance Law Journal 71

Davenport, B, 'The duty of disclosure: *La Banque Financière v Westgate*: the good luck' (1989) Lloyd's Maritime and Commercial Law Quarterly 251

(The Honourable Mr Justice) Derrington, 'Insurance as a cornerstone of civilisation – and another cornerstone' (1994) 7 Corporate and Business Law Journal 1

(The Honourable Mr Justice) Derrington, 'Liability Insurance Contracts Act: where do we stand?' (1990) Queensland Law Society Journal 5

Derrington, D and Ashton, R, 'What have they done to the common law? Disclosure and misrepresentation' (1988) 1 Insurance Law Journal 1

Derrington, S, 'The law relating to non-disclosure, misrepresentation and breach of warranty in contracts of marine insurance: a case for reform', unpublished PhD thesis, 1998, University of Queensland, Australia

Fridman, GHL, 'Annual survey of Canadian law: commercial law' (1981) 13 Ottawa Law Review 571

Goldberg, V, 'Institutional change and the quasi-invisible hand' (1974) 17 Journal of Law and Economics 461

Goetz, C and Scott, R, 'Liquidated damages, penalties and the just compensation principle: some notes on an enforcement model of and a theory of efficient breach' (1977) Columbia Law Review 554

Gravelle, H, 'Insurance law and adverse selection' (1991) 11 International Review of Law and Economics 23

Green and Moore, 'Winter's discontent: market failure and consumer welfare' (1973) 82 Yale Law Journal 903

Hamilton, J, 'The duty of disclosure in insurance law – the effectiveness of self-regulation' (1995) 23 Australian Business Law Review 359

Hasson, R, 'The "basis of the contract clause" in insurance law' (1971) 34 MLR 29

Hasson, R, 'The doctrine of *uberrimae fidei* in insurance law – a critical evaluation' (1969) 32 MLR 615

Hasson, R, 'Misrepresentation and non-disclosure in life insurance – some steps forward' (1975) 38 MLR 89

Hasson, R, 'The special nature of the insurance contract: a comparison of the American and English law of insurance' (1984) 47 MLR 505

Hawke, F, 'Utmost good faith – what does it really mean?' (1994) 6 Insurance Law Journal 2

Henchliffe, SR, 'Insurance claims: fraud and the duty of utmost good faith' (1997) 8 Insurance Law Journal 210

Henderson, R, 'The doctrine of reasonable expectations in insurance law after two decades' (1990) 51 Ohio State Law Journal 823

Henderson, R, 'The formulation of the doctrine of reasonable expectations and the influence of forces outside insurance law' (1998) 5 Connecticut Law Review 69

Hird, N, '*Pan Atlantic* – yet more to disclose?' (1995) Journal of Business Law 608

Hird, N, 'Rationality in the House of Lords' (1995) Journal of Business Law 194

Isaacs, J, 'The standardizing of contracts' (1917) 27 Yale Law Journal 34

Jerry, R, 'Insurance, contract, and the doctrine of reasonable expectations' (1998) 5 Connecticut Law Review 21

Jordan, R and Rubin, P, 'An economic analysis of the law of false advertising' (1978) 8 Journal of Legal Studies 527

Keeton, R, 'Insurance law rights at variance with policy provisions' (1970) 83 Harvard Law Review 961

Keeton, R, 'Insurance law rights at variance with policy provisions: part two' (1970) 83 Harvard Law Review 1281

Kelly, D, 'Amendment to the Insurance Contracts Act 1984: misuse of the omnibus Bill procedure' (1987) 15 Australian Business Law Review 275

Kelly, D, 'The insured's rights in relation to the provision of information by the insurer' (1989) 2 Insurance Law Journal 45

Kelly, D, 'Review of the Insurance Contracts Act 1984', Conference Proceedings, 30 May 1977, Sanctuary Cove, comment at p 7 (text on file with author)

Kelly, D, 'Recent developments in relation to inducement in non-disclosure and misrepresentation' (1998) 1 Insurance Law Journal 30

Kelly, D, 'Towards plain English insurance policies' (1994) 9 Insurance Law Bulletin 48

Kessler, F, 'Contracts of adhesion – some thoughts about freedom of contract' (1943) 43 Columbia Law Review 629

Khan, S, 'A new test of materiality in insurance law' (1986) Journal of Business Law 37

Kimball, S and Pfenningstorf, W, 'Legislative and judicial controls of the terms of insurance contracts: a comparative study of American and European practice' (1964) 39 Indiana Law Journal 675

(The Honourable Justice) Kirby, M, 'Marine insurance: is the doctrine of utmost good faith out of date?' (1995) 13 Australian Bar Review 1

Kornhauser, G, 'Unconscionability in standard forms' (1976) 64 California Law Review 1151

Kronman, A, 'Mistake, disclosure, information, and the law of contracts' (1978) 7 Journal of Legal Studies 1

Lasher, W, 'A common law alternative to the doctrine of reasonable expectations in the construction of insurance contracts' (1982) 57 New York University Law Review 1175

Leff, A, 'Contracts as thing' (1970) 19 American University Law Review 131

Levmore, S, 'Securities and secrets: insider trading and the law of contracts' (1982) 68 Virginia Law Review 117

Liederman, A, 'Insurance coverage disputes in the United States: a period of uncertainty for the insurer' (1986) Lloyd's Maritime and Commercial Law Quarterly 79

Llewellyn, K, 'What price contracts? – an essay in perspective' (1931) 40 Yale Law Journal 704

Llewellyn, K, 'Book review: the standardization of commercial contracts in English and continental law' (1939) 52 Harvard Law Review 700

Luxford, D, 'The Marine Insurance Act: chronologically challenged legislation?' Paper: MLAANZ Annual Conference Wellington 5–8 November 1995

McCarthy, C, 'The "prudent insurer": the test and its impact on section 2' (1997) 8 Insurance Law Journal 125

Mead, P, 'The effect of section 54 of the Insurance Contracts Act and proposal for reform' (1997) 9 Insurance Law Journal 1

Merkin, R, 'Gambling by insurance – a study of the Life Assurance Act 1774' (1980) 9 Anglo-American Law Review 331

Murray, J, 'The standardizing agreement phenomena' (1982) 67 Cornell Law Review 735

Newell, R, 'To disclose or not to disclose: the duty of utmost good faith and Royal Commission findings' (1993) 5 Insurance Law Journal 212

Nicholson, K, '*Advance (NSW) Insurance Agencies Pty Ltd v Matthews* in the High Court' (1989) 2 Insurance Law Journal 214

Nicholson, K, 'Fraudulent non-disclosure under the Insurance Contracts Act 1984 (Australia): the problem of joint and composite policies' (1989) 2 Insurance Law Journal 82

Pengilly, W, 'Section 52 of the Trade Practices Act and insurance contracts' (1990) 3 Insurance Law Journal 60

Pickering, M, 'Proving underwriting practices in court on issues of non-disclosure and breach of contract' (1991) 4 Insurance Law Journal 52

Pincott, A, 'Growing pains: two English decisions on the duty of good faith' (1988) 1 Insurance Law Journal 110

Priest, G, 'Contracts then and now: an appreciation of Friedrich Kessler' (1995) 104 Yale Law Journal 2145

Priest, G, 'A theory of the consumer product warranty' (1981) 90 Yale Law Journal 1297

Procaccia, U, 'Readable insurance policies: judicial regulation and interpretation' (1979) 14 Israel Law Review 74

Rahdert, M, 'Reasonable expectations reconsidered' (1986) 18 Connecticut Law Review 323

Rakoff, T, 'Contracts of adhesion: an essay in reconstruction' (1983) 96 Harvard Law Review 1173

Regan, L and Tennyson, S, 'Agent discretion and the choice of insurance marketing system' (1996) 39 Journal of Law & Economics 637

Rhea, S, 'The economics of insurance law' (1993) 13 International Review of Law and Economics 145

Robertson, B, 'Insurance law: what the consumers had to say' (1979) Policy Holder Insurance Journal 27, 22 June

Rothschild, M and Stiglitz, J, 'Equilibrium in competitive insurance markets: an essay on the economics of imperfect information' (1976) 90 Quarterly Journal of Economics 629

Schoenbaum, T, 'Warranties in the law of marine insurance: some suggestions for reform of English and American law' (1999) 23 Tulane Maritime Law Journal 1

Schwartz, A and Wilde, L, 'Imperfect information in markets for contract terms: the warranties and security interests' (1983) 69 Virginia Law Review 1387

Schwartz, A and Wilde, L, 'Intervening in markets on the basis of imperfect information: a legal and economic analysis' (1979) 127 University of Pennsylvania Law Review 630

Scotford, T, 'The insurer's duty of utmost good faith: implications for Australian insurers' (1988) 1 Insurance Law Journal 83

Seita, A, 'Uncertainty and contract law' (1984) 46 University of Pittsburg Law Review 75

Spigelman, J, 'Knowledge of a corporate insured' (1994) 6 Insurance Law Journal 159

Slawson, WD, 'Standard form contracts and democratic control of lawmaking power' (1971) 84 Harvard Law Review 529

Slawson, WD, 'Mass contracts: lawful fraud in California' (1974) 48 Southern California Law Review 1

Slawson, WD, 'The new meaning of contract: the transformation of contracts law by standard forms' (1984) 46 University of Pittsburg Law Review 21

Stigler, G, 'The economics of information' (1961) 69 Journal of Political Economy 213

Stoljar, S, 'Normal effective and preparatory damages in contract' (1975) 91 LQR 68

Strudler, A, 'Moral complexity in the law of non-disclosure' (1997) 45 University of California Los Angeles Law Review 337

Sutton, K, 'The duty of utmost good faith' (1994) 22 Australian Business Law Review 302

Sutton, K, 'Insurance' (1995) 23 Australian Business Law Review 64

Sutton, K, 'Insurance note' (1984) 12 Australian Business Law Review 215

Sutton, K, 'Insurance note' (1985) 13 Australian Business Law Review 48

Sutton, K, 'Insurance note' (1988) 16 Australian Business Law Review 330

Sutton, K, 'The test of materiality of facts at common law' (1991) 19 Australian Business Law Review 64

Sutton, K, 'An assured's duty of disclosure' (1995) 23 Australian Business Law Review 225

Sutton, K, 'The contract of insurance' (1972) 5 NZULR 123

Tapsell, K, 'Non-disclosure and the rights of parties' (1997) 8 Insurance Law Journal 3

Tarr, AA, 'Insurance law reform' (1985) 11 New Zealand Universities Law Review 362

Tarr, AA, 'The Insurance Contracts Act revisited' (1991) 4 Insurance Law Journal 227

Thomas, JE, 'An interdisciplinary critique of the reasonable expectation doctrine' (1988) 5 Connecticut Institute Law Journal 295

Ware, S, 'A critique of the reasonable expectations doctrine' (1989) 56 University of Chicago Law Review 1461

White, J, 'Consumer protection and the Uniform Commercial Code: form contracts under revised Article 2' (1997) 75 Washington University Law Quarterly 315

REPORTS, CIRCULARS AND WORKING PAPERS

English Law Reform Committee, 5th Report, *Conditions and Exceptions in Insurance Policies*, Cmnd 62, 1957

Contracts and Commercial Law Reform Committee, *Aspects of Insurance Law*, First Report, April 1975; *Aspects of Insurance Law (2)*, 1983

English Law Reform Commission, *Non-disclosure and Breach of Warranty*, Working Paper No 73, 1979

Australian Law Reform Commission, *Report on Insurance Agents and Brokers*, No 16, 1980

English Law Commission, *Report on Insurance Law, Non-disclosure and Breach of Warranty*, Report No 104, 1980

Australian Law Reform Commission, *Report on Insurance Contracts*, No 20, 1982

New South Wales Law Reform Commission, *Insurance Contracts: Non-disclosure and Misrepresentation*, Report No 34, 1983

ASIC Circular No G I/98 *Insurance Laws Amendment Act 1998 – New Duty of Disclosure Provisions and Other Changes*, May 1988

Australian Law Reform Commission, *Report on Multiculturalism and the Law*, 1992

General Insurance Enquiries and Complaints Scheme Annual Report 1993

General Insurance Enquiries and Complaints Scheme Annual Report 1994

General Insurance Enquiries and Complaints Scheme Annual Report 1995

General Insurance Enquiries and Complaints Scheme Annual Report 1996

General Insurance Enquiries and Complaints Scheme Annual Report 1997

National Consumer Council, *Report of Insurance Law Reform*, London, 1997

General Insurance Enquiries and Complaints Scheme Annual Report 1998

Australian Law Reform Commission, *Review of the Marine Insurance Act 1909*, Report No 91, April 2001

INDEX

D

I

K

P

Q

R

S

T

U